Classical Romantic

Identity in the Latin Poetry
of Vincent Bourne

.

Classical Romantic

Identity in the Latin Poetry
of Vincent Bourne

ESTELLE HAAN

American Philosophical Society
Philadelphia • 2007

Transactions of the
American Philosophical Society
Held at Philadelphia
For Promoting Useful Knowledge
Volume 97, Part 1

Library of Congress Cataloging-in-Publication Data

Haan, Estelle.
    Classical romantic : identity in the Latin poetry of Vincent Bourne / Estelle Haan.
        p. cm. – (Transactions of the American Philosophical Society held at Philadelphia
    for promoting useful knowledge ; v. 97, pt. 1)
    Includes bibliographical references and index.
    ISBN-10: 0-87169-971-0
    ISBN-13: 978-0-87169-971-8
    1. Bourne, Vincent, 1695-1747—Criticism and interpretation. 2. Identity (Philosophical
concept) in literature. 3. Identity (Psychology) in literature. I. Bourne, Vincent, 1695-1747.
Poems. English & Latin. Selections. II. Title.

PA8477.B7Z66 2007
871'.04—dc22

                                                                              2007003195

For Tony

CONTENTS

ACKNOWLEDGEMENTS

The present monograph is a product of my ongoing interest in the Latin poetry of eighteenth-century England. I am very fortunate to have had the opportunity to cultivate such an interest at Queen's University, Belfast. At Queen's I have benefited greatly from discussions with Michael McGann. I am grateful to the anonymous readers for the Transactions Series of the American Philosophical Society for their very helpful suggestions.

I wish to thank the Queen's University Research and Scholarships Committee for funding trips to the British Library, London, and the Bodleian Library, Oxford, and the authorities of those institutions for permitting me to consult manuscripts and early printed books relevant to my research. I am indebted also to the Queen's University Library, especially its Special Collections and Inter-Library Loans divisions.

Finally I wish to thank my husband, Tony Sheehan, Humanities Computing Officer at Queen's, not only for his advice in regard to the technical production of camera-ready copy, but also, and especially, for his unfailing care and support at all times. To him I dedicate this study *maximo cum amore*.

ABBREVIATIONS

ODNB	*Oxford Dictionary of National Biography*
OED	*Oxford English Dictionary*
OLD	*Oxford Latin Dictionary*

INTRODUCTION

If any surviving friend will shew his love to my memory by a small tablet, I desire that this, and this only, may be the inscription:

> PIETATIS SINCERAE
> SUMMAEQUE HUMILITATIS,
> NEC DEI USQUAM IMMEMOR
> NEC SUI,
> IN SILENTIUM QUOD AMAVIT
> DESCENDIT
> V.B.[1]

Thus proclaims a certain V.B. in a self-referential epitaph, which envisages its subject as one who, for all his piety and humility, has in death "descended into the silence which he loved." This is a speaker who desires to be remembered by nothing more than a "small tablet"—a tablet whose inscription culminates, not in the envisaged rewards of an afterlife or in the joys of heavenly glory, but in silence (*silentium*) itself. Worthy of comparison perhaps are the sentiments expressed by the same author in his "Letter to a Young Lady":

> Surely in death there is safety, and in the grave there is peace. This wipes off the sweat of the poor labouring man, and takes the load from the bended back of the weary traveller. This dries up the tears of the disconsolate, and maketh the heart of the sorrowful to forget its throbbing. 'Tis this eases the agonies of the diseased, and giveth a medicine to the hopeless incurable. ... This silences the clamours of the defamer, and hushes the virulence of the whisperer.[2]

---

[1] *Poematia Latine Partim Reddita Partim Scripta a Vicentio Bourne*, ed. John Mitford (London, 1840), xxv.

[2] Mitford, ed. *Poematia*, xiii. This letter, together with a further letter by Bourne to his wife, were first printed (but with no indication of their source) in the 1772 edition of his poetry, on which see 9 below. Mitford, ed. *Poematia*, xvi, speculates that the editor of that volume "appears to have had access to some unpublished MSS. of Bourne."

In both instances the speaker is Vincent Bourne (1694–1747), neo-Latin poet and Westminster schoolmaster, whose expression of contentment in the tacit anonymity of the grave is mirrored perhaps by the silence into which he has indeed descended in more ways than one. In that same letter he had stated:

> The churchyard I look on as the rendezvous of the whole parish, whither people of all ages and conditions resort. It is the common dormitory where, after the labours of life are over, they all lie down and repose themselves together in the dust.[3]

The metaphor of the churchyard as dormitory is highly appropriate for one who spent almost all his life at Westminster School, serving as usher (assistant teacher) of the fifth-form until just before his death in 1747. For Bourne then the descent into the "repose" of the grave constitutes a homecoming of sorts. But more than that: Bourne's epitaph seems to epitomize that desire for the suppression of identity that seems to characterize its author's life and works. As the poet's most reliable editor,[4] John Mitford, proclaims:

> Of Vincent Bourne … it may be said, not that what is known of him is devoid of interest, for that is far from being the case, but that scarcely any remembrance of his life has been preserved. "Qui bene latuit, bene vixit," seems to have been the motto of his easy and unambitious mind.[5]

This "concealment," this virtual quest for silence, works on a number of levels: in the express dismissal of longevity as a personal aspiration,[6] in the poet's consistent self-presentation as the observer not the observed,[7] in a whole series of other silences (autobiographical, biographical, critical) that serve to match the silence of the grave and ultimately of the poetic voice. Or as Foucault puts it:

---

[3] Mitford, ed. *Poematia*, xi. Bourne continues: "The little cares and concerns they had when living are here entirely forgotten; nor comes there hither any uneasiness or enmity to disquiet or interrupt their rest. The jealousies and fears, the discontents and suspicions, the animosities and misunderstandings, which embitter men one against another, are all determined. Here end all resentments and contentions."

[4] On Bourne's eighteenth- and nineteenth-century editors, see 9–10 below.

[5] Mitford, ed. *Poematia*, i.

[6] See *Anus Saecularis*, discussed at chapter 4, 122–129.

[7] See chapter 3 passim.

> There is not one but many silences, and they are an integral part of the strategies that underlie and permeate discourses.[8]

It is the purpose of this study to break these "many silences" by constructing another "Bourne identity,"[9] so to speak, that of a prolific and highly skillful neo-Latin poet, whose work merits close critical attention in its classical, neo-Latin and vernacular contexts. Despite the recent surge in neo-Latin studies, a surge that has manifested itself quite specifically in relation to the Latin poetry of seventeenth- and eighteenth-century England,[10] Bourne and his work continue to lie hidden from the scholarly world as if attesting to Mitford's comment: *qui bene latuit, bene vixit*. His Latin poetry has not been edited since the mid-nineteenth century, and no book on the subject has ever been written. In short, critical commentary amounts to Leicester Bradner's seven-page survey of the poet in his *Musae Anglicanae* (1940),[11] a single article, by Mark Storey, written some thirty years later,[12] and, more recently, a five-page discussion by David Money.[13] Thus Storey's concession that "for most people Vincent Bourne might as well not have existed"[14] is still very true

---

[8] Michel Foucault, *The History of Sexuality, Volume I: An Introduction*, trans. Robert Hurley (New York, 1990), 27.

[9] For the phrase I am indebted to Robert Ludlum's novel *The Bourne Identity* (New York, 1980). Cf. the film version, directed by Doug Liman, in 2002.

[10] See in particular Estelle Haan, *From Academia to Amicitia: Milton's Latin Writings and the Italian Academies* (Transactions of the American Philosophical Society 88.6 [Philadelphia, 1998]); Estelle Haan, *Thomas Gray's Latin Poetry: Some Classical, Neo-Latin and Vernacular Contexts* (Collection Latomus 257: Brussels, 2000); Estelle Haan, *Andrew Marvell's Latin Poetry: From Text to Context* (Collection Latomus 275: Brussels 2003); Estelle Haan, *Vergilius Redivivus: Studies in Joseph Addison's Latin Poetry* (Transactions of the American Philosophical Society 95.2 [Philadelphia, 2005]). See also the work of Dana Sutton, whose online bibliography of neo-Latin texts (compiled for The Philological Museum) has made hitherto neglected primary texts accessible to a wide readership.

[11] Leicester Bradner, *Musae Anglicanae: A History of Anglo-Latin Poetry 1500-1925* (New York and London, 1940), 266–273.

[12] Mark Storey, "The Latin Poetry of Vincent Bourne," in *The Latin Poetry of English Poets*, ed. J.W. Binns (London and Boston, 1970), 121–149.

[13] D.K. Money, *The English Horace: Anthony Alsop and the Tradition of British Latin Verse* (Oxford, 1998), 223–227.

[14] Storey, "The Latin Poetry of Vincent Bourne," 122.

in the twenty-first century. And this is not without irony given the publication history of Bourne's Latin verse,[15] and the praise bestowed upon that verse by his contemporaries and indeed by subsequent authors, factors that attest to the immense popularity of this neo-Latin poet in eighteenth-century England.[16]

Storey, while shedding much light on certain aspects of the Latin verse, hardly does justice to the poet's methodology by making such misleading generalizations as "Bourne's Latin is not classical or even imitative."[17] Bradner criticizes the "apologetic tone" of the article in question, and continues: "It takes real poetic genius to turn these little observations of daily life into delightful epigrams, and I am convinced that Bourne had that rare kind of genius."[18] Money remarks on "the discreet charm of Vincent Bourne."[19] Similarly Ross Kennedy correctly notes that "the deceptive simplicity of his verse conceals numerous wry subtleties."[20] If Bradner is correct, that "genius" still remains to be demonstrated to twenty-first-century readers and critics, as indeed do those "wry subtleties" noted but not exemplified by Ross. In fact Bourne's methodology is governed by an author's rare ability to offer perceptive insights into animal, human, and civic behavior, while enshrouding the whole in a superficially simple style. It is a style that constitutes a fusion of the classical and the romantic, a fusion that makes him stand out from his neo-Latin predecessors and contemporaries.

At the outset it should be remarked that virtually nothing of any real significance has been uncovered about Vincent Bourne's life.[21] Born in 1694 to Andrew Bourne and his wife, Anne, he was baptized on 22

---

[15] See Introduction, 9–10.

[16] See Introduction, 14–18.

[17] Storey, "The Latin Poetry of Vincent Bourne," 130.

[18] Leicester Bradner, Review of J.W. Binns, ed. *The Latin Poetry of English Poets* (London, 1974), *Renaissance Quarterly* 29.2 (1976), 293–295, at 294–295. Cf. James Diggle, *Times Higher Educational Supplement* (13 Sept.1974).

[19] Money, *The English Horace*, 223.

[20] Ross Kennedy, *Oxford Dictionary of National Biography*, eds. H.C.G. Matthew and Brian Harrison (Oxford, 2004), 6, 860 (s.v. Vincent Bourne).

[21] Cf. Mitford, ed. *Poematia*, i–ii: "A few meagre dates, which only mark some unimportant areas of his life, have alone been handed down to us, without any accompanying facts; as if the enumeration of the milestones on a road were to form a satisfactory description of the features and scenery of a country."

July 1694 in the church of St Martin-in-the-Fields, Westminster. He was admitted to Westminster School, and in 1710 he became queen's scholar. His teacher was Robert Freind, a minor Latin poet in his day,[22] whose particular forte in the art of the epigram and the epitaph[23] would come to have no slight influence upon his pupil.[24] For central to the educational curriculum of Westminster was of course the study of the classics.[25] As Carleton remarks of the school: "Greek and Latin, and Latin again sometimes even to the exclusion of Greek, were the order of the day."[26] It was here that Bourne received that rigorous drilling in classical languages and literature[27] that would bear fruit in so many different ways in terms of

---

[22] See J.D. Carleton, *Westminster School: A History* (London, 1965), 24. *ODNB* s.v. Robert Freind. Among Freind's rather slight output of original Latin verse are two poems that he contributed to the *Musarum Anglicanarum Analecta* (Oxford, 1699), an ode addressed to the Duke of Newcastle, published in *The Gentleman's Magazine* of 1737, and a panegyric upon the death of Queen Caroline, which appeared in the *Pietas Academiae Oxoniensis* (Oxford, 1738).

[23] See, for example, Freind's Latin inscription adorning the monument of Philip Carteret in Westminster Abbey. Freind's writing of Latin epitaphs was satirized in lines attributed to Alexander Pope: "Freind, for your epitaphs I'm grieved,/Where still so much is said,/One half will never be believ'd,/The other never read." See *ODNB* s.v. Robert Freind.

[24] For Bourne's predilection for these forms, see chapter 4 at 114 and 132–133.

[25] For a neo-Latin poem in praise of Westminster School and its classical curriculum, cf. *Scholae Westmonasteriensis Descriptio, Musae Anglicanae* (Oxford, 1699), II, 231–236. Note in particular references to the study of Ovid, Aesop (*interea aut facilis teritur post prandia Naso,/aut lepidae Aesopi ridetur fabula* [233, lines 51–52]), Virgil (*his sensim gradibus formavit Mantua vatem* [233, line 60]), and Horace (*te, Flacce, tenemus/invicti Britones* [234, lines 73–74]).

[26] Carleton, *Westminster School*, 31.

[27] Central to that "drilling" were such Latin textbooks as *A Short Introduction to Grammar* (London, 1549) by William Lily, and *A Short Institution of Grammar* (Cambridge, 1647) (reprinted as *A Short Institution of Grammar For the Use of the Lower Forms in the King's School at Westminster* [London, 1776]) by Richard Busby, the strict disciplinarian and thrashing headmaster of Westminster School (1638-1695). William Cowper, who was taught by Bourne, conveys in a letter to William Unwin (3 July 1782) his hostility toward Lily: "I am no friend to Lily's grammar, though I was indebted to him for my first Introduction to the Latin language," and continues: "The grammars used at Westminster, both for the Latin and the Greek, are those to which if I had a young man to educate, I should give the preference. They have the merit of being compendious and perspicuous, in both which properties I judge Lily to be defective ... They are called Busby's Grammars." Cf. *The Letters and Prose Writings of William Cowper*, ed. James King and Charles Ryskamp (Oxford, 1986), II, 63.

his own literary output as Latin poet and indeed as translator into Latin of a whole host of vernacular poems. It should be remembered too that the educational curriculum of the day demanded of its pupils skills not only in translation, but also in original verse-composition. The former manifested itself in such pedagogical exercises as the "double translation system," the "turning of verses," "paraphrase," "metaphrase" inter alia;[28] the latter, in the regular composition of original Latin epigrams, generally on a weekly basis. In many ways the objective of such exercises lay in the molding of the budding poet, and in instilling in that poet a whole wealth of compositional skills. In this respect original verse-composition, and especially the composition of Latin elegiacs, constituted the very core of the educational process. It is when such verses transcended mere pedagogy that the neo-Latin poet could come to birth.[29] Indeed it is as the composer of an amazingly eclectic range of Latin poems that Bourne excelled. From the classical rigor of Westminster he proceeded to a scholarship at Trinity College, Cambridge.[30] The register of the college lists his admission under the date 27 May 1714, describes him as the son of Andrew Bourne, from Westminster, with Dr Freind as his *praeceptor*.[31] Bourne is recorded as having received his BA in 1717. And

---

[28] These exercises are recommended by such Renaissance educators as John Brinsley, *Ludus Literarius or The Grammar Schoole*, Charles Hoole, *A New Discovery of the Old Art of Teaching Schoole*, and Roger Ascham, *The Scholemaster*. See D.L. Clark, *John Milton at St Paul's School* (New York, 1948; repr. Hamden, 1964), passim; Estelle Haan, *Andrew Marvell's Latin Poetry*, 33–34, 69–72. See also Estelle Haan, "'The Adorning of My Native Tongue': Linguistic Metamorphosis in Milton," *Metaphrastes or Gained in Translation: Essays in Honour of Robert H. Jordon*, ed. Margaret Mullett (Belfast, 2004), 111–127, at 115–124.

[29] For an earlier example of this, see Estelle Haan, "From Neo-Latin to Vernacular: Marvell's Bilingualism and Renaissance Pedagogy," *Proceedings of the International Andrew Marvell Conference*, ed. Gilles Sambras (University of Reims, forthcoming, 2007).

[30] Cf. Mitford, ed. *Poematia*, iii: "We find from the list of King's scholars, that he was admitted on the foundation at Westminster in the year 1710, at the age of fifteen; and from Mr Welsh's list of Westminster scholars, we have the following Elections, in the year 1714 to the Universities: To Oxford: John Wigan, William Davies, Salusbury Cade, George Toblett, David Gregory; to Cambridge: Richard Cuthbert, Thomas Fitzgerald, Vincent Bourne, Henry Geast."

[31] Cf. Mitford, ed. *Poematia*, ii–iii: "Maii 27, 1714 *Vincentius Bourne, annos natus 19, filius Andreae Bourne, Westmonasteriensis; electus in hoc Collegio, e schola Reg: Westmonasteriensis sub Praeceptore, Doctore Friend. Mro Baker, Tutr.* Robert Freind was appointed headmaster in 1711. See Carleton, *Westminster School*, 24, and 5 above.

it was in this year that he addressed Latin verses to none other than the celebrated Joseph Addison (upon the latter's recovery from sickness),[32] with whom he would establish important literary links later in his career.[33] That Bourne himself had achieved much acclaim as a Latin poet in Cambridge is attested by the fact that in 1717 he was honored by being selected to compose the tripos verses for the spring of that year. The result was the *Mutua Benevolentia Primaria Lex Naturae Est*, Bourne's masterful rendition in Latin elegiacs of the fable of Androcles and the lion.[34] He was made a Fellow in 1720. In 1721 he commenced his MA, in which year he also edited a collection of Cambridge tripos verses (*Carmina Comitalia Cantabrigiensia*). This included his own tripos verses,[35] and also (under *Miscellanea*) two of his other Latin poems,[36] and three of his Latin verse-translations of vernacular pieces.[37] In 1726 he published separately *In Obitum Roussaei Anno MDCCXXI, Carmen Elegiacum Editio Altera*, a witty poem lamenting the death of a Cambridge bed-attendant and oarsman.[38]

After Cambridge Bourne was appointed (certainly by 1727) to the position of usher at Westminster School. The evidence would suggest, however, that as schoolmaster he was unable to maintain an adequate level of discipline. William Cowper, perhaps his most famous pupil, admirer, and imitator,[39] relays a humorous anecdote concerning Charles

---

[32] See Lucy Aikin, *The Life of Joseph Addison* (London, 1843), II, 214, and Appendix 4 in this volume.

[33] On Bourne's links with Addison, see Appendix 4 in this volume.

[34] See chapter 2, 48–53.

[35] *Carmina Comitalia Cantabrigiensia*, ed. Vincent Bourne (London, 1721), 23–24.

[36] *Fanaticus* (*Carmina Comitalia Cantabrigiensia*, 85–86); *Epitaphium in Canem* (*Carmina Comitalia Cantabrigiensia*, 95–96).

[37] *Corydon Querens: Carmen Pastorale, Latine Redditum* (*Carmina Comitalia Cantabrigiensia*, 77–80). This piece, a translation of Nicholas Rowe's "Colin's Complaint," was issued separately both in 1721 and 1726; *Chloe Venatrix* (*Carmina Comitalia Cantabrigiensia*, 87–88), and *Amor Inermis* (*Carmina Comitalia Cantabrigiensia*, 88–91), both of which are Latin versions of original vernacular poems by Matthew Prior.

[38] See chapter 4, 114–121.

[39] Cowper entered Westminster School and remained there until after Bourne's death in 1747. On Cowper's translations of Bourne's Latin poetry, see Appendix 2 in this

Lennox, the future Duke of Richmond, who, according to Cowper, set fire to Bourne's "greasy locks," a fire that he proceeded to extinguish by boxing his schoolmaster on the ears![40] Such pranks played upon Westminster teachers were nothing out of the ordinary. Southey reports, for example, that Pierson Lloyd (who taught the form below Bourne) furnished "matter for innumerable stories,"[41] while Nicholl seems to have been the victim of a drag-act prank whereby the young Lord Higham Ferrers impersonated a lady, requesting that Nicholl give him/her a tour of the school.[42] And pranks were likewise played upon fellow pupils. Such mischievous customs as covering newcomers in ink[43] were typical of schoolboyish behavior of the times.[44]

Despite these antics allegedly played upon Bourne the schoolmaster, Bourne the poet continued to compose Latin verse, in all likelihood, although not exclusively so, as a source of inspiration for his teaching. Several of his Latin poems find their first appearance in print in the *Lusus Wesmonasteriensis* (1730), a multiauthored Westminster volume of Latin verse intended both to entertain and instruct. In the Preface to that volume the editor expresses the hope that the work will be of use to young scholars, and will sharpen and incite their tender minds in their literary studies toward a sense of emulation and love of praise.[45] But

---

volume. On possible points of contact between Bourne's Latin and Cowper's English poetry, see chapter 1, 33–34, 41; chapter 2, 57, 68, 70; chapter 3, 102 and 103.

[40] "Yet such was poor Vinney. I remember seeing the Duke of Richmond set fire to his greasy Locks, and box his Ears to put it out again." *The Letters and Prose Writings of William Cowper*, I, 482: Letter to William Unwin (23 May 1781).

[41] See Carleton, *Westminster School*, 30–31.

[42] Carleton, *Westminster School*, 30–31.

[43] Cf. Carleton, *Westminster School*, 30: "Practical joking and high spirits were not to be suppressed. Frederick Reynolds, launched at the age of eleven into Mrs Jones's boarding house in Dean's Yard, was the victim of one of these jokes on his very first night at school, and wrote a letter home which is moving in its epigrammatic appeal: 'My Dear Dear Mother, If you don't let me come home, I die—I am all over ink, and my fine clothes have been spoilt—I have been tost in a blanket, and seen a ghost.'"

[44] As Carleton states, *Westminster School*, 31: "Readers of the Memoirs of William Hickey, Richard Cumberland, George Colman, and others who have recorded their experience of Westminster in the eighteenth century may think it remarkable that the boys learnt anything at school beyond the knowledge of how to use their fists."

[45] *Lusus Westmonasterienses* (Westminster, 1730), Preface: *et si hi puerorum lusus viros, severioribus paululum depositis studiis, delectare potuerint, proposito ipsius*

it is for his collection of Latin poetry and Latin translations of English poets that he was to achieve much acclaim. His *Poematia* (sic) first appeared in 1734[46] and immediately became a best-seller in its day, going through further editions both during and after the author's lifetime. Thus a second appeared in 1735, and a third in 1743 (which incorporated *adiectis ad Calcem quibusdam novis*).[47] As Mitford notes, this was the last edition printed in the lifetime of the author.[48] A fourth appeared in 1750,[49] a fifth in 1764, a sixth in 1772,[50] a seventh in 1808, another in 1826, and Mitford's own edition in 1840.[51] And there is evidence that he was well connected. There survives in the British Library a letter of Bourne's addressed to his former classmate, Thomas Pelham, Duke of Newcastle (dated 29 June 1734), in which he seeks to be considered for the position of Housekeeper of the House of Commons.[52] Perhaps

---

pulchre respondebunt Tironibus certe erunt usui, et in literarum studiis teneros eorum animos ad aemulationem et amorem laudis acuent et excitabunt.

[46] *Poematia, Latine Partim Reddita, Partim Scripta: a V. Bourne, Collegii Trinitatis Apud Cantabrigienses Aliquando Socio* (London, 1734).

[47] *Poematia, Latine Partim Reddita, Partim Scripta: a V. Bourne, Collegii Trinitatis Apud Cantabrigienses Aliquando Socio Tertio Edita Adiectis ad Calcem Quibusdam Novis* (London, 1743). A copy of this edition was in Cowper's library when he died. See *The Letters and Prose Writings of William Cowper*, I, 272, and Geoffrey Keynes, "The Library of Cowper," *Transactions of the Cambridge Bibliographical Society*, 1959–1961, 47, 53.

[48] Mitford, ed. *Poematia*, xxxiv.

[49] *Poematia, Latine Partim Reddita, Partim Scripta: a V. Bourne, Collegii Trinitatis Apud Cantabrigienses Aliquando Socio* (London, 1750).

[50] As Mitford, ed. *Poematia*, xxxv, notes: "It was published without the name of the editor, and contained no preface or advertisement of any kind. In this edition many poems were introduced which had appeared in no previous one; none of them are sanctioned by any authority that one knows; and some of them were written by other persons." Mitford, ed. *Poematia*, xxxvii–xxxviii, suggests that the editor "inserted the mass of new and unauthorised poems to swell out the volume for the satisfaction of his subscribers." William Cowper, in a letter to Joseph Hill (dated 13 July 1777), requested that he send him a copy of this 1772 edition. Several of the 1772 pieces incorrectly attributed to Bourne are pointed out by Robert Nares in his review (of the 1826 edition), in *The Gentleman's Magazine* 96.1 (1826), 295, who states: "Bourne is rich enough in his own compositions to have no need of borrowing."

[51] See Mitford, ed. *Poematia*, xxxiii–xxxiv.

[52] BL Add 32689, f. 296. The full text of the letter is as follows: "May it please Your Grace, I am inform'd, that the Housekeeper to the House of Commons is either dead

Bourne's dedication of the 1734 volume to him as former *condiscipulus*[53] went beyond typical flattery, and showed for once some sort of single-minded career motivation. Whether or not this is the case, it emerges that he was successful in his request, for in November 1734 he was indeed appointed Housekeeper and deputy Sergeant-at-Arms to the House of Commons.[54] But just as Bourne continued to compose during his Westminster years, so too did he edit other Latin poets. This is evident in his edition (the fifth) of the *Musae Anglicanae*, a volume of Oxonian neo-Latin verse first compiled by Addison and published in 1699. Bourne's edition, published in London in 1741, moves far beyond its Addisonian original in that it includes works by Cambridge as well as Oxford poets.[55] As such it would seem to reflect Bourne's sense of pride in the fact that Cambridge too possessed a wealth of neo-Latin talent.

Concerning Bourne's personal life information is very thin. It is known that on 14 May 1727, he married a certain Lucia, widow of George Jewell,[56] and that the wedding took place in St Margaret's,

---

or past Hopes of Recovery; and should think it the greatest Favour I could receive, if by Your Grace's Recommendation, I might succeed him. I have been very punctual in my Promise, not to leave Westminster School till your Grace should be pleas'd to remove me; And I the rather make this Application to Your Grace, that by this Means I shall still continue in the Neighbourhood of a Place Your Grace has so great an Affection for. I am, with the greatest Duty, Your Grace's most obedient humble Servant, Vincent Bourne, June 29 1734."

[53] *Nobilissimo Principi Thomae Duci Novocastrensi Otium Hoc Poeticum, Nullo Potius Quam Condiscipuli Nomine Commendatum, Humillime Offert et Dedicat Vincentius Bourne* (*Poematia, Latine Partim Reddita, Partim Scripta a V. Bourne, Collegii Trinitatis apud Cantabrigienses Aliquando Socio* [London, 1734], Dedication).

[54] Cf. *The Gentleman's Magazine* 4 (November 1734), 628: "Mr Vincent Bourne, made Housekeeper and Dep. Serjeant at Arms to the H. of Commons."

[55] Note Bourne's comment at *Musae Anglicanae*, I, A3[r] that he has included Cambridge poems: *Praemonendus es, Lector Quintae huiusce Editionis, priorum Quattuor retineri omnia, locis transponi quaedam, mutari vero perpauca. Adiici Cantabrigiensium invenies multa: novi pleraque, nec ingrati fortasse, Argumenti; exercitationes scilicet Academicas, de Quaestionibus praecipue Philosophicis; Juvenilium Studiorum Testimonia simul et Ornamenta.* Thus the volume anthologizes inter alia William Dillingham's *Sphaeristerium Suleianum* (*Musae Anglicanae*, I, 109–112) and *Campanae Undellenses* (*Musae Anglicanae*, I, 244–248), on which see 100 below, and Robert Creyghton's *Iter Occidentale* (*Musae Anglicanae*, I, 133–136).

[56] George Jewell was a contemporary of Bourne at Westminster and Trinity, and was likewise an usher at Westminster School. He died in 1725 at the age of thirty-one. See *ODNB* s.v. Vincent Bourne.

Westminster. By 25 December of the same year Bourne had already written his will, in which "he describes himself as of St Margaret's Westminster; desires to be buried in privacy in some neighbouring church of England; and gives all his worldly goods to Lucia, his wife."[57] It is a will that Bourne was to amend, for sometime after 1727 it is evident that the couple had a son, Thomas (who would later join the merchant navy),[58] and a daughter, Lucia. This is attested by the fact that in 1745 Bourne made a codicil to his will stating that he had two children, Thomas and Lucia, by his wife, Lucia. He also mentions a farm near Bungay in

---

[57] Mitford, ed. *Poematia*, iv. A contributor to *Notes and Queries* 12 (27 October 1855), 327, cites an extract from the *Illustrated London News* (13 October 1855), which points out that Mitford misquoted "church" for "country churchyard": "Vinny's last and best biographer, the Rev. John Mitford, informs us that Vinny, in his will, records his desire 'to be buried in privacy in some neighbouring church of England.' For this information he tells us he is indebted to the present Garter King-at-Arms (Sir Charles Young), then only York Herald. But the wording of the desire is not what Mr Mitford has made it. Vinny, a parishioner of St Margaret's Westminster, desires 'to be interred with privacy in some neighbouring *country churchyard*.' And how beautifully does this agree with the sentiments expressed by him in a letter to a lady: 'I am just come from indulging a very pleasant melancholy in a *country churchyard*, and paying a respectful visit to the dead, of which I am one day to increase the number. Every monument has its instruction, and every hillock has its lesson of mortality. I have by this means, in a short space of time, read the history of the whole village.'"

[58] On 12 November 1746 Bourne wrote a letter to Andrew Stone concerning the involvement of his son, Thomas, in the War of the Austrian Succession. The manuscript survives (among the papers of Thomas Pelham, Duke of Newcastle) in the British Library (BL Add. 32713, f. 428). The full text is as follows: "Sir, Having receiv'd a Letter from my Son, who at the time of his writing was return'd to Portsmouth, and is since order'd to Plymouth, where he now is, I call'd at Your House to communicate the Contents of it. Within a few Days after I have receiv'd another from a Relation in Commissioner Vanbrugh's Family at Plymouth with a Confirmation of what he had told me in his: that he was on Board the Exeter, in an Engagement of near L'Isle with a French Ship of 64 Guns nam'd L'Ardent, which was drove on Shore, and afterwards burnt. That he was likewise With his Command of Marines a Shore, and order'd to an advanc'd Post at two Miles Distance from the rest of the Troops, where at Midnight he was attack'd by a French Party which he repuls'd with the Loss of one of his Men, and his Serjeant's being wounded, himself unhurt. As I believe his Account is true, I was desirous of acquainting you with it, in the hope that you will represent it, where you shall think proper, that he may meet with due Encouragement, and be further advanc'd either in the Service he is now in, or where else you shall please to recommend him. I am Sir, your most oblig'd humble Servant, Vincent Bourne, Nov 12 1746." Storey, "The Latin Poetry of Vincent Bourne," 122, incorrectly states that this letter was addressed to the Duke of Newcastle.

Suffolk and a house that he had built in Westminster.[59] In 1747 he made a second codicil granting to his son Thomas the farm near Bungay (in the event of his mother's death).[60] By at least September 1747 he had resigned from his position as usher at Westminster School,[61] most likely on the grounds of his declining health.[62] Several weeks before his death he addressed a letter to his wife, which constitutes in several respects a quasi-deathbed confession. In it he reviews his past life, laments "the offences of my youth and the transgressions of my riper years," and begs forgiveness from his Saviour.[63] While the letter conveys something of his fear of death, it is characterized for the most part by an extremely grim sense of despondency whereby "the prospect into futurity is all darkness and uncertainty" for one who is "ever so much wearied with life."[64] As a

---

[59] Mitford, ed. *Poematia*, iv–v.

[60] Mitford, ed. *Poematia*, v. Bourne states that his son was a second Lieutenant in the Marines, and going to India on Government Service. As Mitford notes, "the widow proved the will the 22nd December, 1747."

[61] Bourne's resignation is mentioned in *The Gentleman's Magazine* 17 (September, 1747), 448, which includes among its list of promotions for the year 1747: "Rev. Mr Lloyd, an usher in Westminster school, in room of Mr Vincent Bourne, famous for his Latin poems, who has resign'd."

[62] The gradual nature of Bourne's declining health is suggested in his letter to his wife written a few weeks before his death: "Being warned by the hand of God that my dissolution draweth nigh, I thank the Divine Goodness for giving me this timely notice, and not cutting me off suddenly in the midst of my sins: that he has granted me leisure, and a due sense of my follies and corruptions, and thereby enabled me to make my reconciliation with Him before that I am no more seen." Cf. Mitford, ed. *Poematia*, v–vi.

[63] Mitford, ed. *Poematia*, vi: "Upon recollection, I find the offences of my youth and the transgressions of my riper years are so many, that, were not the mercy of God as infinite as His justice, I might despair of pardon. But, through the merits and intercession of a crucified Saviour, I humbly hope forgiveness. ... For that part of my behaviour that relates to my fellow-creature, man; if that should happen to be less exceptionable; if I have not willingly and deliberately injured my neighbour, by calumny, oppression, or extortion, not unto me, but unto God, be the praise."

[64] Cf. Mitford, ed. *Poematia*, viii–ix: "The most pleasing and the dearest engagements of this world, as having nothing in them solid, sincere, or lasting, I could readily forego: but the looking-for that unknown state into which I am to enter when I put off this body of frailty and corruption, is confounding and terrible. The prospect into futurity is all darkness and uncertainty nor can the nearest relative or friend who is gone before me repass the gulf that is fixed between us, to give me the least notice or intimation of it. 'Tis this thought that forbids me, polluted as I now am, though ever so much wearied with life, to wish for dissolution: this reminds me, that though the

letter, it suggests a life of unhappiness, perhaps even depression, and certainly conveys a paranoid sense of unworthiness. Part of that unworthiness seems to have arisen from the fact that at some point Bourne had seriously considered entering the church, but had ultimately decided against the idea. Mitford regards the consequence of this as "clos[ing] up the road which would have led to preferment and worldly advantage," and alludes to the rumor that the Duke of Newcastle had "offered him very valuable ecclesiastical preferments."[65] In that letter to his wife he confesses that it was his own sense of inadequacy coupled with the importance of such an undertaking that were responsible for his decision.[66] Finally, just three weeks later (2 December 1747)[67] Vincent Bourne at the age of fifty-three "descended into the silence that he loved": *in silentium quod amavit descendit.* He was buried in Fulham Churchyard in Middlesex.[68]

---

body be sleeping and mouldering in the grave, the soul dieth not, nor yet slumbereth: the place and condition of unbodied spirits, who of all mankind knoweth? ... Where shall I, who have spent many years in idleness and vanity, and have no merit of my own to plead for me, where shall I, who have not treasured up one good work to bespeak the favour of the Almighty, and have only the sufferings of Jesus Christ, and those very sufferings often slighted, trampled upon, and rejected by me, to offer in my behalf?"

[65] Cf. Mitford, ed. *Poematia*, v: "By declining to enter into holy orders, Vincent Bourne closed up the road which would have led to preferment and worldly advantage. It has been said that the Duke of Newcastle offered him very valuable ecclesiastical preferments."

[66] Cf. "Letter to his Wife," Mitford, ed. *Poematia*, vii: "There is one thing which I have often heard myself charged with; and that is, my neglect of entering into holy orders, and a due preparation for that sacred office. Though I think myself in strictness answerable to none but God and my own conscience, yet for the satisfaction of the person that is dearest to me, I own and declare that the importance of so great a charge, joined with a mistrust of my own sufficiency, made me fearful of undertaking it: if I have not in that capacity assisted in the salvation of souls, I have not been the means of losing any."

[67] *The Gentleman's Magazine*, 17 (December, 1747), 592, lists as among the deaths for the year 1727 "Dec. 2: Mr Vincent Bourne, late usher in Westminster school, author of the ingenious Latin poems, call'd *Poematia*."

[68] On nineteenth-century interest in discovering Bourne's place of burial, cf. *Notes and Queries* 12: October 27 1855, 327, which quotes a query from the *Illustrated London News* (13 October 1855): "Now where was Vincent Bourne buried? What, in December 1747 (when Vinny died), was the neighbouring country churchyard in which Vinny's bones were laid? — in Surrey or in Middlesex? at Camberwell or Kensington? at Hampstead or Hendon? at Wandsworth or Wimbledon? Some of our readers who reside near country churchyards in the neighbourhood of London will

Despite such sparse biographical details, the paradox remains that this lover of silence was one of the most, if not *the* most, popular neo-Latin poet of his day. Indeed if Bourne's initial emergence from silence is attested by the publication history of the *Poematia*, so too is it verified by the comments of later writers, chiefly though not exclusively so by William Cowper and Charles Lamb.

Cowper's comments in regard to Bourne's pedagogical methods (or the lack of such) have already been noted.[69] In 1788 he alludes to Bourne in a letter to Samuel Rose, contrasting "the neatness of his versification" with the slovenliness of his person and his apparent indifference as a teacher in regard to the quality of written exercises produced by his pupils.[70] But Cowper frequently qualifies such remarks by stating that these vices were compensated for by the written word itself.[71] The latter point is particularly pertinent to the purposes of this study and to ways in which Bourne was in fact regarded as excelling both classical and neo-Latin poets. In short, Cowper regards Bourne as a better Latin poet than Tibullus, Propertius or Ausonius. The compliment is a great one:

---

assist us, perhaps, in discovering the grave of a very delightful poet." This was answered by J.R (of Wandsworth) in *Notes and Queries* 12: Nov. 10, 371: "Bourne was buried at Fulham, in Middlesex; and the entry of his interment stands in the books of that parish thus: '1747. Mr Vincent Bourne, 5 December.'" Cf. a contribution by a certain "Oxoniensis" to *Notes and Queries* 3.4 (26 Dec. 1863), 515: "Can any correspondent of 'N & Q' tell me whether the following epitaph, composed by Vincent Bourne himself, is inscribed upon his tombstone? He was buried in 1747 at Fulham, I believe, and not in the cloisters at Westminster: PIETATIS SINCERAE/ SUMMAEQUE HUMILITATIS/NEC DEI USQUAM IMMEMOR/NEC SUI,/IN SILENTIUM QUOD AMAVIT/DESCENDIT/V.B. The epitaph aptly describes the 'secretum iter et fallentis semita vitae,' in which the classic poet and friend of Cowper delighted."

[69] See 7–8 above.

[70] *The Letters and Prose Writings of William Cowper*, III, 233–234: "I shall have great pleasure in taking now and then a peep at my old friend Vincent Bourne, the neatest of all men in his versification, though when I was under his ushership at Westminster, the most slovenly in his person. He was so inattentive to his boys, and so indifferent whether they brought him good or bad exercises, or none at all, that he seem'd determined, as he was the best, so to be the last Latin poet of the Westminster line; a plot which I believe he executed very successfully, for I have not heard of any who has at all deserved to be compared with him" (Letter to Samuel Rose, 30 Nov. 1788).

[71] *The Letters and Prose Writings of William Cowper*, I, 481: "He was so good natur'd and so indolent, that I lost more than I got by him, for he made me as idle as himself. He was such a Sloven, as if he had trusted to his Genius as a cloak for every thing that could disgust you in his person; and indeed in his Writings he has almost made amends for all" (Letter to William Unwin: 23 May 1781).

> I love the Memory of Vinny Bourne. I think him a better Latin poet than
> Tibullus, Propertius, Ausonius, or any of the Writers in his way, except Ovid,
> and not at all inferior to Him.[72]

And Cowper's knowledge and explicit admiration of Bourne's
Latin poetry are attested in several ways: by laudatory references in his
correspondence, by his own translations, and less directly by possible
ways in which his vernacular poetry interacts with Bourne's Latin.[73]
Writing to Joseph Hill on 13 July 1777, Cowper requests the most recent
edition of Bourne's Latin poems.[74] And he takes particular delight in
translating his former schoolmaster's work, announcing that: "[I] shall be
glad of my Translations of Bourne, when you can conveniently restore
them, for I am making a Collection, not for the Public, but for Myself."[75]
Later, in a particularly insightful letter (insightful in terms of the
methodology of translation), he announces: "it is but seldom however,
and never except for my Amusement, that I translate,"[76] and continues:

---

[72] *The Letters and Prose Writings of William Cowper*, I, 481 (Letter to William
Unwin: 23 May 1781). Contrast Landor's negative reaction as summarized by
Mitford, ed. *Poematia*, xxv–xxvi: "Of Bourne's poetical powers, and of the somewhat
exaggerated praise bestowed upon them by Cowper ... Mr W.S. Landor thus
expresses himself: *Novimus quem Tibullo ac Propertio praetulit bonus Cuperus.
Mirum est, perperam, ne dicam stolide iudicavit, Poeta paene inter summos
nominandus. Vinnius autem, ita appellabant eum familiares, nihil admodum habet
suum, et quum aliena quam Latina faceret, frigida est plerumque concinnitatis
affectatio, Propertii contra sincera saltem sunt omnia &c.*"

[73] See Introduction, note 39.

[74] *The Letters and Prose Writings of William Cowper*, I, 272: "If when you are most at
leisure you can find out Baker upon the Microscope, or Vincent Bourne's Latin
Poems the last Edition, and send them, I shall be obliged to you." Cf. I, 273 (Letter to
Joseph Hill: 23 Oct. 1777) as Cowper returns the same: "The Basket contains besides
Bourne's Poems and Baker on the Microscope with thanks."

[75] *The Letters and Prose Writings of William Cowper*, I, 375 (Letter to William
Unwin 6 August 1780). Cf. I, 267: Cowper's Letter to John Newton 25 April 1781:
"To these I would add those copies I translated from Vincent Bourne, but having no
transcript of them myself, I must beg you to take the trouble either to send them
hither, or to get them written out for me. The whole together will amount nearly to a
thousand lines, and as I suppose Mr Johnson will not allot more than one page to one
piece, they will fill more paper than the same number of lines written in continuation
and upon the same Subject."

[76] *The Letters and Prose Writings of William Cowper*, I, 481 (Letter to William
Unwin: 23 May 1781).

> A translator of Bourne would frequently find himself obliged to supply what is called the Turn, which is in fact the most difficult and the most expensive part of the whole Composition, and could not perhaps, in many instances, be done with any tolerable Success.[77]

He praises Bourne as translator, describing his versions of "ballads" as more "beautiful" than their originals, and as surpassing even Ovid and Tibullus:

> The Ballads that Bourne has translated, beautifull in themselves are still more beautifull in his version of them, infinitely surpassing in my judgment, all that Ovid or Tibullus have left behind them. They are quite as elegant, and far more touching and pathetic than the tenderest strokes of either.[78]

Nor was Cowper alone in his admiration of Bourne. Eighteenth-century reviews of Bourne's Latin poetry are glowing in their praise of his "refined taste and elevated genius," the "remarkable felicity" and "classical purity in his language," all of which render him "at the time in which he wrote, the best Latin poet in Europe."[79] The latter is a stunning remark given the proliferation of Latin verse-composition in England and on the continent. Charles Lamb, writing to Wordsworth in 1815, describes as a "treat" the very act of reading Bourne's Latin verse. Highlighting the poet's sensitive depiction of urban scenes,[80] and his

---

[77] *The Letters and Prose Writings of William Cowper*, I, 481 (Letter to William Unwin: 23 May 1781).

[78] *The Letters and Prose Writings of William Cowper*, II, 155 (Letter to William Unwin: 4 August 1783).

[79] Cf. *Critical Review* xxxiii, April 1772, 318, as quoted by Mitford, ed. *Poematia*, xxi–xxii: "Notwithstanding ... the remarkable diffidence of his own abilities, his writings will be an everlasting testimony of his refined taste and elevated genius. There is such a remarkable felicity, such a classical purity in his language, such ease and harmony in his versification, that he was, perhaps, at the time in which he wrote, the best Latin poet in Europe. He has translated some of the most elegant little poems in the English language with admirable grace and delicacy." Cf. Mitford, ed. *Poematia*, xxii–xxiii: "*The Monthly Review* (August 1772, vol. xlvii) gave only the following short note of the same edition: 'These ingenious Latin poems are well known by every schoolboy that can read the *Carmina Quadragesimalia*. There is a peculiar beauty and harmony in the structure of Mr Bourne's versification, and we may say of it, what he says of the river Tweed, in his translation of the famous old song: – *Non, quae subrepens blando interlabitur agros/Flumine, tam suavi Tueda decore nitet.*'"

[80] See chapter 3 passim.

unpretentious manner, he regards his work as an admirable fusion of Latin diction and English sentiment:

> Since I saw you, I have had a treat in the reading way, which comes not every day:—the Latin poems of Vincent Bourne, which were quite new to me. What a heart that man had, all laid out upon town-scenes, a proper counterpart to some people's extravagancies ... what a sweet, unpretending, pretty-mannered, matterfull creature! Sucking from every flower, making a flower of everything. His diction all Latin, and his thoughts all English. Bless him! Latin was not good enough for him; why was he not content with the language which Gay and Prior wrote in? [81]

while Bourne himself is the "most classical, and at the same time most English, of the Latinists."[82] In a further letter to Wordsworth dating to 1815 Lamb promises to "look out" Vincent Bourne for him.[83] And Bourne continued to appeal in a hitherto unnoticed way to a wide range of poets over the "long eighteenth century," several of whom, including Shelley, translated some of his epigrams,[84] and may even have appropriated to a vernacular level aspects of that neo-Latin romanticism peculiar to his verse. And it is a reputation that would last into the nineteenth century.[85] Thus Lord Macaulay in an intriguing discussion of

---

[81] *The Letters of Charles Lamb*, ed. Alfred Ainger (London, 1904), I, 341.

[82] "Well fare the soul of unfastidious Vincent Bourne, most classical, and, at the same time most English, of the Latinists!" (Charles Lamb, "A Complaint of the Decay of Beggars in the Metropolis," *The Essays of Elia* in *The Works of Charles and Mary Lamb*, ed. E.V. Lucas [London, 1903], II, 117). Cf. Mitford, ed. *Poematia*, xxi.

[83] "Dear Wordsworth,—The more I read of your two last volumes, the more I feel it necessary to make my acknowledgments for them in more than one short letter. The 'Night Piece,' to which you refer me, I meant fully to have noticed; but the fact is, I come so fluttering and languid from business, tired with thoughts of it, frightened with fears of it, that when I get a few minutes to sit down and scribble (an action of the hand now seldom natural to me,—I mean voluntary pen-work), I lose all presential memory of what I had intended to say, and say what I can, talk about Vincent Bourne or any casual image, instead of that which I had meditated (by the way, I mast look out V. B. for you)," *The Letters of Charles Lamb*, ed. Ainger, I, 342.

[84] For Shelley's English verse translation of Bourne's epigram *Si Propius Stes, Te Capiet Minus*, see chapter 3, 102.

[85] On Bourne's nineteenth-century reputation, as reflected in favorable comments in *Notes and Queries*, see 11, 13–14 above. See also *Notes and Queries* 1 [16] (16 Feb. 1850), 253 (an English translation of Bourne's *Si Propius Stes*, on which see 102 below); 3 [65] (25 Jan. 1851), 76, on Bourne's translation "Lucy and Colin," which "will always be admired, both in the original and the translation;" 3 [78] (26 April 1851), 324–325, on Bourne's *Ad Davidem Cook*, on which see chapter 3, 80–85; 2.25

the comparative status of classical and neo-Latin literature, begins by defending Boileau's so-called contempt for "modern Latin" as neither "injudicious" nor "peevish" and by highlighting the potential grounds for such criticism in a range of "modern" authors. Noteworthy, however, is his ensuing comment, in which Bourne is viewed (alongside Thomas Gray, no less) as an exception to such criticism:

> But does it follow, because we think thus, that we can find nothing to admire in the noble alcaics of Gray, or in the playful elegiacs of Vincent Bourne? Surely not.[86]

Such praise is augmented by that of Beattie, who comments favorably upon Bourne's Latin translations: "in sweetness of numbers, and elegant expression, they are at least equal to the originals, and scarce inferior to anything in Ovid or Tibullus."[87] Whether as original Latin poet or translator of vernacular works into Latin, Bourne is seen as excelling in his chosen field.

(30 Aug. 1856), 168, in praise of Bourne's translation of "Colin and Lucy": "Your readers are doubtless familiar with the exquisite paraphrase of these lines by Vincent Bourne;" 2 [44] (1 Nov. 1856), 355: "Who does not recall the Latin poems of Vinny Bourne: *Cicindela*, *Cornicula*, and his pupil Cowper's English version of them?"; 4.83 (1 Aug. 1863), 96, in which Bourne as editor of *Musae Anglicanae* is described as "of classic fame;" 5.127 (4 June 1864), 461, which alludes to "the choice Latin of the amiable scholar Vincent Bourne," and 3.58 (6 Feb. 1869), 129, which describes him as "that celebrated Latinist," and proceeds to quote in full his Latin poem *Hobsoni Lex*.

[86] Macaulay, "Life and Writings of Addison," *Critical and Historical Essays* (London, 1877), 741. It is interesting to note that Macaulay proceeds to include the Latin poetry of Joseph Addison (and Boileau's praise of the same) in this category of exceptions: "For these reasons we feel assured that the praise which Boileau bestowed on the *Machinae Gesticulantes* and the *Gerano Pygmaomachia*, was sincere. He certainly opened himself to Addison with a freedom which was a sure indication of esteem." See Haan, *Vergilius Redivivus: Studies in Joseph Addison's Latin Poetry*, 8–9.

[87] Cf. Mitford, ed. *Poematia*, xix–xx: "To this we may add the opinion of Dr Beattie, who, after noticing that Boileau did not know that there were any good poets in England, till Addison made him a present of the *Musae Anglicanae*, remarks that 'Those foreigners must entertain a high opinion of our pastoral poetry who have seen the Latin translations of Vincent Bourne, particularly those of the ballads of Tweed-side, William and Margaret, and Rowe's Despairing beside a clear Stream; of which it is no compliment to say, that in sweetness of numbers, and elegant expression, they are at least equal to the originals, and scarce inferior to anything in Ovid or Tibullus.'"

What is it about Bourne's Latin verse that appealed to early-eighteenth-century and indeed Romantic sensibilities? In what ways did that verse enable him to stand out from both his predecessors and his contemporaries? Was his poetry really, as Storey remarks, neither classical nor imitative?[88] Or does it not interact in an intriguingly complex way with a whole spectrum of classical, neo-Latin and vernacular literature? To what extent did it exert a formative influence upon subsequent authors including Charlotte Smith, William Cowper, Charles Lamb, Thomas Gray, and even William Wordsworth? In the light of such questions Ross Kennedy's observation that Vincent Bourne "merits ... a central place in discussions of *Anglo-Latin* literature"[89] does not seem to go far enough. The present study does not aim to provide a full-scale overview or critique of Bourne's Latin poetry as a whole, nor does it examine his Latin translations of vernacular pieces. Instead it seeks to open up such discussions by examining a selection of his Latin verse[90] in its classical, neo-Latin and vernacular contexts, with particular attention to the theme of identity (and differing forms of identity). Its aim is to initiate the resurrection from silence of an author, for whom eighteenth-century "self-fashioning" (in a reinvention of Greenblatt's use of the term) is achieved by investigating the identity of the self in relation to the other and by foregrounding multiple attempts to fashion other selves.[91] Or to approach this from an essentially postmodern perspective, the establishment of another "Bourne identity," so to speak, may, it is hoped, lead to critical acknowledgement of another "Bourne supremacy."[92]

---

[88] See Introduction, 4.

[89] See *ODNB* s.v. Italics are mine.

[90] For Latin text and English translation of all of Bourne's poems discussed in this study, see my edition in Appendix 1 in this volume. For relevant verse-translations by Cowper and Lamb, see Appendices 2 and 3 in this volume.

[91] See Stephen Greenblatt, *Renaissance Self-Fashioning From More to Shakespeare* (Chicago and London, 1984), passim, and especially 3: "Self-fashioning ... invariably crosses the boundaries between the creation of literary characters, the shaping of one's own identity. The experience of being molded by forces outside one's control, the attempt to fashion other selves."

[92] See note 9 above, and Robert Ludlum's novel *The Bourne Supremacy* (New York, 1986). Cf. the film version, directed by Paul Greengrass, in 2002.

CHAPTER 1

The Quest for Identity: Reflections of the Self

It is something of a paradox that while Bourne expressed contentment in the envisaged silence and anonymity of the grave, his Latin poetry is frequently characterized by the quest for and ultimate recognition of identity. Such themes lie at the heart of four short pieces which treat of mirror-imaging, reflection, mimicry, and assimilation. In so doing they interrogate from the interrelated perspectives of both animal and human the reaction of the self when confronted with an *imago* that is both self and other, and, as will be illustrated, can be manifested on a vocal, visual, aural, and psychosomatic level.

1.1   Echoing the Self: *Canis et Echo*

Bourne's Latin poem on a Dog and Echo (*Canis et Echo*)[1] takes as its subject a mirror-image that cannot quite be understood or assimilated by the self. The piece transcends the apparent simplicity of its theme by presenting an *imago* that can be both vocal and visual. Thus the reflection of the moon on a river's surface is juxtaposed with, and indeed mirrored by, Echo's reiteration (from beneath the same river) of a dog's barking. Both images moreover coalesce in a series of intertextual links with aspects of the Echo and Narcissus myth as delineated by Ovid in *Metamorphoses* 3. 359–510. In this respect this piece, like many of the Latin poems discussed in this study, strikingly contradicts Storey's claim that Bourne's poetry is neither classical nor imitative.[2] For, as argued below, both dog and Echo would seem to mirror, albeit ironically, their Ovidian counterparts of Narcissus and Echo, respectively; on other occasions, however, they exchange roles in a pseudochiasmic fashion whereby each seems to assume characteristics of its Ovidian opposite half. The result is a cross-comparison of sorts, which is reflected quite literally in the structure of the piece, and not least in the use of language whereby

---

[1] *Canis et Echo* was first published in *Poematia* (1734), 133.

[2] See Introduction, 4.

verbal and thematic reminiscences of Ovid are matched by the quasi-narcissistic self-reflexivity of a poem built upon its own internal echoes.

Read on the simplest of levels *Canis et Echo* describes how the moon's reflection on the Thames is noticed by a rather mischievous dog, who responds by barking violently at both the moon in the sky and the moon on the water. The commotion is heard by the sportive nymph Echo, who is lying hidden beneath Thames's waters. Her reaction to the uproar is to determine to avenge this savagery with savagery of her own. Thus she echoes the dog's barking, which in turn becomes more and more intense as her echo replicates it. Eventually, the dog's jaws grow weary, as do his breath and voice. His savagery abates and he falls silent, his anger thereby rendered futile.

Worthy of comparison perhaps is a much neglected Latin poem by Jonathan Swift. Entitled *Fabula Canis et Umbra* and first printed in 1765,[3] this hexameter piece retells the Aesopian fable[4] of how a puppy, carrying food in his mouth, beholds, and is captivated by, a reflection of even better food (*praedae melioris imago* [2]) in a pool.[5] This captivation is depicted in terms of narcissistic wonderment (*dum ... diu ... admiratur* [3]), but the object of such admiration constitutes in fact the puppy's loss, conveyed by Swift in the oxymoronic *speciosa ... damna* (3). As the puppy gapes in awe at the water, the food falls from his mouth to the bottom of the pool, and the reflected image snatches it up (4–5). Eager to recuperate his loss, the puppy greedily attacks the reflection, but in so doing is, like Ovid's Narcissus (*deceptus imagine* [*Met.* 3. 385]) the victim of deception (*occupat ille avidus deceptis faucibus umbram* [6]) as the image deludes him and he bites at mere air (*illudit species, ac dentibus aera mordet* [7]). Swift's puppy, like its Aesopian model,

---

[3] See *The Poems of Jonathan Swift*, ed. Harold Williams (Oxford, 1958), III, 947.

[4] Cf. *Aesop's Fables*, translated by Laura Gibbs (Oxford World's Classics 2002), no. 263: "The Dog, the Meat and the Reflection": "A dog seized some meat from the butcher shop and ran away with it until he came to a river. When the dog was crossing the river, he saw the reflection of the meat in the water, and it seemed much larger than the meat he was carrying. He dropped his own piece of meat in order to try to snatch at the reflection. When the reflection disappeared, the dog went to grab the meat he had dropped but he was not able to find it anywhere, since a passing raven had immediately snatched the meat and gobbled it up. The dog lamented his sorry condition and said, 'Woe is me! I foolishly abandoned what I had in order to grab at a phantom, and thus I ended up losing both that phantom and what I had to begin with.' *This fable is about greedy people who grasp at more than they need.*"

[5] *ore cibum portans catulus dum spectat in undis,/apparet liquido praedae melioris imago* (1–2). All quotations are from *The Poems of Jonathan Swift*, ed. Williams, III, 947.

clearly epitomizes the moral of the *fabula* in question: the dangers of excessive admiration and the deceptive powers of the *imago* itself.

From the outset the dog of Bourne's poem is presented in essentially narcissistic terms, and, more specifically, in ways that seem to interact with Ovid's version of the Echo and Narcissus myth.[6] And in this instance parallels are suggested not merely by the occurrence of Echo as one of the poem's *dramatis personae*, so to speak, but also and especially by a series of verbal, thematic, and methodological "echoes" of Ovid's account.

In *Metamorphoses* 3 the Echo and Narcissus myth is narrated by the seer Tiresias, who begins by explaining the punishment imposed by Juno upon Echo. Realizing that Echo was in the habit of detaining her with garrulous chatter while Jupiter was philandering with nymphs on the mountainside, Juno decides to punish her by threatening to curtail the power of the tongue that had tricked her, and by allowing Echo to possess only the briefest use of her voice. It is a threat that the goddess ruthlessly carries out.[7] The practical consequences of this are that Echo can repeat only the last part of any sentence she hears, resulting in her "echoing" that particular section.[8] One day, however, the nymph catches sight of Narcissus, and falls in love with him. When he calls out, all she can do is echo the end of his sentences, and a series of confusions ensues. In short, Narcissus is deceived by what he thinks is someone else's voice, and when Echo eventually emerges from the woods to embrace him, he flees. Thus spurned, Echo hides herself in the woods, and wastes away, until

---

[6] For vernacular examples of the reworking of the myth, see in particular Eve's gazing into the Edenic lake in Milton, *Paradise Lost* 4. 449–491; Andrew Marvell, "To his Coy Mistress," on which see R.H. Ray, "Marvell's 'To His Coy Mistress' and Sandys's translation of Ovid's *Metamorphoses*," *Review of English Studies*, 44 (1993), 386–389, who argues that the poem's speaker corresponds to Echo, while the "coy mistress" reflects (via Sandys's translation) aspects of Ovid's Narcissus. For further examples in vernacular literature, see among others D.J. Palmer, "*Twelfth Night* and the Myth of Echo and Narcissus," *Shakespeare Survey* 32 (1979), 73–78; A.T. Harrison, "Echo and her Medieval Sisters," *The Centennial Review* 26.4 (1982), 324–340; Gina Bloom, "Localising Disembodied Voice In Sandys's 'Narcissus and Echo'" in G.V. Stanivukovic, ed. *Ovid and the Renaissance Body* (University of Toronto, 2001), 129–154; Jeffrey Berman, *Narcissism and the Novel* (New York, 1990); Lieve Spaas and Trista Selous, eds. *Echoes of Narcissus* (New York, 2000). For the interpretation of the myth by psychoanalytical theorists and others, see Herbert Marks, "Echo and Narcissism," *University of Toronto Quarterly* 51.3 (1992), 334–354.

[7] "*huius*" ait "*linguae, qua sum delusa, potestas/parva tibi dabitur vocisque brevissimus usus,*"/*reque minas firmat* (*Met.* 3.366–368).

[8] *tantum haec in fine loquendi/ingeminat voces auditaque verba reportat* (368–369).

there is nothing left but her echoing voice. Another love victim likewise spurned by Narcissus prays that the gods will bring vengeance upon him. One day Narcissus sees a clear pool with its silvery waters. Exhausted from hunting and the heat, he seeks to quench his thirst, when suddenly he is enchanted by the beautiful image that he sees. Thus does he fall in love with an insubstantial *imago*. Mistaking his own reflection for a real person, he gazes in admiration, but his love is not reciprocated. Then as he utters a lengthy love lament, he disturbs the waters with his tears. Seeing the image blurring and his passion unrequited, he gradually wastes away with love, as his complexion and strength fade. Echo, while pitying his long lamentation, can do nothing more than reiterate his pathetic "alas." And so Narcissus dies on the river bank, transformed into a soul that even in the underworld can only gaze upon his own reflection in the waters of the Styx.

The themes of echoing and mirroring that lie at the heart of Ovid's lines are cleverly reflected in linguistic and syntactical repetition. Thus at various points in the myth Ovid captures linguistically the very substance of Echo's reiteration: Narcissus's *"ecquis adest"* (380) is met by Echo's *"adest"* (380); his *"huc coeamus"* (386) by her *"coeamus"* (387); his *"ante ... emoriar quam sit tibi copia nostri"* (391) by her *"sit tibi copia nostri"* (392), and so on.[9] This is replicated syntactically also through balanced repetition, in, for example, the descriptions of Echo (*natura repugnat/nec sinit, incipiat, sed, quod sinit ...* [376–377]; *vocat illa vocantem* [382]) and of Narcissus (*qui probat, ipse probatur* [425]); *dumque petit, petitur* [426]).

---

[9] Something of the same mirroring effect achieved by syntactical repetition is evident in a neo-Latin poem entitled *Echo* by Antonius Tebaldeius Ferrariensis: *dic Echo, quid vult, ut semper vivam ego moestus?/aestus: non facit hoc spes moriens? oriens/mene urit facies: acies, aciesque favilla?/illa; diu miserum me fore reris? eris* (1–4). Text is that of *Carmina Illustrium Poetarum Italorum*, ed. G.G. Bottari (Florence, 1719–1726), 9, 239. Cf. Milton's depiction of Eve's account of her self-reflection in Eden at *Paradise Lost* 4.460–464: "As I *bent* down *to look*, just opposite,/A shape within the watery gleam appear'd/*Bending to look* on me, I started back, but *pleas'd I soon returnd,/Pleas'd it returnd as soon* ...." Italics are mine. It is noteworthy that in Milton, this visual echoing pattern is followed by vocal echoing: "What thou seest,/What there thou seest fair Creature is thy self" (*Paradise Lost* 4. 467–468). Ultimately, however, the self-reflection seen and admired by Eve is displaced by the image of Adam himself, who in turn functions as a Narcissus figure, with Eve as his visual *imago*: "he/Whose image thou art" (*Paradise Lost* 4. 471–472). From Eve's point of view Adam is "less fair,/Lest winning soft, less amiable mild,/Than that smooth watry image" (*Paradise Lost* 4. 478–480). Cf. also Pope's reworking of the Miltonic episode at *Rape of the Lock* 1.125–126: "A heav'nly Image in the Glass appears,/To that she bends, to that her Eyes she rears."

It should be remarked at the outset that in terms of its linguistic methodology Bourne's poem mirrors on a microcosmic level that "echoing" device so central to Ovid's treatment. This is achieved through a series of internal echoes effected by the repetition or juxtaposition of nouns (*lunamque ... lunamque* [5]; *rabie rabiem* [9]; *latratus ... latratibus* [13], adjectives (*parque referre pari* [10]), and verbs (*audiit et .../audiit et* [8–9]). At the same time Bourne reworks and develops the Ovidian myth itself into something quite new.

Where Ovid's tale is located in a remote Aonian past, and upon the river banks of an essentially sylvan setting, Bourne transposes the whole from country to city: more precisely to eighteenth-century London[10] and the banks of the river Thames. Whereas in Ovid the spurned Echo lay hidden in the woods (*spreta latet silvis* [393]), here she hides beneath those very London waters (*sub ripis latuit ... ultoribus Echo* [7]). Most obvious, of course, is the substitution of a dog for the Ovidian Narcissus, a dog, however, whose personified behavior echoes with comic irony that of Narcissus himself.[11] Furthermore, the self-reflection as observed by the latter in a pool is now transmuted into the *imago* of a moon, which, as noted below, elicits an altogether different reaction from its beholder.[12]

Central to Ovid's version of the myth is the contrast between the substantial and the insubstantial, and the emphasis upon the futile attempts to grasp the incorporeal on both a literal and figurative level. Echo is initially depicted as an essentially corporeal being. Thus, according to Tiresias, in those early stages she still had a body, and was not a mere voice (359).[13] And even when she falls in love with Narcissus,

---

[10] On the role of London in Bourne's Latin poetry, see chapter 3 in this volume.

[11] The substitution of an animal for the Ovidian Narcissus likewise occurs in a contribution to *The Gentleman's Magazine* 15 (August, 1745), 439. Entitled "The Lyon and the Echo," this anonymous poem (dated Dublin, 15 August 1745) may even look back to Bourne's treatment. The piece describes how a lion's growl is echoed by Echo herself: "As o'er his wide domains he prowl'd,/And in pursuit of booty growl'd,/An echo from a distant cave/Re-growl'd, articulately grave." (9–12). Like Narcissus, the lion investigates the source of such mimicry; as in Ovid, his words are answered by an echo that cannot fully articulate them: "Whose voice is that which growls at mine?/(His highness ask'd) says echo—mine!" (17–18); "Know I'm a lyon, hear and tremble,/Reply'd the king—cry'd echo, tremble!" (21–22). The whole leads to a series of comic misunderstandings "Come forth (says lyon) shew thy self;/Laconic Echo answer'd—Elf/Elf durst thou call me, vile pretender!/Echo as loud reply'd—pretender!" (23–26). The piece concludes with a fox offering the lion a rational explanation for the echo.

[12] See 27–28 in this chapter.

[13] *corpus adhuc Echo, non vox erat* (359).

her passion is described in tangibly physical terms—as a flame consumes her body (371).[14] However, this is offset by the intangible, for when at last she seeks that longed-for physical embrace (389),[15] the object of her very real passion eludes her in flight. This intangibility, this incorporeality, are mirrored in turn by her own fading into physical nothingness, the gradual stages of which are described in graphic terms: she becomes thin (396),[16] wrinkled, and wasted (397–398);[17] then only her bones and voice survive (398);[18] eventually all that remains is her voice (*vox manet* [399]), her bones allegedly transformed into stone.

But if Echo epitomizes a tension between the physically real and the insubstantial, and the dissolution (rather than the resolution) of the former, it is a tension that is replicated in the language and behavior of Narcissus himself, who is both tangible and intangible, both a self and an *imago*, or, to put it another way, *both* Narcissus and Echo. Ironically it is as a consequence of Narcissus's very real physical exhaustion from hunting and the heat (413),[19] and a basic corporeal need to quench his thirst that the whole *imago* episode is set in motion. Narcissus's mistake, however, is to regard (quite literally) the incorporeal as corporeal (417).[20] This ultimately results in a futile attempt to kiss a deceptive pool (427),[21] to plunge his arms into its waters, and to clasp the neck of the beloved image (428–429).[22] What is evident here is that Narcissus's very actions are in themselves reflective of Echo's behavior (*ut iniceret sperato bracchia collo* [389]). Likewise Ovid's rhetorical question aimed at Narcissus and his vain attempt to capture what flees (*Quid frustra simulacra fugacia captas?* [432]) assumes additional poignancy when it is remembered that Narcissus had asked the mysterious Echo "*quid ...*/me

---

[14] *vidit et incaluit* (371). Cf. *flamma propiore calescit* (372).

[15] *ut iniceret sperato bracchia collo* (389).

[16] *extenuant vigiles corpus miserabile curae* (396).

[17] *adducitque cutem macies et in aera sucus/corporis omnis abit* (397–398).

[18] *vox tantum atque ossa supersunt* (398).

[19] *et studio venandi lassus et aestu* (413).

[20] *spem sine corpore amat, corpus putat esse, quod umbra est* (417).

[21] *fallaci ... dedit oscula fonti* (427).

[22] *in mediis ... visum captantia collum/bracchia mersit aquis* (428–429).

fugis?" (383–384),[23] and later had himself fled from her (*ille fugit fugiensque* [390]). And just as Echo wasted away gradually, so too is Narcissus *attenuatus amore* (489), as he is gradually consumed by a hidden fire (490),[24] loses his complexion, his *vigor et vires* (492),[25] and in a way mirrors the eventual incorporeality of Echo herself (*nec corpus remanet* [493]). In a sense then Ovid's Narcissus is echoing Echo.

Such tensions between the corporeal and the incorporeal and between inter-echoing characters, so to speak, likewise underlie Bourne's piece. These are ironically heightened by a series of parallels and contrasts between the two episodes in question. For example, the "silver" pool (*fons ... argenteus* [407]) in which Narcissus beheld his reflection is transmuted by Bourne into the "silver" moon (*argentea luna* [1]), which now comes to constitute the reflection itself (*in Tamisis tremula luce refulsit aquis* [2]) as the moon in the sky (*lunamque in coelo* [5]) is also the moon in the water (*lunamque ... in undis* [5]).[26] Juxtaposed with the motif of reflection in Bourne is the personification of the dog, whose reaction to the reflection is described in physical terms, as he *solvit ... ora proterva* (4) and launches an attack (*aggressus* [5]), raging against "both planets" (*in sidus pariter saevus utrumque furit* [6]). The latter phrase assumes particular force when seen as a possible inversion of Narcissus's wonderment as he gazes in the pool upon the "twin stars," which are his own eyes (*spectat humi positus geminum, sua lumina, sidus* [420]). Later the dog is overcome by *rabies* (9) and is unable to control his anger (*irarum impatiens* [12]). But countering the seeming physicality of the dog's aggression is the insubstantial nature of the very threats he utters—at least those threats as heard and replicated by Echo herself (*audiit et vanas ludicra nympha minas* [8]). While *vanas* encapsulates the futility of

---

[23] Cf. Adam to Eve at *Paradise Lost* 4.482: "Whom fli'st thou? Whom thou fli'st, of him thou art."

[24] *et tecto paulatim carpitur igni* (490).

[25] Of course this sees its culmination in the depiction of Narcissus as a ghost in the underworld yet still gazing at his reflection in the waters of the Styx (*se.../in Stygia spectabat aqua* [504–505]).

[26] On the parallelism between sky and water in the context of the latter as providing a mirrored reflection of the former, cf. Eve's comment at *Paradise Lost* 4. 456–459: "I thither went/With unexperienc't thought, and laid me downe/On the green bank, to look into the clear/Smooth lake, that to me seemd another Skie." Cf. also Thomas Traherne, "Shadows in the Water," 44–48: "'tis a world indeed,/Where skies beneath us shine,/And Earth by art divine/Another face presents below,/Where people's feet against ours go."

the dog's actions, it also hints at the theme of incorporeality. In this regard the dog's empty threats function as the direct antithesis of Juno's threats against Echo in Ovid, which far from being *vanae*, were fully realized and effected by the angry goddess (*reque minas firmat* [368]).[27] And now the moon's reflection is in a sense usurped by the echo of the dog's own "reverberating voice," as visual *imago* becomes vocal (*ille repercussae deceptus imagine vocis* [11]). The line seems to fuse two aspects of Ovid's description. On the one hand, it recalls the deception experienced by Narcissus upon hearing the vocal *imago* for the first time (*alternae deceptus imagine vocis* [385]);[28] on the other hand, it is also reminiscent of the poet's authorial intervention at line 434, rebuking Narcissus's misconception in regard to his own visual *imago* (*ista repercussae, quam cernis, imaginis umbra est.*) And at the same time Echo herself matches the dog's madness, highlighted by the juxtaposition of *rabie rabiem* (9) as the *lepidissima* Nymph becomes the *vindex*. It is almost as though Echo has become a second Juno figure punishing a victim for her/his chattering (*garrula* [360]) loquacity, except that now the barking dog has ironically been substituted for Echo herself. And more than that. This dog as a second Echo will ultimately become a silenced Echo, dispossessed of his *vox* (15) as by the end of the poem *siletque canis* (16). As if to reinforce these constantly shifting equations the poem's final lines in their mock-heroic description of the dog's eventual weariness (*lassatae fauces* [15]),[29] and his loss of both *spiritus* (15) and *vox* (15) convey something of that gradual enervation and emasculation of both Echo and Narcissus through love and loss, with the underlying subtext perhaps of a dog's exhausted *spiritus* epitomizing and mirroring the physical draining (in Ovid) of life itself.[30]

The theme of mirror-imaging unites three of Bourne's other Latin poems, namely, *Idem Agit Idem*, *Simile Agit in Simile*, and *Agens et Patiens Sunt Simul*. That these are variations upon a single theme is suggested not only by the comparative similarity in terms of their respective headings, but also by the fact that the pieces were grouped

---

[27] Indeed the dog's savagery and relentless anger are quite reminiscent of the behavior of Juno (toward Echo) in the Ovidian extract.

[28] Cf. (of Narcissus) *visae correptus imagine formae* (416); (of Narcissus) *oculos idem, qui decipit, incitat error* (431).

[29] Cf. (of Narcissus) *et studio venandi lassus et aestu* (413).

[30] On *spiritus* as life, consciousness, cf. *OLD* 3 b, and, for example, Virgil, *Aeneid* 4. 336: *dum spiritus hos regit artus*.

together in the 1734 edition of Bourne's poetry.[31] Individually, however, the pieces treat of reciprocal reflection in ways that are very different, as the *imago* comes to operate on visual, aural, and psychosomatic levels.

1.2 Mirroring the Self: *Idem Agit Idem*

Bourne's short elegiac poem *Idem Agit Idem* seems to move beyond similar pieces included in the *Lusus Westmonasterienses* under the general heading *Idem cum duo faciunt non est idem.*[32] Indeed Bourne, in an apparent inversion of the theme in question, conveys the complexity of emotions and behavior that may ensue when the self comes face to face with the other, and also, and especially, when the other mirrors the self. The basic *argumentum* of the poem can be summarized as follows: a playful kitten frisks and dances before its mistress's mirror,[33] only to see a kitten behaving in an identical fashion.[34] The piece conveys a sense of wonderment as a black kitten sees a black kitten reflected:[35] the two-toned snout confronting its equivalent;[36] the grey-eyed gaze matched by the same.[37] And it depicts the variety of emotions that ensue as the kitten reacts to that mirror-image, so to speak: its curving tale and gentle movement of its paw inviting its potential playmate to sportive fun and abandonment;[38] then by contrast its provocative summons to a fight as its claws are unfolded, its back arches into a curve, and wrath is spewed

---

[31] *Idem Agit Idem* (*Poematia*, 1734, 112); *Simile Agit in Simile* (*Poematia*, 1734, 113); *Agens et Patiens Sunt Simul* (*Poematia*, 1734, 114).

[32] See *Lusus Westmonasterienses*, 49: *Idem cum duo faciunt non est idem.* The poem is as follows: *causam agit agrestis sic coram iudice, vaccam/bos meus occidit, vir venerande, tuam./iratus iudex, dabitur mihi pro bove taurus./occidit vaccam bos tuus, erro, meam./currat lex igitur. iudex venerandus, at ipse/erravi, dixit; lex vetat hoc fieri.*

[33] *felicula ad speculum saltu lascivit erile* (1).

[34] *lascivam saltu feliculamque videt* (2).

[35] *nigra videt nigram* (3).

[36] *bicolor naso, bicolorem* (3).

[37] *glaucaque torquentem lumina, glauca tuens* (4).

[38] *et sociam ad lusus lentae incurvamine caudae/provocat et lepidi mobilitate pedis* (5–6).

forth,[39] all of which actions are replicated by its mirror-image.[40] Then
from playfulness and anger the emotion changes to one of intense
curiosity as the kitten actively investigates the source of such mimicry:[41]
perhaps the reflected kitten exists inside or behind the mirror,[42] and yet its
reflection (*imago*) investigates precisely the same phenomenon.[43] The
poem concludes in a couplet that provides a summary of the whole: each
kitten investigates and deludes the other; in short, two kittens perform the
action of one.[44]

Like *Canis et Echo*, superficial simplicity belies the poem's
complex subject matter. In this instance the poet interrogates from a
number of perspectives animal behavior upon a face-to-face encounter,
whereby, in the words of Levinas, "the identity of the I envelops the
alterity of the object."[45] And this is encapsulated by the poem's language
and syntax, which mirror the very mirroring that lies at its core. The
parallel behavior of kitten and *imago* is reflected in the linguistic and
syntactical movement of the elegiacs themselves, and especially in the
careful use of rhetorical balance, repetition, and wordplay. This manifests
itself in a series of paired or repeated phrases: *saltu* (1) ... *saltu* (2);
lascivit (1) ... *lascivam* (2); *felicula* (1) ... *feliculam* (2); *nigra videt
nigram* (3); *bicolor naso, bicolorem* (3); *glauca ... glauca* (4); *utra
utramque, ... utraque ... utramque* (7); *iam tumet* (9) ... *et tumet* (10);
simulated anger: *et simulatas exspuit iras* (9) with the reciprocally
punning *similes exspuit ... minas* (10); *mima ... mimica* (11); *in
speculo ... speculumne* (12); *praesentem praesens* (13); with line 12
repeated virtually verbatim in line 14; *alterutra alterutram* (15); *facitis
quod facis* (16).

---

[39] *utraque utramque lacessit et utraque palpat utramque,/et molle oppositos explicat
unguiculos./iam tumet in tergum et simulatas exspuit iras* (7–9).

[40] *et tumet et similes exspuit umbra minas* (10).

[41] *quaenam haec sit, mima unde sui tam mimica quaerit* (11).

[42] *te quoque, praesentem praesens quam quaeris et illa/quaerit an in speculo post
speculumne sies* (13–14).

[43] *... an in speculo post speculumne sies.* (14)

[44] *alterutra alterutram quaeritque et decipit; idque/feliculae facitis quod facis una
duae* (15–16).

[45] Emmanuel Levinas, *Totality and Infinity*, trans. Alphonso Lingis (1969), 194–202,
in Philip Rice and Patricia Waugh, eds. *Modern Literary Theory: A Reader* (London,
2002), 422–429, at 422.

Reciprocal reflections then are central to the poem's very language as language becomes its own mirror, so to speak. In this respect the cat's behavior and experience would seem to run contrary to the comments of Shuger (vis-à-vis the methodology of Shakespearean mirroring [46] in Sonnet 24): "The presence of both subject and object is challenged by the reciprocal reflections that mark acts of social exchange." [47] On the contrary, it is through such linguistic parallelism that the other (the *imago* or mirror-image) serves to reaffirm rather than to negate the I. Assuming a Lacanian perspective, one might argue that for Bourne's kitten "the mirror-image would seem to be the threshold of the visible world," [48] especially as the very function of the *imago* is "to establish a relation between the organism and its reality." [49] True as this may be, the subject nonetheless sees the self as other, yet it is an "other" that manages to retain something of its own absolutism: "The fact that the face maintains a relation with me by discourse does not range him in the same; he remains absolute within the relation." [50] Moreover that level of indeterminacy, which characterizes the poem's conclusion (after all, the kitten, rather like the dog in *Canis et Echo*, seeks to know yet fails to understand the nature of the *imago*), [51] is facilitated by a Levinasian reading: "What we call the face is precisely this exceptional presentation of self by self." [52] Is it not the case that this particular self—a kitten—is

---

[46] For an excellent discussion of the mirror as motif and methodology in Shakespeare, see Philippa Kelly, "Surpassing Glass: Shakespeare's Mirrors," *Early Modern Literary Studies* 8.1 (May 2002), 2, 1–32. See also Sabine Melchior-Bonnet, *The Mirror: A History*, trans. K.H. Jewitt (New York: Routledge, 2001), 112–113.

[47] Cf. Deborah Shuger, "The 'I' of the Beholder: Renaissance Mirrors and the Reflexive Mind," *Renaissance Culture and the Everyday*, eds. Patricia Fumerton and Simon Hunt (Philadelphia, 1999), 19–36, at 26.

[48] Jacques Lacan, "The Mirror Stage as Formative of the Function of the I as Revealed in Psychoanalytic Experience," *Ecrits, A Selection* (1949), trans. Alan Sheridan, 1–7 as anthologized in *Modern Literary Theory*, 189–195, at 191.

[49] Lacan, "The Mirror Stage," *Modern Litarary Theory*, 192.

[50] Levinas, "Totality and Infinity," *Modern Literary Theory*, 423.

[51] Contrast a fable by Florian on the same theme, in which the cat examines both sides of the glass in an effort to find the other cat, after which he settles back quite satisfied: "Que m'importe, dit-il, de percer ce mystère?/Une chose que notre esprit,/Après un long travail, n'entend ni ne saisit,/Ne nous est jamais nécessaire." Text is that of *Fables de Florian* (Paris, 1846), 27–28, at 28.

[52] Levinas, "Totality and Infinity," *Modern Literary Theory*, 428.

enabled to coexist with the other without detracting from the *imago*'s alterity? In this face-to-face encounter the other, through *not* being fully comprehended and hence not incorporated into the same, is left to some degree with its otherness intact.[53]

In presenting a kitten as its subject, Bourne's piece takes its place within a miniature genre of cat poems—a genre most fully represented, however, by a body of vernacular[54] rather than neo-Latin poetry.[55] Perhaps the most striking example is *Lagrime in Morte di Un Gatto*, a multilingual collection of eulogies on a dead cat, commissioned and compiled by Domenico Balestieri and published at Milan in 1741, although long since passed into oblivion.[56] And it is a subject that has continued to inspire poets through the ages. Among more modern examples are of course T.S. Eliot's, *Old Possum's Book of Practical Cats*, or Chase Twichell's "Cat and Mirror," which merits quotation if only to show a methodological simplicity that is very dissimilar to Bourne's more complex treatment:

> I'd like to turn my eyes
> on the mirror's hard water

---

[53] Cf. another mirror poem at *Lusus Westmonasterienses*, 11. Entitled *Caecus Amor Sui Est*, this piece depicts an old woman Lais, who looks in the mirror for several hours but fails to see an old woman in the mirror. Quite the contrary, she is unable to see a single grey hair on her whole head nor a wrinkle on her brow. Whether the mirror is true or lying, she loves her reflection: *Lais anus speculum per longas consulit horas,/nec tamen in speculo Laida cernit anum./nec capite in toto canum reperire capillum,/nec rugam in tota fronte videre potest./seu verum est speculum, quod amanti ostendit amatam,/seu speculum est mendax, Laida Lais amat.*

[54] For a general survey of representations of the cat in literature, see Carl Van Vechten, *The Tiger in the House* (New York, 1922), chapter 11: "The Cat and the Poet." This albeit cursory analysis usefully lists allusions to the cat in Goldsmith, Herrick, Skelton, Chaucer, Shakespeare, Gay, Gray, Cowper, Prior, Wordsworth et al.

[55] The cat does occur as a theme in the *Lusus Westmonasterienses*, although the poem in question discusses such commonplaces as the nine lives possessed by the creature. Cf. *Lusus Westmonasterienses*, 19: *Blandior indulsit, felis, tibi Parca, novena/nam tibi net Lachesis fila novena colo./hinc, si missa voles celsi de culmine tecti,/volveris in tutos praecipitata pedes./nec, miseram licet infestent laniique, canesque,/te lanii exanimant, exanimantve canes./si moriare semel, si bis, si terve quaterve,/plus quam dimidia parte superstes eris.*

[56] Domenico Balestieri, *Lagrime in Morte di un Gatto* (Milan, 1741) (which became known as *La Gatteide*). This collection, running to no fewer than 285 pages, perpetuates the memory of a single cat.

> and not see myself,
> not know myself to be me.
> My young brown tiger-cat can do it —
>
> he sniffs a little smear
> where someone touched the glass,
> happy to be on the bureau, so high up.
> From there he can survey the entire
> kingdom of the moment and rule it.[57]

Turning to our "kingdom of the moment," that of eighteenth-century England, it might be wondered whether the recurrence of the theme in the work of Bourne's pupil and admirer, William Cowper, is more than a coincidence.[58] Cowper's animal fable "The Retired Cat" depicts the dilemma of a subject who seems to possess something of that appealing inquisitiveness (*quaerit*) of Bourne's equivalent:

> A poet's Cat, sedate and grave,
> As poet well could wish to have,
> Was much addicted to inquire
> For nooks, to which she might retire,
> And where, secure as mouse in chink,
> She might repose, or sit and think. (1–6)[59]

Like Bourne's kitten, this cat is depicted in essentially human terms, and as experiencing a variety of conflicting emotions. Possessed by a "love of change," (21) which "cats also feel, as well as we" (23), and in search of "some place of more serene repose" (30), she seeks to find rest and protection from the cold in a half-opened drawer "within her master's snug abode" (34). However, the chambermaid inadvertently closes the drawer, trapping the sleeping cat inside. Roused by the shock, the cat, now given a voice, laments her unfortunate fate. The hours pass by—sunset, evening, night—until her scratching is heard by "the poet" (77), who comes looking for her, and after much searching, eventually finds and rescues her. As a consequence the cat's self-conceit turns into quiet contentment:

---

[57] Text is that of Chase Twichell, *The Snow Watcher* (Princeton, 1998), 15: "Cat and Mirror."

[58] On literary parallels between Bourne and Cowper, see chapter 1, 41; chapter 2, 57, 68, 70; chapter 3, 102 and 103. For Cowper's translations of Bourne, see Appendix 2 in this volume.

[59] Text is that of *Cowper: Poetical Works*, ed. H.S. Milford (Oxford, 1971), 407–409.

> Forth skipp'd the cat; not now replete
> As erst with airy self-conceit,
> Nor in her own fond apprehension
> A theme for all the world's attention,
> But modest, sober, cur'd of all
> Her notions hyperbolical,
> And wishing for a place of rest
> Anything rather than a chest. (99–106)

The whole comes to function for the poet as a fable demonstrating the folly of self-importance.[60] Unlike Bourne's poem, this piece ends with neat resolution. It is possible that the manifold feline emotions conveyed in Cowper's poem owe something to Bourne's depiction of a kitten that can be both playful and angry; both inquisitive and subject to an ultimate deception. Worthy of comparison also are Cowper's remarks in a letter of 1787 addressed to Lady Hesketh, as he describes the playful behavior of a kitten in his possession. As in Bourne's poem, this is a playfulness that is only transient:

> I have a kitten my Dear, the drollest of all creatures that ever wore a Cat-skin. Her gambols are not to be described, and would be incredible if they could. She tumbles head over heels several times together, she lays her cheek to the ground and presents her rump at you with an air of most supreme disdain, from this posture she rises to dance upon her hind feet, an exercise that she performs with all the grace imaginable. ... In point of size she is likely to be a kitten always, being extremely small of her age, but time I suppose, that spoils every thing, will make her also a Cat. You will see her I hope, before that melancholy period shall arrive, for no wisdom that she may gain by experience and reflection hereafter, will ever compensate the loss of her present hilarity. She is dress'd in a tortoise-shell suit, and I know that you will delight in her.[61]

But perhaps the most famous eighteenth-century cat poem is the mock-heroic "Ode on the Death of a Favourite Cat, Drowned in a Tub of Gold Fishes" by Thomas Gray, himself a highly accomplished neo-Latin poet.[62] Composed in 1747 (i.e., just thirteen years subsequent to the

---

[60] "Then stept the poet into bed,/With this reflexion in his head:/Beware of too sublime a sense/Of your own worth and consequence!/The man who dreams himself so great,/And his importance of such weight,/That all around in all that's done/Must move and act for him alone,/Will learn in school of tribulation/The folly of his expectation" (107–116).

[61] *The Letters and Prose Writings of William Cowper*, III, 51 (Letter to Lady Hesketh [10 Nov. 1787]).

[62] See Haan, *Thomas Gray's Latin Poetry*, passim, and Introduction, 18 in this volume.

publication of *Idem Agit Idem* in Bourne's *Poematia* [1734]) Gray's poem bears a number of hitherto unnoticed resemblances to Bourne's piece, not least in providing, as Edgecombe has noted, "a cat's-eye view of the landscape."[63] Like Bourne, Gray treats to some degree of mirror-imaging as his cat in quasi-narcissistic fashion gazes at its reflection, but the mirror of Bourne's poem has become the surface or "lake" of water in a goldfish bowl:

> 'Twas on a lofty vase's side,
> Where China's gayest art had dyed
> The azure flowers, that blow;
> Demurest of the tabby kind,
> The pensive Selima reclined,
> Gazed on the lake below. (1–6)[64]

In both, the cat, gazing upon its *imago*, surveys with wonder individual parts of its own reflected anatomy, an anatomy that is in fact two-toned. Bourne's cat is black (*nigra videt nigram* [3]), but has a two-toned snout (*bicolor naso* [3]); Gray's has a white face "fair round face" (8) with "snowy beard" (8), black ears ("ears of jet" [11]) and a "coat that with the tortoise vies" (10). Bourne's cat possesses grey eyes (*glaucaque torquentem lumina* [4]) while Gray's has "emerald eyes" (11). Both pieces convey in a gradual crescendo the complexity of emotions experienced by the cat. The initial emotion is one of pleasure, as is reflected in the curving of the tail (*lentae incurvamine caudae* [5]; "her conscious tail her joy declared" (7),[65] "she saw: and purred applause" [12]). Gray's emphatic "she saw"[66] mirrors Bourne's *videt* (2; 3). This leads ultimately to curiosity (*quaerit* [11]) in Bourne and to wonderment

---

[63] Cf. Rodney Edgecombe, "A Reading of Gray's 'Ode on the death of a Favourite Cat, Drowned in a Tub of Gold Fishes,'" *English Studies in Africa* 26.2 (1983), 99–104, at 99.

[64] Text is that of Roger Lonsdale, ed. *The Poems of Thomas Gray, William Collins, Oliver Goldsmith* (London and New York, 1992).

[65] Cf. Edgecombe, "A Reading of Gray's 'Ode on the death of a Favourite Cat,'" 100: "By placing 'tail' in the nominative case, and by foregrounding the direct object so as to make possible their collation, the poet suggests the continuity between the consciousness of the tail and the emotion it registers."

[66] On the emphatic effect of Gray's verb, cf. Edgecombe, "A Reading of Gray's 'Ode on the death of a Favourite Cat,'" 100, who notes: "all the substantives are governed by the verb 'saw,' the mirror image superbly realized in the reflective inversion of the syntax, and by the masterly transition from the shadowed eyes to the verb of perception."

in Gray "the hapless nymph with wonder saw:/A whisker first and then a claw" [19–20]), a wonderment that will of course prove fatal as "With many an ardent wish/She stretched in vain to reach the prize" [21–22]), resulting in her tumbling in and drowning in the goldfish bowl. As in Bourne, the cat's actions mirror her mental reasoning.[67]

Ultimately Gray's poem moves far beyond Bourne's in its mock-heroic satire and in its personification of the cat as an overly vain female. This is conveyed through intertextual links with a range of literary females: 1) Camilla, Virgil's doomed warrior huntress, whose death in *Aeneid* 11 was the consequence of her pursuit of golden spoil;[68] 2) Eve, whose quasi-narcissistic gaze into an Edenic lake is described by Milton in *Paradise Lost* 4;[69] 3) Belinda, the heroine of Pope's *Rape of the Lock* (1712), whose performative self-gazing adumbrates aspects of both the Virgilian[70] and Miltonic passages.[71] In all of this the cat is equated with the feminine. Or, in the words of Edgecombe: "Selima is *both* a female and a cat."[72] Frequently the equation is made explicit: "hapless nymph" (19), "female heart" (23), "presumptuous maid!" (25), as the poem becomes an eighteenth-century Aesopian fable of sorts on the folly of female vanity,[73] typical of the fable genre in its "lightly moralistic application of the story to humanity."[74] Thus by application the "lake" or the surface of water in a goldfish bowl becomes perhaps two types of symbolic mirror: the mirror into which such an eighteenth-century

---

[67] Cf. D.B. George, "An Etymological Reading of Thomas Gray's 'Ode on the Death of a Favourite Cat,'" *Classical Journal* 82.4 (1987), 329–330, at 330: "... For the last time her body mirrors her mind. Her looks which have been reaching for the fish ('looks intent'; *in-* to or toward, *tent-* to stretch) are transformed into a literal physical action: 'Again she stretch'd, again she bent.'"

[68] See in particular *Aeneid* 11. 768–782; 801–806.

[69] See *Paradise Lost* 4.460–464, quoted at 24 in this chapter.

[70] See, for example, *Rape of the Lock* 1. 132: "And decks the Goddess with the glitt'ring Spoil." Cf. *Rape of the Lock* 2. 19–22.

[71] See in particular *Rape of the Lock* 1.125–126: "A heav'nly Image in the Glass appears,/To that she bends, to that her Eyes she rears."

[72] Edgecombe, "A Reading of Gray's 'Ode on the death of a Favourite Cat,'" 102.

[73] Edgecombe, "A Reading of Gray's 'Ode on the death of a Favourite Cat,'" 103, interestingly views the "fabular conclusion of the poem" as "Cowperish in tone."

[74] Roger Lonsdale ed., *Gray, Collins and Goldsmith: The Complete Poems*, 80.

gentlewoman as Belinda and her equivalents ("ye beauties" [37]) might gaze, and the looking glass of temptation that might befall the "wandering eyes" (40) of the female self in its doomed attempt to achieve an elusive *imago* that is in effect the unattainable other.

1.3   Mimicking the Other: *Simile Agit in Simile*

Where *Canis et Echo* depicts the ultimate silencing of the *vox* (*siletque canis* [16]), a silencing that establishes an ironic equation between Bourne's dog and Ovid's Echo, *Simile Agit in Simile* conveys the very opposite: the gradual acquisition of voice, of language itself. In this instance the subject is a parrot, who gradually acquires language as a consequence of careful instruction on the part of its owner, and close assimilation on the part of the bird itself. Once again Bourne turns to the animal world to produce a poem that, as its title clearly indicates, concerns mimicry and mirroring (linguistic), a poem that is, moreover, analogous of human, or in this case, pedagogical behavior.

In generic terms the piece takes its place alongside a variety of parrot poems, both Latin and vernacular.[75] For example, Ovid in *Amores* 2.6 laments the death of the parrot belonging to his *domina* Corinna.[76] The theme recurs in Statius's *Silvae* 2.4.[77] Worthy of comparison also is a short poem by Sir William Scott (1674–1725) entitled *Psittacus ad D[ominam] E—B—, Dominam Suam.*[78] And despite the fact that Bourne's parrot, unlike its classical counterparts, is very much in the world of the vibrant living, his poem seems to interact with a variety of such intertexts (Ovid in particular). As might be expected, the allusion in

---

[75] For a very comprehensive survey, see John Gilmore, "Parrots, Poets and Philosophers: Language and Empire in the Eighteenth Century," *Entertext* 2.2 (2003), 84–102.

[76] Cf. Catullus 3, in which the speaker laments the death of Lesbia's pet sparrow.

[77] Gilmore, "Parrots, Poets and Philosophers," 97, notes that "a neo-Latin echo of Statius may be found in the poems (*Carmina*, II, vi) of the German writer Petrus Lotichius Secundus (1528–1560), where a parrot belonging to the nobleman Daniel Stibar is praised as a means of praising his owner."

[78] Scott's poem is included in *Selecta Poemata Archibaldi Pitcarnii ... et Aliorum*, ed. Robert Freebairn (Edinburgh, 1727), 126. Cf. Gilmore, "Parrots, Poets and Philosophers," 101.

the opening line to the bird's colorings (*pictis ... alis* [1]) finds a parallel in Ovid, who refers to the parrot's *rari forma coloris* (17). The depiction of the parrot as a gift to a *domina* from her oriental suitor (*missus ab Eoo munus amante venit* [2]), draws upon the traditional association of the parrot with the orient as denoted by Ovid (*Eois imitatrix ales ab Indis* [*Am.* 2.6.1]) and Statius (*plagae viridis regnator Eoae* [*Silv.*2.4.25]),[79] while the specific notion of the bird as a gift from a lover likewise occurs in Ovid (*extremo munus ab orbe datum* [*Am.* 2.6.38]).[80] Likewise the emphasis upon the bird's loquacity and linguistic ingenuity[81] as it impersonates the sick, and makes offensive jokes (*multa scurratur mendax et multa iocatur* [13]) merits comparison with Ovid's remarks on the variety of accents that Corinna's parrot used to assume (*quid vox mutandis ingeniosa sonis* [2.6.18]).[82] Indeed for Ovid the parrot itself constituted the loquacious *imago* of the human voice (*illa loquax humanae vocis imago* [*Am.* 2.6.37]).[83] As is true of Bourne's methodology, this *imago* serves to function on an essentially linguistic level.

But Bourne's piece differs from its classical and neo-Latin counterparts in two striking ways: first, in the emphasis upon the theme of pedagogy; second, in the focus on language itself, and on linguistic assimilation as mirrored by the poem's self-conscious use of repetition, wordplay, and emphatic juxtaposition. Throughout the poem the relationship between the pet's owner and her charge, so to speak, is described in terms reminiscent of eighteenth-century pedagogy, with, however, a humorous shift of gender as the traditional school*master* (*archididascalus*)[84] becomes a school*mistress* (*archididascalia* [4]; *era* [9;

---

[79] Cf. Scott 1: *India me genuit, fuscis tibi mittor ab Indis.*

[80] Cf. Scott 2: *Hesperio munus ab orbe ... datum.*

[81] On the parrot's attractive linguistic ingenuity, cf. Pliny, *Historia Naturalis* 10. 117: *imperatores salutat et quae accipit verba pronuntiat, in vino praecipue lasciva.*

[82] Cf. Ovid, *Amores* 2.6.23–24: *non fuit in terris vocum simulantior ales:/reddebas blaeso tam bene verba sono!* Cf. Scott: *garrula lingua mihi est* (3).

[83] Cf. Ovid, *Amores* 2.6.29: *sermonis amor*; 2.6.37: *loquax*; Cf. Statius, *Silvae* 2.4.1–2: *domini facunda voluptas/humanae sollers imitator psittace, linguae*; *Silvae* 2.4.31–32: *monstrataque reddere verba/tam facilis.*

[84] For *archididascalus* as the traditional Latin term for Westminster headmaster, cf. the inscription on the bust of Robert Freind (by John Michael Rysbrack): *Robertus Friend, S.T.P. Scholae Westmon: Per XXI Annos Archididascalus.* See also *ODNB* s.v. Robert Freind.

10] *magistra* [19]). Here Bourne seems to play upon and develop a topos exemplified in Ovid, Statius, and others of the classical *domina* as recipient of a parrot as an exotic gift from her suitor. But this is a *domina* turned schoolmistress, who imparts through careful instruction (*docenti* [21] *doceat* [22]) the power of language to a pupil (*tirunculus* [7] *alumno* [9]),[85] who is in turn a very apt learner (*discenti* [21]) or, as the poet proclaims of both: *quando fuit melior tiro, meliorve magistra!* (19). In some respects the poem might be seen to replicate the pedagogical experience itself, an experience so central to Bourne's personal life. The noun *tiro* (19) (and *tirunculus* [7]), which he uses to describe the parrot, is the usual word to denote an eighteenth-century school pupil. It is, for example, the term used in the preface to the *Lusus Westmonasterienses* as the poems contained in that anthology are envisaged as being of use to Westminster school pupils: *Tironibus certe erunt usui.*[86]

But in the course of Bourne's poem this particular *tiro* transgresses the boundaries of decorum, using the language he has learned to abuse others. In short, the school pupil (*tiro*) becomes the scoundrel (*nebulo* [18]), a transformation all too familiar no doubt to the usher of a Westminster fifth-form who, as noted previously, seems himself to have encountered many difficulties in disciplining his own parroting pupils, and was purportedly the target of a cruel schoolboy prank.[87] Furthermore the description of the parrot (*et nebulo es* [18]) merits comparison with a poem anthologized in the *Lusus Westmonasterienses*. Included under the heading *Maledicta Spreta Exolescunt*,[88] this piece describes a parrot that, to the amusement of many, used to call passersby by the name of a scoundrel (*nebulo*), and call down curses upon their heads.[89] But one of the victims of this abuse retaliates by denying that he is such (*"non ego sum nebulo"* [7]) and by uttering threats against the parrot himself.[90] The

---

[85] Contrast the depiction of "Belinda's Canary-Bird" in *The Gentleman's Magazine*, III (February 1733), 93 as "delightful, airy, skipping thing,/To charm *by nature taught*" (102). Italics are mine.

[86] *Lusus Westmonasterienses*, ii[r]. See Introduction, 8–9.

[87] See Introduction, 7–8.

[88] Cf. *Lusus Westmonasterienses*, 154–155.

[89] *hanc repetit vocem dum praeterit unus et alter,/heus! nebulo, nebulo, pro nebulone crucem!* (3–4).

[90] *unus, cui mens est conscia, sistit iter./"non ego sum nebulo, me non impune lacesses,"/inquit, et improbulae multa minatur avi* (6–8).

moral of the story is to ignore such words of abuse.[91] It is certainly the case that Westminster School possessed its own parroting scoundrels. That said, the concluding lines of Bourne's poem emphasize the apparent ease attendant upon the teaching and learning process as experienced by schoolmistress and parrot alike (*ardua discenti nulla est, res nulla docenti/ardua, cum doceat femina, discat avis* [21–22]).[92]

The mirroring of language itself is central to the poem's methodology. Initially the acquisition of language on the part of the parrot is depicted as a gradual process.[93] This is conveyed through the repetition of *iam* (7; 11).[94] But as the parrot acquires the skill of mimicry, *iam* changes to a confident *nunc* (15; 17).[95] Throughout the poem the parrot's mimicry or attempted mimicry is mirrored by the poem's language mimicking itself. This manifests itself in internal repetition and syntactical balance: *molle/ ... molle* (5–6); *alumno/ ... alumnus* (9–10), *era .../ ... erae* (9–10), *argutae ... argutulus* (17), *ardua ... /ardua* (21–22). The effect of this is strikingly humorous and more than that. In at least one instance the "mirroring" effect is rather reminiscent of Echo's habitual practice (and punishment) in Ovid of sounding only the last parts of a sentence. Thus the schoolmistress's *"Psittace mi pulcher pulchelle"* (9) is "echoed" and replicated by the parrot as *"Psittace me pulcher"* (10) —the omission of that *pulchelle* indicative perhaps of the inability of a mere parrot to achieve complete verbal assimilation (*dimidiat tirunculus* [7]). It may grasp at a vocal *imago*, but, as in the instance of Echo, the replication is bound to be imperfect in itself.

---

[91] The piece concludes: *parce minis, non haec solum te opprobria tangunt,/praeteriere alii qui meruere crucem./nil nocuere illis spretae convicia linguae,/at, tibi quod psittacus, omen habet* (9–12).

[92] This is almost an inversion of Pliny's remark that when a parrot has learned something it is then hit upon the head with an iron rod: *hoc, cum loqui discit, ferreo verberatur radio* (*Historia Naturalis* 10.117). Gilmore correctly notes that the use of the passive voice "neatly ignores the question of who is beating Latin words into the poor bird's head."

[93] Cf. in general the description of the gradual acquisition of language in primitive man and beast at Lucretius, *De Rerum Natura* 5. 1028–1090. Noteworthy are the points of contrast established between two *genera* in terms of their articulation of sound: *ergo si varii sensus animalia cogunt,/muta tamen cum sint, varias emittere voces,/quanto mortalis magis aequumst tum potuisse/dissimilis alia atque alia res voce notare!* (5. 1087–1090).

[94] *iam captat, iam dimidiat tirunculus; et iam ...* (7); *iamque canit* (11).

[95] *nunc tremulum illudit fratrem* (15); *argutae nunc stridet anus argutulus instar* (17).

Ultimately this emerges as the poet's prerogative. For hand in hand with such verbal echoing is the poem's celebration, self-consciously and comically, of a variety of ways in which language can be acquired, used and ultimately abused. In contrast to Echo's fateful punishment is the unbridled loquacity of this speaking subject, as poet, like parrot, seems to usurp the very privilege of voice. In so doing, he is the direct antithesis of the "hard-working, peace-loving, *pius* psittacus-poeta" of Ovid, *Amores* 2.6.[96] In fact Bourne's piece rejoices in the power of the Latin language to encapsulate its subject matter whether through use of the diminutive (*tirunculus* [7], *pulchelle* [9] *argutulus* [17]), internal rhyme (*multaque scurratur mendax et multa iocatur* [13]), and most notably perhaps in the clever use of wordplay, exemplified by the macaronic pun in *pol!* (15) as Bourne plays on the Latin interjection ("by Pollux!") used to lend emphasis to a particular assertion, and the vernacular "Polly," the traditional name for a parrot. In view of the poem's treatment of mirroring, the interjection would seem highly appropriate. Pollux, after all, was a twin. In several respects the parrot is the twin of a *domina* who could be seen in turn to assume the role of Castor. Both parrot and schoolmistress are, after all, *gemini* of sorts.

It is interesting to note that Cowper's "translation" of this piece expands the closing lines, applying them specifically to the education of children, and their gradual acquisition of language:

> When children first begin to spell,
> And stammer out a syllable,
> We think them tedious creatures;
> But difficulties soon abate,
> When birds are taught to prate,
> And women are the teachers.[97]

Cowper's expansion is not without a satiric irony of its own. A parrot's linguistic acquisition is facilitated by having a female teacher. Is this because the female sex (rather like Ovid's Echo) possesses a garrulous loquacity of its own, a loquacity which can be all the more readily assimilated by the parrot? Perhaps the trained parrot is ultimately a mirror-image of womankind.

---

[96] See Leslie Cahoon, "The Parrot and the Poet: The Function of Ovid's Funeral Elegies," *Classical Journal* 80 (1984–85), 27–35, at 35.

[97] See Appendix 2 in this volume.

1.4   The Self as Other: *Agens et Patiens Sunt Simul*

Mirroring the female is a theme that recurs in Bourne's strikingly modern poem *Agens et Patiens Sunt Simul*. Turning to the human world of marital relationships, this piece describes the couvade, or the psychosomatic condition of sympathetic pregnancy, whereby a husband (here named Acon) suffers the pregnancy symptoms of his wife (Leonilla). For this is a world in which the male of the species now *becomes* the poem's *imago*, an *imago* that transcends the boundaries of gender, and is presented in the poem's closing conceit as perhaps the most idealized form of reciprocity.

Couvade signifies either a ritual or a syndrome that traces its origins back to classical times. The former operates on a postnatal, the latter on a prenatal level. The ritualistic couvade entails a male taking to his bed either during or after his partner goes into labor. In this instance the male is treated as the patient and is tended to by the female. The existence of this ritual among the Iberians of Northern Spain, the Corsicans, and the Tibareni is attested by, among others, Strabo,[98] Diodorus Siculus,[99] and Apollonius Rhodius,[100] respectively, while modern writers have noted the prevalence of the custom in Biscay, China, India, Africa, and the Americas among others.[101] But, as Lundell points

---

[98] Strabo, 3.4.17, notes the following custom prevalent among the Basques: "For example, these women till the soil, and when they have given birth to a child they put their husbands to bed instead of going to bed themselves and minister to them." Cf. *The Geography of Strabo*, trans. H.L. Jones (Harvard, 1969), II, 113.

[99] Diodorus Siculus notes the prevalence of the practice among the Corsicans: "But the most amazing thing which takes place among them is connected with the birth of their children; for when the wife is about to give birth she is the object of no concern as regards her delivery, but it is her husband who takes to his bed, as though sick, and he practises couvade for a specified number of days, feigning that his body is in pain." (Diodorus of Sicily, trans. C.H. Oldfather [Cambridge, Mass., 1939], III, 135).

[100] Apollonius Rhodius, noting the existence of the custom among the Tibareni, states: "Here when wives bring forth children to their husbands, the men lie in bed and groan with their heads close bound; but the women tend them with food, and prepare child-birth baths for them." (*Argonautica* II, 1011–1014. See *Apollonius Rhodius: The Argonautica*, trans. R.C. Seaton [London, 1930], 171).

[101] See, among others, H.L. Roth, "On the Signification of Couvade," *Journal of the Anthropological Institute of Great Britain and Ireland* 22 (1893), 204–243; E.S. Hartland, "Birth (Introduction)," *Encyclopedia of Religion and Ethics*, ed. James Hastings (New York, 1928); W.D. Hand, "American Analogues of the Couvade," *Studies in Folklore*, ed. W. Edson (Indiana, 1957), 213–229; Alan Dundes, "Couvade

out, couvade "can refer to pre-natal as well as post-natal customs,"[102] and to the sense of "mystic sympathy" that can exist between male and pregnant female.[103] The ability of the male of the species to experience a sympathetic pregnancy is a theme that had occurred in vernacular literature[104] from the Elizabethan period onward. As a syndrome it is certainly not confined to a distant or primitive past:

> Actual or imagined transference of pain from the mother in confinement to the father is also part of the couvade system of customs and may well be the best known. This phenomenon is not limited to "primitive" societies. An investigation of birth customs in East Anglia as well as other parts of England (1939) revealed that nearly all midwives agreed that husbands' pains were quite common.[105]

It is in this psychosomatic, prenatal context of the couvade that Bourne's poem assumes a hitherto unnoticed place, as it develops the whole to epitomize that predilection for mirror-imaging and reciprocity noted above in his other pieces on the *imago*.[106] Such themes are suggested in the title's potential alignment (*sunt simul*) of the agent and the sufferer, *agens et patiens*, and also in the choice of protagonists (Acon and Leonilla), a couple associated in other neo-Latin epigrams with various types of sharing or fellow-feeling.[107]

---

in Genesis," *Parsing Through Customs: Essays by a Freudian Folklorist* (Madison, 1987), 145–166.

[102] Torborg Lundell, "Couvade in Sweden: Customs for New Fathers," *Scandinavian Studies* 3.22 (1999), 93–104, at 95.

[103] Lundell, "Couvade in Sweden," 94, quoting Hartland, *Encyclopedia of Religion and Ethic*, 635: "Couvade might also be an expression of the close relationship between husband and wife which engenders a 'mystic sympathy' between them so 'the acts of one are reflected in the enterprises of the other.'"

[104] See L.L. Newman, "Some References to Couvade in Literature," *Folklore* 53–54 (1943), 148–157.

[105] Lundell, "Couvade in Sweden," 95.

[106] See chapter 1, 21–22, 27–32, and 38–41.

[107] Thus the Italian humanist Hieronymus Amaltheius depicts them both as sharing the disability of blindness in one eye: *Lumine Acon dextro, capta est Leonilla sinistro,/et potis est forma vincere uterque deos./blande puer lumen, quod habes, concede sorori:/sic tu caecus Amor, sic erit illa Venus* (*Carmina Illustrium Poetarum Italorum*, 1, 143). This epigram later generated much eighteenth-century interest. It occurs in *The Gentleman's Magazine* 15 (March 1745), 101, where it is described as an

As is typical of Bourne's methodology, the poem's language and syntax reflect its subject matter. Leonilla's pregnancy symptoms of pallor (*os pallet* [3]) are mirrored in her husband's pale countenance (*pallidus est pariter vultus* [6]); her languishing eyes (*languent oculi* [3]) in his *ocellus hebes* (6); her nausea (*stomacho fit ista/nausea quae gravidas denotat esse nurus* [3–4]) in the sickness that he also suffers (*eadem quoque nausea Aconti est* [5]). Likewise, the remedies prescribed for the husband and wife are identical (*cardiacum uxori cardiacumque viro* [8]). But juxtaposed with the seeming rationality reflected in carefully balanced syntax is a tone of anticipated wonderment matched by sardonic comment. For the speaker urges the reader to believe his words (*esto fides dictis* [5]), and utters a series of three rhetorical questions addressed to the nurse: what is this new disease? (9),[108] whence did the shared pains originate? (9),[109] culminating in the emphatically concise: How can men be pregnant? (*quave sumus gravidi conditione viri?* [10]). In that telling *sumus*, the speaker includes himself in the masculine world order, an order which seems to be shattered by the transgression of gender inherent in the very concept of the couvade. Ultimately, however, it is the female who gains the upper hand, for the poem's *sedula anus* (7) is also a *callida anus* (11),[110] replying with reasoned logic yet also with a "wit" that constitutes the piece's final conceit: just as both parties enjoyed the pleasures of sex (11) so is it fitting that they should share the pain of

---

"epigram by a monk of Winchester." *The Gentleman's Magazine* 15 (March 1745), 159, contains a version emended by a certain I.T. That emended version is translated (by a certain W.W.) in *The Gentleman's Magazine* 15 (April 1745), 213, while a further corrected version of the piece occurs at *The Gentleman's Magazine* 15 (June 1745), 327. Amaltheus composed a further epigram on the pair. In this piece Acon tries to avoid the scorching heat and so he swims naked in a cold river. He sees Leonilla on the shore, which causes him to burn metaphorically despite the coldness of the water: Hieronymus Amaltheus: *De Acone et Leonilla*: *ut fugeret fervorem aestus sub sidere Cancri,/nudus in algenti flumine nabat Acon./qui simul ac alto Leonillam in litore vidit,/ah miser, in gelidis ferbuit ustus aquis* (*Carmina Illustrium Poetarum Italorum*, 1, 143). Cf. Amaltheus, *De Leonilla et Lydia*: *me laetus Leonilla oculis, me Lydia torvis/aspicit: haec noctem nuntiat, illa diem./has Cytherea meo stellas praefecit amori:/haec meus est Vesper, Lucifer illa meus* (*Carmina Illustrium Poetarum Italorum*, 1, 144).

[108] *quis novus hic, nutrix, morbus?* (9).

[109] *socii unde dolores* (9).

[110] On the role of the old woman (*anus*) in Bourne's Latin poetry, cf. chapter 4, 122–129.

pregnancy (12).[111] It is in this characteristically epigrammatic tour de force that the poem's shared themes of reflection and reciprocity are united. If through the couvade syndrome the male as an *imago* of the female can transcend the boundaries of gender, so, in an oxymoronic chiasmus, that shared prenatal *dolor* (12) functions as the obverse *imago* of *voluptas* (11) itself.

---

[111] *nutrix, callida anus, "fuit," inquit, "utrique voluptas;/aequa satis lex est ut sit utrique dolor"* (11–12).

CHAPTER 2

Reciprocal Identities: Human and Beast

Just as Bourne reverts to the animal world to foreground an essentially human impulse to investigate the *imago*, so too does he establish points of contact and contrast between human and beast. At times his poetry conveys a series of reciprocal identities, so to speak, whereby these two worlds seem perfectly in tune through acts of mutual kindness and companionship. Thus a man may alleviate the pain of a lion by gently removing a thorn from its paw, an act of kindness that will later be repaid by the lion in the amphitheater,[1] or a dog may serve a blind master, functioning as his faithful guide, and posthumously rewarded for such fidelity in the form of an eternal memorial.[2] Or the cricket can enhance human existence through affording cheerful companionship.[3] On the other hand, the possible dichotomy between the two worlds is suggested in a variety of ways: by a nightingale aspiring to match a shepherd's song, but doing so with tragic consequences;[4] by the detachment of a jackdaw perched aloft in carefree abstraction, willfully oblivious to the trials and tribulations of human civilization;[5] by a caged bird, exiled from its surroundings, yet finding solace in song as it accustomizes itself to imprisonment;[6] and not least by the poet himself in his exasperated attempt at detachment upon perceiving the apparent death wish of a fly flitting about his candle.[7] But perhaps it is in the reconciliation of these

---

[1] See *Mutua Benevolentia Primaria Lex Naturae Est*, discussed at 48–53 in this chapter.

[2] See *Epitaphium in Canem*, discussed at 53–56 in this chapter.

[3] See *Ad Grillum*, discussed at 56–60 in this chapter.

[4] See *Stradae Philomela*, discussed at 60–64 in this chapter.

[5] See *Cornicula*, discussed at 64–65 in this chapter.

[6] See *Levius Fit Patientia Quicquid Corrigere Est Nefas*, discussed at 65–66 in this chapter.

[7] See *Suicida*, discussed at 66–67 in this chapter.

potential tensions that the animal world of Bourne's poetry can in itself serve as a model for human existence and behavior. This manifests itself in, for example, the beauty and functional practicality of the glowworm,[8] or in the bee community, which, like its Virgilian counterpart, epitomizes an ideal human civilization.[9]

2.1   *Mutua Benevolentia*: From Kindness to Blindness

It was in the academic year 1716–17 that Vincent Bourne, at the age of twenty-two, was given the honor of composing the Cambridge tripos verses. It is an honor that reflects not only his distinction as Latin poet, but also the increasing esteem in which he was held at the university. The result was a reworking of the fable of Androcles and the Lion. Cast in Latin elegiacs, and exemplifying the prescribed dictum: *Mutua Benevolentia Primaria Lex Naturae Est*, the poem first appeared in printed form in the *Carmina Comitalia Cantabrigiensia* of 1721, a miniature anthology of such tripos verses compiled and edited by none other than Bourne himself.[10] While shedding interesting light on Bourne's early editorial practices,[11] the collection seems to evince a rather

---

[8] See *Cicindela*, discussed at 67–71 in this chapter.

[9] See *Apes, Ignavum Fucos Pecus a Praesepibus*, and *Innocens Praedatrix*, discussed at 71–75 in this chapter.

[10] *Carmina Comitalia Cantabrigiensia*, ed. V.B. Coll. Trin. Socius (London, 1721). Bourne's tripos verses occur on pages 23–24.

[11] In the Preface to the edition Bourne concedes that the number of poems included is very small and that some have indeed been edited before, but he highlights the usefulness of making them available in a single *libellus* (*Carmina Comitalia Cantabrigiensia*, A2[r]: *Poeticas hasce Exercitationes tibi, Lector benevole, in manus tradimus; perpaucas quidem atque olim editas, sed chartulis sparsim mandatas, et in Libellum iam demum congestas.*) Anticipating the criticism that this is a very small collection, he demonstrates a striking sensitivity in regard to the difficult task faced by an editor in both soliciting such poems from a variety of sources and in causing offence by omitting others (*Carmina Comitalia Cantabrigiensia*, A2[r]: *Quod ad Paucitatem spectat, qui in opusculis huiusmodi colligendis versantur, satis norunt quam arduum Editoribus obeundum sit munus; quae in aliis rogitandis fuerint solicitationes, quae in aliis non rogitandis offensiones*). The latter point he promises to redress by producing another such volume in the near future (*Carmina Comitalia Cantabrigiensia*, A2[v]: *optandum restat ut reliqua ea, quae desiderantur Poemata, ad nos transmittantur, cum iis, quae nobis in manu sunt, in alterum huiusmodi*

uncharacteristic attempt at self-promotion on the part of Bourne. For appended to the whole, and included under the heading *Miscellanea*, are no fewer than five of his other Latin poems.[12] This act reflects a sense of pride in his youthful achievements, indicating perhaps that Bourne, or at least the twenty-two-year-old Bourne, was *not* content with the silence of anonymity for which he seemingly yearned in his twilight years.[13] The collection itself moreover provides an important eighteenth-century context in which to view his contribution.

Even from a brief glance at the poems anthologized therein it is evident that such tripos verses were normally cast in Latin hexameters, and treated of scientific and inanimate themes, founded for the most part upon the rhetoric of logic, and expounding, for example, the rational basis

---

Fasciculum continuo colligenda). Although the second project does not seem to have been realized—at least not as a discreet Cambridge *fasciculum*—, Bourne did fulfil his promise some twenty years later by including a whole host of Cambridge tripos verses in his two-volume edition of the *Musae Anglicanae Editio Quinta* (London, 1741). Bourne expands what was originally an exclusively Oxonian anthology (edited by Joseph Addison) to include Cambridge as well as Oxford poems. As he states in the Preface to the Reader, I, A3[r]: *adiici Cantabrigiensium invenies multa*. Several of the *Carmina Comitalia Cantabrigiensia* poems recur here, and further Cambridge tripos verses are also included. The 1721 Cambridge collection also demonstrates what would appear to be Bourne's careful editorial judgement. As Bradner remarks: "The taste and good sense of Bourne's selection thoroughly justified the publishers' choice of him as editor" (*Musae Anglicanae*, 291). It is hardly a coincidence that Bourne's verses, treating of the virtue of mutual benevolence and reciprocity (as man and lion recline together in a quasi Golden Age of their own), are preceded by a piece that looks back to the Golden Age as the ultimate ideal: *Rationes Boni et Mali Sunt Aeternae et Immutabiles* (1706–7) (*Carmina Comitalia Cantabrigiensia*, 18–22). Cf. in particular lines 14–15: *aurea cum primis acta est mortalibus aetas/necdum Astraea hominum commercia fugerat insons*, and the hymn to *Virtus* in the poem's concluding lines. Composed some ten years previous, and thus, it would seem, deliberately placed out of chronological order, this piece on the perennial theme of good versus evil dovetails neatly into its Bournian successor. (Another instance of this apparent departure from chronological order is the sandwiching of the 1710–11 tripos verses [*Tubus Torricellianus*] between the 1721 and 1698 contributions. See *Carmina Comitalia Cantabrigiensia*, 51–63). However, the essentially inanimate and pseudo technical content of the collection is mirrored in the piece that follows Bourne's lines. Composed in 1717–1718 and entitled *Lockius Non Recte Statuit de Particula Anglicana But*, this very odd poem treats of Locke's misinterpretation of the English word "but."

[12] See Introduction, 7. Among other poems appended are two by Matthew Prior, on whom see Introduction, 7.

[13] Contrast Bourne's self-referential epitaph discussed at Introduction, 1–2. See also chapter 4, 131–133.

for the existence of incorporeal beings,[14] or the ebbing and flowing of the tides,[15] or the inhabitability of the planets,[16] or the workings of the telescope.[17] In fact the characteristic tone of the collection as a whole is probably most accurately describable as neo-Lucretian throughout. Read in this context, Bourne's poem is noteworthy for its striking *difference*. Characterized by its superficial simplicity, this piece attests to his typical predilection for elegiacs over hexameters, and also to his seemingly perennial tendency to focus on animate (and indeed animal) themes as opposed to the purely abstract. But it is in the unusual reconciliation of the inanimate "theme" or dictum with the essentially animate subject that this fable of man and beast comes to exemplify the foremost law of Nature (*Primaria Lex Naturae*) upon which it is founded.

The tale selected by Bourne to exemplify the tripos theme in question is one that traces its origins back to Aesop:

The Shepherd and the Lion

While he was wandering in the fields, a lion got a thorn stuck in his paw. He immediately went to a shepherd, wagging his tail as he said, "Don't be afraid! I have come to ask your help; I'm not looking for food." The lion then lifted his paw and placed it in the man's lap. The shepherd pulled out the thorn from the lion's paw and the lion went back into the woods. Later on, the shepherd was falsely accused of a crime and at the next public games he was released from jail and thrown to the beasts. As the wild animals rushed upon him from all sides, the lion recognized that this was the same man who had healed him. Once again the lion raised his paw and placed it in the shepherd's lap. When the king understood what had happened, he commanded that the lion be spared and that the gentle shepherd be sent back home to his family. *When a man acts righteously, he can never be defeated by the punishments inflicted on him by his enemies.*[18]

---

[14] *Existentia Entium Incorporeorum Colligi Potest Lumine Naturae* (1714) (*Carmina Comitalia Cantabrigiensia*, 15–17).

[15] *Fluxus et Refluxus Maris Pendent ab Actionibus Solis et Lunae* (1719–20) (*Carmina Comitalia Cantabrigiensia*, 27–30).

[16] *Planetae Sunt Habitabiles* (1718–19) (*Carmina Comitalia Cantabrigiensia*, 31–34). On links between this piece and Thomas Gray's tripos verses *Luna Habitabilis*, (1736), see Haan, *Thomas Gray's Latin Poetry*, 42–45.

[17] *Tubus Torricellianus* (1710–11) (*Carmina Comitalia Cantabrigiensia*, 55–61).

[18] *Aesop's Fables*, trans. Laura Gibbs, no. 69.

It is hardly coincidental that study of Aesop's fables had formed a central part of the educational curriculum from the Renaissance period onward,[19] as pupils sought to replicate the sense of the original in eloquent vernacular verse[20] or else they "double translated" the Greek into Latin, and the Latin back into Greek.[21] The fable in question had already been reworked into Latin prose by the grammarian Aulus Gellius in *Noctes Atticae* 5.14.[22] Gellius replicates many of the details of the Aesopian version, but he expands the whole in a number of ways. Most notably perhaps, he inverts the order of events whereby the episode actually commences with Androcles in the arena, having already been thrown to the lion. This is then followed by the mutual recognition and fawning scene, culminating in a flashback narrative whereby Androcles, assuming the first person, recounts to the Emperor details of his previous kindness toward the wounded lion. The effect of this inversion is to intensify the drama and suspense of the episode, while also highlighting the themes of reciprocity and mutual kindness that would come to be so central to Bourne's poem. Indeed, as noted below, Bourne's treatment is much more akin to that of Gellius than to Aesop.

The title of his piece (*Mutua Benevolentia Primaria Lex Naturae Est*) sets it within the genre of the moralizing fable exemplified by Aesop's concluding dictum: "When a man acts righteously, he can never be defeated by the punishments inflicted on him by his enemies." The title's emphasis upon reciprocity finds a parallel in Gellius's pseudo-heading outlining the mutual recognition between man and beast,[23] a

---

[19] On the inclusion of Aesop in the educational curriculum, cf. Charles Hoole, *A New Discovery of the Olde Arte of Teaching Schoole*, ed. E.T. Campagnac (London, 1913), 158: "You may cause them to turn a Fable of Aesop into what kinde of verse you please to appoint them."

[20] See, for example, William Bullokar, *Aesop's Fables in True Orthography* (London, 1585). On Milton's possible debt to Bullokar as manifested in a school exercise dating to his period at St Paul's School, London, cf. Estelle Haan, "Mantuan, Milton and 'The Fruit of That Forbidden Tree,'" *Medievalia et Humanistica* 25 (1998), 75–92.

[21] On this and other such pedagogical methods, see Introduction, 5–6.

[22] The fable would of course be immortalized in the highly imaginative play of the same name by George Bernard Shaw.

[23] *quod Apion, doctus homo, qui "Plistonices" appellatus est, vidisse se Romae scripsit recognitionem inter sese mutuam ex vetere notitia hominis ac leonis.* Text is that of *A.Gellii: Noctes Atticae*, ed. P.K. Marshall (Oxford, 1968), I, 202–208, at 202.

reciprocity reflected in the fable proper.[24] And the setting of the whole in the desert (*per Libyae ... siccas errabat arenas* [1]) likewise looks back to Gellius, who had developed the Aesopian location of fields[25] to embrace *arenarum solitudines*.[26] As in Gellius, the human protagonist is a slave who has fled from his master. Bourne's emphasis upon the exiled status of the slave (*fugerat exsul* [2]) and the anger of the master (*iratum ... erum* [2]; *furor ultoris ... eri* [20]) finds a parallel in Gellius as Androcles describes the unjust beatings he endured at the hands of his master, and the violence that forced him to go into exile.[27] Gellius transports the initial encounter to a cave itself,[28] and Bourne follows suit.[29] Further parallels between the two Latin treatments include the emphasis upon the fear experienced by Androcles[30] and the careful attention he paid to the wounded animal. Thus whereas in Aesop, Androcles merely "pulled out the thorn from the lion's paw," the protagonist in both Gellius and Bourne scrutinizes the thorn, pulls it out, and dries off the blood as the skin begins to heal.[31] Both Gellius and Bourne depict the lion fetching food and sharing it with Androcles,[32]

---

[24] *"tum quasi mutua recognitione facta laetos"* inquit *"et gratulabundos videres hominem et leonem"* (*Noctes Atticae* 5.14.14).

[25] "While he was wandering in the fields." (*Aesop's Fables*, trans. Laura Gibbs, no. 69).

[26] *in camporum et arenarum solitudines concessi* (*Noctes Atticae* 5.14.17).

[27] *iniquis eius et cotidianis verberibus ad fugam sum coactus* (*Noctes Atticae* 5.14.17).

[28] *specum quandam nanctus remotam* (*Noctes Atticae* 5.14.18); *ad eandem specum* (*Noctes Atticae* 5.14.19).

[29] *ad scopuli patuit caeca caverna latus* (4); *rugit ad antra leo* (6).

[30] *territum ... ac pavefactum animum* (*Noctes Atticae* 5.14.20); *perculsus novitate rei* (9); *incertusque timore* (9) *vix tandem admovet erro manus* (10).

[31] *ego stirpem ingentem vestigo pedis eius haerentem revelli conceptamque saniem vulnere intimo expressi accuratiusque sine magna iam formidine siccavi penitus atque detersi cruorem* (*Noctes Atticae* 5.14.22). Cf. Bourne, 11–12: *et spinam explorans (nam fixa in vulnere spina/haerebat)*; 13–14: *taeter fluit humor,/et coit, absterso sanguine, rupta cutis* (13–14).

[32] Thus Gellius: *triennium totum ego et leo in eadem specu eodemque et victu viximus. nam quas venabatur feras, membra opimiora ad specum mihi subgerebat* (*Noctes Atticae* 5.14.24–25); Bourne, 15–16: *et affert/providus assiduas hospes ad antra dapes*; 17–18: *iuxta epulis accumbit homo conviva leonis,/nec crudos dubitat participare cibos*.

while Gellius's emphasis on the host/guest relationship (*hic est leo hospes hominis, hic est homo medicus leonis*)[33] is mirrored in Bourne's use of *hospes* (16; 27). In both, Androcles begins to experience the tedium (*pertaesum est*; *taedia* [19]) of such a savage way of life.[34] But whereas both Aesop and Gellius describe the consequences of the mutual recognition scene in the arena (in Aesop the shepherd and lion are spared;[35] in Gellius the slave is freed and rewarded with the lion as a pet),[36] Bourne maintains a tantalizing silence about the outcome, replacing it with two rhetorical questions concerning the source of fear experienced by the Romans (29–30),[37] and concluding in a gnomic, pseudo Aesopian moral, which takes the whole back to the tripos theme of *Natura: unius naturae opus est: ea sola furorem/sumere quae iussit, ponere sola iubet* (31–32).

While Bourne's tripos verses clearly take their place within a Greco-Roman tradition, they also move outside that tradition by establishing a series of internal echoes. The final product is a Latin poem that sets up, in typical Bournian fashion, several types of mirror-images, so to speak: between the sand (*arena*) of the Libyan desert (*Libyae ... siccas ... arenas* (1) and the formal arena (*tristis arena* [24]) at Rome in which human and beast meet for a second time; between the wanderings of man (*errabat* [1]) and those of an animal (*peragrat* [15]); between the lion's cave (*caeca caverna* [4]) and the lion's cage (*e caveis* [25]); between the lion's wounded foot (*pedem ... laesum* [7]) and the feet of Androcles later recognized by the reclining beast (*notos ... ante pedes* [28]); between the shock of Androcles (*perculsus novitate rei* [9]) as the lion begs for help and that of the Roman spectators (*perculsi animis stupuere, Quirites* [29]) upon beholding the fawning animal. As such, the very language of Bourne's poem both expresses and reflects the reciprocity that it celebrates.[38]

---

[33] *Noctes Atticae* 5.14.30.

[34] *vitae illius ferinae iam pertaesum est* (*Noctes Atticae* 5.14.26); *quis tamen ista ferat desertae taedia vitae?/vix furor ultoris tristior esset eri* (19–20).

[35] "He commanded that the lion be spared and that the gentle shepherd be sent back home to his family."

[36] *cunctis petentibus dimissum Androclum et poena solutum leonemque ei suffragiis populi donatum* (*Noctes Atticae* 5.14.29–30).

[37] *quid vero perculsi animis stupuere Quirites?/ecquid prodigii, territa Roma, vides?* (29–30).

[38] Cf. 51 in this chapter.

That sense of *mutua benevolentia* that lies at the heart of Bourne's verse fable on Androcles and the lion underlies another of his Latin poems likewise included in the *Carmina Comitalia Cantabrigiensia*.[39] The *Epitaphium in Canem* takes as its subject the mutual sense of fidelity and kindness that can exist between a dog and its blind owner. Now in death the dog is given a voice with which, as speaker of the poem,[40] he offers a flashback of the life he has just departed. As Storey perceptively notes, "the idea of the poem as inscription permeates the structure."[41] And the life "inscribed" is one that is characterized by a series of reciprocal events and gestures. Both master and dog are ultimately the victims of old age: thus the dog, who was his master's *columen ... senectae* (2), has himself been overtaken by that same eventuality (*senecta/quae tandem obrepsit* [19–20]). But during his lifetime he proved an excellent guide— a fact conveyed in the mock heroism of lines 5–7 where, in language reminiscent of Ovid's Ariadne, he provided a metaphorical thread (*filum*), directing the footsteps of his Theseus-like master (*sed fila secutus/quae dubios regerent passus, vestigia tuta/fixit inoffenso gressu* [5–7]).[42] Like Androcles and the lion,[43] this man and animal partake of the same food (15–16).[44] And in sharp contrast to the canine guardian of the underworld, Cerberus, who could be put to sleep by the Sibyl's offering of a heavily drugged morsel,[45] this dog is ever wakeful (*vigil* [14]), his ears pricked

---

[39] *Carmina Comitalia Cantabrigiensia*, 95–96.

[40] For a deceased dog as the poem's speaker, cf. Giovanni Cotta, *Carmina Illustrium Poetarum Italorum*, 3, 14: *Epitaphium Canis*. For further neo-Latin examples of the genre, cf. Andrea Navagero, *Augonis Venatici Canis Epitaphium*, Nathan Chitraeus, *Epitaphium Canis*, Anonymous, "Margaret: A Dog's Epitaph" (*The Oxford Book of Latin Verse*, ed. H.W. Garrod [Oxford, 1934], no. 308). For vernacular treatments of the subject, see, among others, Eugene O'Neill, "The Last Will and Testament of an Extremely Distinguished Dog."

[41] Storey, "The Latin Poetry of Vincent Bourne," 134.

[42] Cf. Ovid, *Heroides* 10 (Ariadne's epistle to Theseus), in which she states: *cum tibi, ne victor tecto morere recurvo/quae regerent passus pro duce fila dedi* (46–47). Cf. also (of Daedalus) Virgil, *Aen.* 6.30 *caeca regens filo vestigia*.

[43] See 52 in this chapter.

[44] *seu frustula amice/porrexit sociasque dapes* (15–16).

[45] Cf. Virgil, *Aeneid* 6. 419–423: *cui vates horrere videns iam colla colubris/melle soporatam et medicatis frugibus offam/obicit. ille fame rabida tria guttura pandens/corripit obiectam, atque immania terga resolvit/fusus humi totoque ingens extenditur antro.*

and alert to his master's commands, as he receives the crumbs (*frustula* [15]) given to him. Strikingly juxtaposed with such canine heroism, however, is the essential vulnerability of the human, who as a member of a marginalized social group is disadvantaged by both blindness and poverty.[46] For it emerges that the blind man in question is a beggar, lamenting his disability and, as though in search of his own *frustula*, living off the charity of passersby. But it is precisely because of this marginalization that such reciprocity between human and animal behavior is rendered all the more precious.

Despite the element of hope afforded by the subtext of this canine Ariadne guiding the footsteps of an heroic Theseus, it is clear that this master can never in fact be rescued from the metaphorical labyrinth that is his own blindness (*noctemque oculis ploravit obortam* [10]), nor, it is implied, can he escape his very social status (or the lack of such). Instead, he is ironically depicted as in an underworld of his own, as a pseudo-Charon figure, at the mercy of whatever coin (*obolus*) the charitable decide to bestow upon him (*obolum dedit alter et alter* [11]).[47]

In the following century Charles Lamb would convey with a sense of wistful reminiscence something of the vulnerability, dignity, and meaning of that now lost and long forgotten "human and quadrupedal alliance, this dog and man friendship:"[48]

> Above all, those old blind Tobits that used to line the wall of Lincoln's Inn Garden, before modern fastidiousness had expelled them, casting up their ruined orbs to catch a ray of pity, and (if possible) of light, with their faithful Dog Guide at their feet,—whither are they fled? or into what corners, blind as themselves, have they been driven, out of the wholesome air and sun-warmth? immersed between four walls, in what withering poor-house do they endure the penalty of double darkness, where the chink of the dropt half-penny no more consoles their forlorn bereavement, far from the sound of the cheerful and hope-stirring tread of the passenger? Where hang their useless staves? and who will farm their dogs? Have the overseers of St. L—caused

---

[46] On Bourne's predilection for treating of marginalized groups, cf. chapter 3, 85–94.

[47] On the *obolus* as payment to Charon for transportation across the Styx in his ferry, cf. Bourne, *In Obitum Roussaei*, 25–26: *nec poscas naulum, loculos nam vivus inanes/gessit, et haud obolum quem tibi solvat habet.* See also chapter 4, 114–121.

[48] Charles Lamb, "A Complaint of the Decay of Beggars in the Metropolis," *Essays of Elia*, ed. Lucas, II, 117. Lamb praises Bourne's *Epitaphium in Canem* as "the sweetest of his poems," and continues: "Reader, peruse it; and say, if customary sights, which could call up such gentle poetry as this, were of a nature to do more harm or good to the moral sense of the passengers through the daily thoroughfares of a vast and busy metropolis."

them to be shot? or were they tied up in sacks, and dropt into the Thames, at the suggestion of B—, the mild rector of—?[49]

Perhaps Lamb's series of rhetorical questions may be answered, at least in part, by the power of art itself, a power that can immortalize this bond and recreate its identity[50] by rescuing that "alliance" from a literal and metaphorical labyrinth. In the closing lines of Bourne's poem we learn that the master has repaid the dog in a way that transcends both life and death, by constructing a tomb for the deceased animal[51] *prisci ... gratia facti/ne tota intereat* (21–22). Though small and inexpensive, it is depicted as the *non ingratae munuscula dextrae* (24) and is equipped with an epitaph[52] aptly commemorating a faithful dog and a kind master:

> carmine signavitque brevi dominumque canemque
> quod memoret: fidumque canem dominumque benignum (25–26).[53]

It is in this *carmen* that the ultimate reconciliation between man and dog is inscribed for all eternity.

2.2   Vocal *Imitatio*: The Poet and the Cricket

The theme of a shared *carmen* likewise underlies Bourne's Latin poem on the cricket. Entitled *Ad Grillum Anacreonticum*,[54] this piece takes its place within the miniature genre of *Anacreontea*, highly self-conscious imitations of the lyric verse of Anacreon, a Greek poet of the sixth

---

[49] Lamb, "A Complaint of the Decay of Beggars in the Metropolis," *Essays of Elia*, ed. Lucas, II, 116–117.

[50] On the theme of art recreating identity, see below, chapter 4 passim.

[51] Cf. Giovanni Cotta, *Epitaphium Canis*, 2: *tumulum post dedit et titulum.*

[52] On Bourne's own recourse to the genre of the Latin epitaph, see chapter 4, 114 and 132.

[53] Cf. Nathan Chitraeus, *Epitaphium Canis: Parve canis, tibi parva domus et corpore parvus. et brevis est tumulus, et breve carmen habe.*

[54] The poem first appeared in Bourne's *Poematia* (1734), 93.

century B.C. It was a genre that exerted a formative influence upon English lyric poetry from the Renaissance period onward. Abraham Cowley, for example, translated eleven such pieces, which he appended to his *Miscellanies* (1656).[55] *Anacreontea* 34 constitutes a hymn to the cicada, and as such functions as an interesting classical forerunner of *Ad Grillum*.[56] Bourne's poem would of course be immortalized in the translation of Cowper,[57] via which it was known to and celebrated by Charlotte Smith.[58]

In the Greek original the cicada is envied by the speaker for its blessedness,[59] or, in Cowley's translation: "Happy insect, what can be/In happiness compared to thee?" (1–2). Central to the piece is the notion of kingship and dominion that the creature enjoys ("Thou dost drink, and dance, and sing;/Happier than the happiest king!" [9–10]) as "Man for thee does sow and plough;/Farmer he, and landlord now" (15–16).[60] It owns everything in the fields and in the woods, and is beloved of the Muses and Apollo.[61] Indeed it seems to approximate the gods themselves, impervious as it is to the distresses of old age.[62]

Bourne's piece moves beyond its "Anacreontic" predecessor in several respects, not least in its motif of reciprocity. Here the *cantus* (6)

---

[55] This later appeared as *Anacreon Done into English Out of the Original Greek* (Oxford, 1683).

[56] See *Greek Lyric, II: Anacreon, Anacreontea, Choral Lyric From Olympus to Alman*, trans. D.A Campbell (Loeb: Harvard, 1988), 204–207.

[57] See Appendix 2 in this volume.

[58] Cf. Charlotte Smith, *Conversations Introducing Poetry: Conversations the Fifth*, I, 179: "Mrs Talbot: Well! I have a bird or two hatching for you, but they are not yet in a state to make a figure in our Museum of animals. Let us have recourse therefore to some expedient to fill up our time, if not our book. Come, read to me Cowper's translation of Vincent Bourne's verses 'to the Cricket,' in which, tho' it is something like sacrilege to change a word of his, you will see I have made a few alterations." Text is that of *Charlotte Turner Smith: Conversations Introducing Poetry* (London, 1804).

[59] "We count you blessed, cicada" (*Greek Lyric*, II, 205).

[60] Cf. "You sing like a king: you own everything that you see in the fields, everything that the woods produce" (*Greek Lyric*, II, 205–207).

[61] "The Muses love you and Phoebus himself loves you and has given you a clear song" (*Greek Lyric*, II, 207).

[62] See 60 in this chapter.

of a cricket renders this particular animal an *argutulus choraules* (2),[63] the chirping musician of the speaker's kitchen, songful (*canorus* [3]), as it greets him with delightful music (6).[64] It is a *cantus* that can be replicated by the poet himself through the power of his muse (*musa* [10]) as these verses are presented as a reciprocal exercise in music-making.[65] Most striking perhaps is the way in which the poem itself seems to mirror the very nature of the cricket's measured yet chirping song. This is evident in its carefully balanced structure (forty lines in four ten-line stanzas), choice of meter (iambic dimeter), and lilting rhythm throughout. This also works on a metaphorical, syntactical, and linguistic level: in the metaphor of repayment (*rependam* [8], *remunerabo* [10]), and in the homely yet hymnic use of balance and repetition (*et ipse ... et ipse* [8–9]; *quae te ... quae ...te* [22–23]; *te nulla ... te nulla* [31–32]; *quin amplies ... quin amplies* [35–36]); onomatopoeia (*meae culinae/argutulus choraules* [1–2]), rhyming gerunds (*canendo,/fruendo* [35–36]),[66] and cumulative alliteration, particularly at line-endings (*choraules, canorus, commoreris* [2–4]; *siquando ... salutes* [7]; *contentus et calore* [20]).

True to its nature, and like its Dickensian successor,[67] this cricket occupies the hearth,[68] loves warmth,[69] possesses a shrill voice,[70] is

---

[63] On *choraules*, cf. Bourne's Latin poem entitled *Optimum Est Convivium In Quod Choraules Non Venit*, at *Lusus Westmonasterienses*, 139. See in particular lines 13–14: *Heus, dapifer, quid cena iuvat, cessante Choraule;/vel mihi redde fides, vel tibi sume dapes.*

[64] *iucundiore cantu/siquando me salutes* (6–7).

[65] On the theme of reciprocity in Bourne's Latin poetry, cf. chapter 1 passim.

[66] Cf. *querendo* (39).

[67] Charles Dickens, *The Cricket on the Hearth* (1845).

[68] *meae culinae* (1); *in camini/recessibus* (18–19). Cf. Dickens, *The Cricket on the Hearth*, passim.

[69] *contentus et calore* (20).

[70] *argutulus* (2). Cf. Dickens, *The Cricket on the Hearth*: "Good Heaven, how it chirped! Its shrill, sharp, piercing voice resounded through the house, and seemed to twinkle in the outer darkness like a Star." Text is that of *Charles Dickens: The Christmas Books*, ed. Michael Slater (Penguin, 1971), 21–119, at 25. Cf. Charlotte Smith, *Conversations Concerning Poetry: Conversation The Fifth*, I, 182: "In the warmer countries of Europe, Italy, Spain, and the South of France, these cicada or cicala make such a clamorous chirping of an evening that it is very disagreeable; and they are less pleasant to hear, because they are such devourers of the green leaves, as to disfigure the country, and are besides very prejudicial."

associated with cheer,[71] and functions as a good omen.[72] Like the verse fable on Androcles and the lion,[73] this too is a poem that concerns itself with animal as the *hospes* (3) of man,[74] a fact conveyed with homely intimacy. Bourne takes pains to contrast the cricket, a welcome lodger (*gratus inquilinus* [12]), with such domestic pets as rodents and mice (11–20).[75] And he reworks the Anacreontic hymning of the cicada as "the sweet prophet of summer,"[76] by explicitly stating that unlike the cicada, which is similar in appearance to the cricket, but which possesses a song that lasts just for a single summer (*unius, haud secundae,/aestatis est chorista* [25–26]), the cricket renews his song and stores it up for December (21–30).[77] Throughout the piece the cricket's miniature size is mirrored via the use of diminutives: *argutulus* (2), *aetatulam* (37). But in the final lines the perspective seems to shift via the use of ironic comparatives (*amplies* [35–36]; *longiorem* [40]), and also by means of a telling contrast that reworks the tradition in which the poem is cast.

---

[71] *iucundiore cantu* (6); *laetus* (29). Cf. Dickens, *The Cricket on the Hearth*, 32–33: "The first time I heard its cheerful little note. ... Its chirp was such a welcome to me! It seemed so full of promise and encouragement;" cf. 33: "its Chirp, Chirp, Chirp, has cheered me up again, and filled me with new trust and confidence."

[72] *felicitatis omen* (5). Cf. Dickens, *The Cricket on the Hearth*, 32: "And it's sure to bring us good fortune. ... It always has done so. To have a Cricket on the Hearth is the luckiest thing in all the world!" Cf. Charlotte Smith, *Conversations Introducing Poetry: Conversations the Fifth*, I, 181: "You may remember when we were talking of these insects one morning, while Mary Ambrose was in the room helping me to measure some linen, she said it was 'counted' to use her expression, 'very bad luck indeed when the Crickets all went away from an house'—and this superstition is, I believe, still very general among the cottagers."

[73] See 52–53 in this chapter.

[74] Cf. *Mutua Benevolentia Primaria Lex Naturae Est*, 15–16: *et affert/providus assiduas hospes ad antra dapes* (15–16); *et veterem agnoscens vetus hospes amicum* (27).

[75] Cf. Bourne's description of the bee as an *Innocens Praedatrix* in the poem of that title. See also 73–74 in this chapter.

[76] *Greek Lyric* II, 207.

[77] On the speaker's differentiation between the cricket and other such creatures, cf. Keats, "On the Grasshopper and Cricket," especially 9–14: "The poetry of earth is ceasing never:/On a lone winter evening, when the frost/Has wrought a silence, from the stove there shrills/The Cricket's song, in warmth increasing ever,/And seems to one in drowsiness half lost,/The Grasshopper's among some grassy hills." Text is that of *The Works of John Keats* (The Wordsworth Poetry Library [Denmark, 1994]), 41.

Where the Anacreontic cicada was seen as impervious to the distresses of age, and thus approximating the gods themselves,[78] the Bournian cricket is compared not to the gods but to man. Thus it enjoys much more fully a little span of life that is envisaged as in fact longer than the lifetime that "little men" (*homunciones* [38]) waste in complaining. And it is in this contrast that the poem achieves its ultimate tour de force. Whereas initially this creature in its possession of *cantus* seemed to be much more akin to the human speaker than to its fellow creatures, so too is it very different. If in their possession of a shared *carmen* man and beast can function as reciprocal mirrors, so too can that *imago* be distorted by a realistically painful acknowledgement of the trials and tribulations of human existence.

2.3   Human Versus Beast: Forms of Detachment?

Despite such patterns of *imitatio*, several of Bourne's animal poems would seem to deconstruct that very notion of reciprocity between the human and the bestial. In these instances attempted *imitatio* or *aemulatio* give way to detachment and withdrawal from the troubled world of humanity.

Bourne's short epigrammatic piece *Stradae Philomela* epitomizes the dangers that may accompany a shared *carmen*. In so doing it succinctly reworks a much lengthier *Prolusio* on the subject by the Jesuit Famianus Strada (1572–1647). First published in 1617,[79] Strada's poem, in professed imitation of the style of Claudian, and running to 58 Latin hexameters, depicts a *certamen musicum*,[80] in which a nightingale hears the skillful music of a lyre-player, which it strives to replicate in its own

---

[78] Cf. "Age does not distress you, wise one, earth-born, song-lover! You who do not suffer, you whose flesh is bloodless, you are almost like the gods" (*Greek Lyric*, II, 207).

[79] *Prolusiones Academicae, Oratoriae, Historicae, Poeticae R.P. Famiani Stradae Romani e Societate Iesu ... Coloniae Agrippinae* (Rome, 1617), II, *Prolus. VI. Poet Academia* II, 351. The text is usefully reproduced in L.C. Martin, ed. *The Poems, English, Latin and Greek of Richard Crashaw* (Oxford, 1927), 438–439.

[80] On Bourne's *Certamen Musicum*, see chapter 3, 100–101.

song.[81] The musician acknowledges the nightingale's *imitatio*, and challenges it to a contest (11–12)[82] by intensifying the quality and standard of the music produced. This is balanced by the nightingale, which likewise seeks to perfect its imitation. That sense of *aemulatio* that underlies the contest is conveyed by Strada in excited rhythms and breathless syntax as art is matched by art (23–24).[83] The musician is amazed at the nightingale's ability to produce so sweet a melody from its small throat (30–31).[84] Once again he augments his music, and when this is replicated by the nightingale, the whole is depicted in terms of an epic battle (31–40). Suddenly, however, the tone changes as the musician becomes angry (41) and strives to intensify his music even more. When the nightingale tries to match this, it proves unequal to the task (55),[85] and dies (56).[86] In short, Strada's fable explicitly exemplifies the spirit of emulation that is possessed even by slight creatures (58).[87]

Strada's poem had already exerted no slight an influence upon vernacular poets. Most notable perhaps is Richard Crashaw's replication of the tale in "Musicks Duell,"[88] which moves beyond the original in outlining the contest and in emphasizing the increasing and ultimately fatal power of the nightingale's imitative song. Among others to reinvent Strada's piece were John Ford in *The Lovers Melancholy* (1629),[89]

---

[81] *et quos/ille modos variat digitis, haec gutture reddit* (9–10). For other neo-Latin poems on the nightingale, see, for example, Giovanni Battista Amaltheus, *In Philomelam* (*Carmina Illustrium Poetarum Italorum*, 1, 163); Petrus Angelus (*Carmina Illustrium Poetarum Italorum*, 1, 233); Augustinus Fortunius, *De Garrula Philomela* (*Carmina Illustrium Poetarum Italorum*, 4, 441).

[82] *sensit se fidicen philomela imitante referri,/et placuit ludum volucri dare* (11–12).

[83] *illa modis totidem respondet, et artem/arte refert* (23–24).

[84] *miratur fidicen parvis e faucibus ire/tam varium tam dulce melos* (30–31).

[85] *impar magnanimis ausis, imparque dolori* (55).

[86] *vitam summo in certamine linquens* (56).

[87] *usque adeo et tenues animas ferit aemula Virtus* (58).

[88] See *The Poems, English, Latin and Greek of Richard Crashaw*, ed. Martin, 149–153.

[89] John Ford, *The Lover's Melancholy*, ed. R.F. Hill (Manchester, 1985), Act I, Sc. i.

Vilvain in *Enchiridion Epigrammatum* (1654),[90] William Strode in "A Translation of the Nightingale Out of Strada" (1656),[91] and John Wilson in *Poems by Several Hands* (1685).[92] And there also exists an anonymous version of the whole, entitled *Strada's Musical Duel, ... In Latine, Much Enlarg'd in English* (1671).[93] Later reworkings would include a contribution to *The Gentleman's Magazine* of 1791.[94] Such is the vernacular context in which Bourne's neo-Latin lines take their place.

That Strada's piece should have appealed to the youthful Bourne is hardly surprising. Here once again are the motifs of replication and reciprocity that so frequently lie at the heart of his poetic output. In this instance the lengthy hexameter original is recast in the form of a ten-line epigram composed in the elegiac meter. The epigram develops the pastoral potential of Strada's *ilice ... nigra* (5)[95] by replacing his lyre-player (*fidicen* [3]) with a shepherd (now explicitly referred to as a *pastor* [1, 5, 10]), while the music of the lyre (*explorat citharam* [13]) is transformed into that of the shepherd's pipe (*calamis ... canentem* [1]). The effect of this is to locate this particular *certamen musicum* within a genre in which rival music-making between two shepherds played a central role. In this instance, however, one of those human competitors is transmuted into the nightingale itself, whose attempts to replicate a shepherd's music are rendered all the more pathetic and pitiable. Thus in the spirit of *aemulatio* that characterizes pastoral performance, the

---

[90] Robert Vilvain, *Enchiridion Epigrammatum Latino-Anglicum: An Epitome of Essais, Englished Out of Latin Etc.* (London, 1654), 177.

[91] William Strode, *The Academy of Pleasure* (London, 1656), 123, ed. Bertram Dobell (London, 1907), 16–18.

[92] Nahum Tate, ed. *Poems by Several Hands, and On Several Occasions* (London, 1685), 405. The author of the verses is designated as "Mr Wilson." It is clear from the same author's preceding verses in the volume that this is John Wilson (1626–1695), the dramatist, lawyer, and recorder of Londonderry.

[93] *Strada's Musical Duel ... In Latine, Much Enlarg'd in English* (London, 1671). Cf A3[r]: "Strada's Musical Duel, In Latine; First Imitated in English by Mr Crashaw, then by Mr Hinton; and now by a third hand so enlarg'd, and the whole Frame of the Poem so alter'd, that little of Strada is preserv'd, save only the Scene and Issue of the Duel: All in a more familiar Style than that of Claudian imitated by Strada." A manuscript version exists in the British Library: Add. MS. 19268. See *The Poems, English, Latin and Greek of Richard Crashaw*, ed. Martin, 440.

[94] By an unidentified I.M. See *The Gentleman's Magazine*, August 1791.

[95] *ilice defensus nigra scaenaque virenti* (Strada, 5).

nightingale wishes to replicate the shepherd's *tenues ... modos* (2), an attempted replication conveyed by such infinitives as *referre* (2)[96] and *reddere* (4),[97] but does so only to produce an *argutum ... melos* (4).[98] And if one of the traditional pastoral participants has become a bird, the other is presented as a shepherd who is rather atypical of the genre in that he is unaccustomed to having a rival (5).[99] But a rival he does indeed have. Thus the comparatives *plenius* (12), *nec segnius* (15), *maioraque tentans* (31)[100] with which Strada had conveyed the participants' subsequent attempts to augment their music-making are replicated in Bourne's *grandius* (6) as the shepherd rather ruthlessly urges (*urget* [6])[101] the bird to match his music. It is an invitation that proves fatal. Despite the potential heroism of the nightingale's elevation of its song (*tuque etiam in modulos surgis* [7]),[102] the bird, like its Stradian equivalent proves to be unequal to the task, succinctly conveyed in the repetition of *impar* (7–8).[103] But this inequality is lamented by the speaker himself as he moves beyond Strada in expressing his twofold sense of empathy and pity for the bird. This is reflected in the use of the diminutive *misellam ... avem* (5–6), the impassioned direct address to the creature itself (*tuque ... surgis ... sed ... cadis* [7–8]),[104] in the emotional *heu* (8), and in the double rhetorical exclamation (*durum certamen! tristis victoria!* [9]). The tone in

---

[96] Cf. *sensit se fidicen philomela imitante referri* (Strada, 11).

[97] Cf. *ille modos variat digitis, haec gutture reddit* (Strada, 10).

[98] Cf. *venturi specimen praefert argutula cantus* (Strada, 17).

[99] *pastor inassuetus rivalem ferre* (5). Contrast Crashaw, "Musicks Duell," 15: "The man perceiv'd his Rivall."

[100] Cf. Crashaw, "Musicks Duell" 45–47: "a voyce, whose melody/Could melt into such sweet variety/*Straines higher yet*"; 107–108: "now reach a straine my Lute/*Above her* mocke"; 135–136: "The Lutes light *Genius* now *does proudly rise*,/Heav'd on the *surges of swolne Rapsodyes*." Italics are mine.

[101] Cf. *digitisque micantibus urget/fila minutatim* (Strada, 21–22); *non imitabilibus plectrum concentibus urget* (Strada, 44).

[102] Cf. Crawshaw's brilliant expansion of the original in his rendition of the actual musical contest in "Musicks Duell," 57–156.

[103] *sed impar/viribus, heu impar* (7–8). Cf. *impar magnanimis ausis, imparque dolori* (Strada, 55).

[104] Contrast Strada's use of the third person: *deficit et vitam summo in certamine linquens/victoris cadit in plectrum* (56–57).

which the speaker's sympathy for the bird is cast may owe some debt to Crashaw's dramatic rendition of the nightingale's final moments and ultimate end:

> Alas! In vaine! For while (sweet soule) shee tryes
> To measure all those wild diversities
> Of chatt'ring stringes, by the small size of one,
> Poore simple voyce, rais'd in a Naturall Tone;
> Shee failes, and failing grieves, and grieving dyes.
> Shee dyes; and leaves her life the Victors prise,
> Falling upon his Lute; o fit to have
> (That liv'd so sweetly) dead, so sweet a Grave!
>   ("Musicks Duell," 161–168)

As Bourne's *certamen musicum* becomes a *durum certamen*, the epigram becomes an elegy, lamenting the potentially tragic consequences of replication between the human and the animal worlds. In that climactic *exanimisque cadis* (8) the animal is significantly deprived of the *anima*. Attempted assimilation has resulted in the annihilation of identity itself.

This potential dichotomy between the human and the animal worlds of Bourne's poetry resurfaces in *Cornicula*.[105] Here a jackdaw is literally and symbolically positioned "above" human concerns. The piece is founded upon two contrasting perspectives: the bird's-eye view and that of man. And more than that. The physical height enjoyed by the jackdaw perched upon a church tower is mirrored by its associated sense of sublimity (*nil tam sublime est* [3]) and moral superiority (*spernens inferiora* [4]), conveyed in the literal and metaphorical meanings of the phrases. The bird sits *quo nemo ascendat* (5). Whereas the human being can hardly look up at this spot without a sense of trepidation (7),[106] the bird occupies it fearlessly and in safety (8).[107] Now with no sense of danger (*secura pericli* [11]) this creature is completely oblivious both to the very possibility of its falling (12) and especially to the human affairs that it beholds beneath (13–14).[108] His is a state of carefree ease and willful abstraction. The repetition of *spectat* (13; 15) emphasizes the role of the bird as observer of humankind,[109] watching in every street below

---

[105] The poem first appeared in the 1743 edition of Bourne's poetry (p. 192).

[106] *quo vix a terra tu suspicis absque tremore* (7).

[107] *metus expers incolumisque sedet* (8).

[108] *res inde humanas sed summa per otia spectat,/et nihil ad sese quas videt esse videt* (13–14).

[109] For Bourne's comparable stance in his Latin poetry, see chapter 3, 77–79.

essentially human *concursus* (15) and *negotia* (15) in striking contrast to the *otia* (13) that it enjoys, and wisely regarding everything as a trifle (*pro nugis* [16]). Indeed even if it happens to hear the shouting below (17), it ignores such as worthless (*pro rebus nihili negligit* [18]), and simply resorts to clamor of its own—its raucous croaking, a potential impertinence reflected in the abrupt yet climactically prosaic line-ending *crocitat* (18). And it is in this state of abstracted detachment that the bird is depicted as *felix* (19), its wings envied by the troubled man who, perhaps like that "lover of silence," Bourne himself,[110] would seek to withdraw and absent himself from human affairs (19–20).[111] In this respect the envied detachment of the Bournian jackdaw anticipates perhaps that of the Keatsian nightingale:

> Fade far away, dissolve, and quite forget
>   What thou among the leaves hast never known,
> The weariness, the fever, and the fret
>   Here, where men sit and hear each other groan;
> Where palsy shakes a few, sad, last gray hairs,
>   Where youth grows pale, and spectre-thin, and dies;
>   Where but to think is to be full of sorrow
>   And leaden-eyed despairs,
> Where Beauty cannot keep her lustrous eyes,
>   Or new Love pine at them beyond to-morrow.
>   (Keats, "Ode to a Nightingale," 21–30)[112]

If a carefree jackdaw serves to symbolize the ultimate dichotomy that can exist between the human and the animal worlds, so a caged bird can epitomize the virtue of human patience and suffering. Such is the theme of Bourne's epigrammatic lines on the Horatian topic *levius fit patientia quidquid corrigere est nefas*.[113] The topos constitutes the gnomic conclusion of *Odes* 1.24, a poem of consolation addressed by Horace to Virgil on the death of their mutual friend Quintilius. Central to the Ode in question is the speaker's emphasis upon the inevitability and finality of death. Thus even if Virgil could play the lyre more charmingly than Orpheus himself, blood would not return to the lifeless corpse of his friend (13–15). Hence although it is a difficult task, suffering is the ultimate means of alleviating whatever it is forbidden to amend.

---

[110] See Introduction, 1–3.

[111] *ille tibi invideat, felix cornicula, pennas,/qui sic humanis rebus abesse velit* (19–20).

[112] *The Works of John Keats*, 231.

[113] Cf. Horace, *Odes* 1.24.19–20.

Bourne transforms the grief-stricken mortal (Virgil) into an imprisoned bird. Ensnared by a human noose (that of the *auceps* [1]), this prisoner is initially reduced to silence (*et silet* [2]). It is a silence, however, that rapidly turns into lugubrious mourning as the encaged creature laments a different type of *fatum*—not the death of an acquaintance, but its own fate of imprisonment (*et fatum lugubre plorat avis* [2]). It does so in terms rather reminiscent of Horace's invocation to Melpomene (*praecipe lugubris/cantus, Melpomene* [2–3]) and of the especial grief experienced by Virgil himself (*nulli flebilior quam tibi* [10]). Central to the bird's *fatum* is its deprivation of liberty as conveyed by language of enclosure (*clauditur* [1]) and narrowness (*angustus carcer* [3]) in dramatic contrast to the unbridled freedom it once enjoyed (*quam limite nullo/aerias nuper iuverat ire vias* [3–4]). But exactly halfway through this eight-line poem, negatives become positives in a quasi-symbolic birth of *patientia* as though the virtue of long-suffering were in itself hatching from a metaphorical egg. Now patience is born (*nascitur* [5]) and increases (*crescit* [5]) with the result that the tedium of imprisonment is no longer such. Instead lamentation turns to consolation as the captive bird finds solace in song (7). Unlike its Horatian equivalent (Virgil in relation to Orpheus), it can in fact outdo its peers. The exemplary music of Orpheus is replaced in Bourne's poem by the birdsong produced by creatures who enjoy the freedom of the open plains. And the winner of this particular *certamen musicum*, as it were, is the captive bird. Thus the Horatian rhetorical question *quid si Threicio blandius Orpheo/auditam morderere arboribus fidem?* (13–14) is confidently answered: *nec ulla/suavius in campis libera cantat avis* (7–8), as this bird ultimately reconciles and unites Orphic *cantus* and Horatian *consolatio*: *se solatur cantu* (7).

Where song and *patientia* enable a caged bird to achieve some form of detachment from its sufferings, such is hardly the case of the human who observes the apparent death wish of a fly. Bourne's brief epigram *Suicida*, first published in the *Lusus Westmonasterienses* under the heading *Sunt Qui Servari Nolunt*,[114] describes the speaker's essentially troubled reaction to the sight of a fly flitting all too closely about his candle and as a consequence almost scorching its wings.[115]

---

[114] *Lusus Westmonasterienses*, 120. Mitford, ed. *Poematia*, 231, incorrectly states that *Suicida* first appeared in ed. 1743, p. 219.

[115] *musca meam volitat circum importuna lucernam,/alasque amburit iam prope iamque suas* (1–2). For a parallel treatment of the theme in neo-Latin literature, cf. Nicol. L'Estrange, *Transactio Philosophica Sive Metamorphosis Atomistae in Muscam*, *Musae Anglicanae*, I, 46: *per spatia incertis alis tenebrosa vagatur,/ad sese attonitam donec trahit aurea lampas* (136–137); *Musae Anglicanae*, I, 47: *flectitur in*

Given the imminent danger,[116] all he can do is repel the creature with his hand (3)[117] while asking this *ineptula musca* (3) why it longs for death (4).[118] When the fly returns and replicates its behavior, the speaker likewise endeavors to save it, but as it persists in rushing toward the flame, he surrenders in an exasperated exclamation: *si sis certa perire, peri!* (8). Perhaps there is only so much that the human can do to save such a creature. And yet is such detachment really possible? For is not the Bournian animal also to some degree a mirror-image of the Bournian human?

2.4 Models of Existence: From Glowworm to Bee

The inherent grandeur of even the smallest of creatures is a recurring leitmotif in Bourne's Latin poetry. In several instances he turns to the insect world, which can in its own way function as a model for human behavior. *Cicindela* takes as its subject the glowworm,[119] as investigated and analyzed by the curious eye of Bourne, the meticulous observer[120] of the created world. While the poem finds an interesting neo-

---

gyrum, spatiisque remotus iisdem/usque videt praedam, ductis per nubila spiris:/lampada sic torto levis ambit turba volatu,/lucentesque pyras et non ignobile bustum/ascendit demens, quaesitisque ignibus ardet (140–144).

[116] On the theme of the dangers encountered by a fly, cf. the description of the *musca* falling into the spider's web at *Lusus Westmonasterienses*, 18: *implicat innocuum volitantis aranea muscae/corpus, et implicitum dira venena necant.* Cf. Gabriel Faernus, *Musca: in cranium ollam musca quondam decidit:/ubi quum cibo, potuque distenta, ac madens,/paullatim in alto iure se se cerneret/pessum ire, mortemque imminere iam sibi,/interrito, atque composito animo oppetens:/"ego tantum," ait, "bibi, et comedi, et lavi, ut hunc/satura exitum ferre haud moleste debeam"* (*Carmina Illustrium Poetarum Italorum*, 4, 133). Cf. Gabriel Faernus, *Musca et Quadrigae: starent quadrigae quum paratae cursui,/musca advolans, temoni earum insederat,/misso ergo signo, illisque procurrentibus,/pulsu rotarum, et quadripedantis ungulae/pulverea nubes mota opacavit diem./tum in se ipsa musca gestiens: "dii magni," ait,/"quantum profundi vim excitavi pulveris"* (*Carmina Illustrium Poetarum Italorum*, 4, 146).

[117] *saepe repello manu venientem* (3).

[118] *"quae te," inquam, "impellit tanta libido mori?"* (4).

[119] The poem first appeared in the 1743 edition of Bourne's poetry (p. 203).

[120] See chapter 3, 77–79.

Latin parallel in a piece of the same title by the Italian humanist Antonius Thylesius (although the piece in question actually describes a firefly),[121] the tradition to which it belongs (and which perhaps it helped to establish) is essentially a vernacular one. Cowper, for example, not only translated Bourne's poem into English verse,[122] but also seems to have drawn upon it in his own poetry,[123] while the glowworm is likewise the subject of poems by Marvell,[124] Charlotte Smith,[125] Blake,[126] Wordsworth,[127] among others.

In the opening lines the speaker remarks on the fact that the glow worm has the appearance of a "worm" (3),[128] yet derives its name from "light" (3).[129] Then as etymologist turns entomologist, he considers the source of the "glow" (whether from the creature's tail or head [5–6]), and the purpose for its shining in the dark (perhaps to prevent its being trodden underfoot, or perhaps to prevent humans from losing their way at night [9–12]). In so doing, he attributes to the worm what Marvell had described as an "officious flame," which can have its own practical usefulness.[130] But Bourne also moves beyond earthly practicalities.

---

[121] See Antonius Thylesius, *Cicindela*, in *Carmina Illustrium Poetarum Italorum*, 9, 263–264. That the piece describes the firefly is conveyed via a series of homely details. This *cicindela* possesses wings (*summa petens commotis emicat alis* [8]) and thus can fly (*nocte volans* [1]; cf. *volat* [11]).

[122] See Appendix 2 in this volume.

[123] Cf. Cowper, "The Nightingale and the Glow Worm," on which see 70 below.

[124] See Andrew Marvell, "The Mower to the Glow Worms."

[125] See Charlotte Smith, Sonnet 58 (of the *Elegiac Sonnets*), entitled "The Glow Worm."

[126] See Blake, "A Dream."

[127] See Wordsworth, "The Pilgrim's Dream Or The Star and the Glow worm," and 70–71 in this chapter.

[128] *vermis habet speciem* (3).

[129] *sed habet de lumine nomen* (3). Cf. Thylesius, *Cicindela*, 5–7: *quae quoniam noctu lucet, cognomen adepta est/aut incensa nitet quoniam; velut ignea lampas,/cauda sit una licet, nomen non est tamen unum.*

[130] Cf. Marvell, "The Mower to the Glow Worms," 9–12: "Ye Glo-worms, whose officious Flame/To wandering Mowers shows the way,/That in the Night have lost their aim,/And after Foolish Fires do stray;" Blake, "A Dream," 17–18: "I am set to light the ground,/While the beetle goes his round."

Throughout the piece the speaker conveys the paradoxical fusion of earthy realism and noble splendor of a reptile (*reptile* [2]), whose nocturnal radiance is in tune with the celestial. Whereas Thylesius had compared the *cicindela* to a spark of fire, which as a child he was afraid to touch for fear of being burned,[131] Bourne elevates the whole to the fires of the heavens. Thus his *cicindela* seems to mirror on a microcosmic level the very stars in the sky (7–8).[132] Although unable to approximate the luminosity of the stars above, it is depicted as playing its own part in Nature's cosmic plan. For this is a created realm in which "mother Nature" (*natura parens* [13]) is the prime mover.[133] And the whole is described in pseudo-Lucretian terms. Thus as the speaker speculates that Nature perhaps wished that the glowworm's tiny light be emitted (*exiguam ... /praetendi voluit forsitan illa facem* [11–12]) lest anyone should falter his way in the dark (*in tenebris ne gressum offenderet ullus* [11]), the language is rather reminiscent of Lucretius's hymn to Epicurus, who raised a light out of the darkness, and whose footsteps the speaker professedly follows.[134] As is typical of Bourne's methodology, the whole concludes in a gnomic couplet: thus the fact that even this tiny creature possesses a source of light (16)[135] functions in itself as a warning to the

---

[131] *ardenti similes scintillae, quam puer olim/aequales inter metuebam tangere, ne me/ureret* [2–4]). The homely intimacy of these lines finds a rather striking parallel in Charlotte Smith, "The Glow Worm," 1–8: "When on some balmy-breathing night of Spring/The happy child, to whom the world is new,/Pursues the evening moth, of mealy wing,/Or from the heath-bell beats the sparkling dew;/He sees before his inexperienc'd eyes/The brilliant Glow-worm, like a meteor, shine/On, the turf-bank; amazed and pleased, he cries/'Star of the dewy grass!—I make thee mine!'" Text is that of *The Poems of Charlotte Smith*, ed. Stuart Curran (Oxford, 1993), 51–52.

[132] *nam superas stellas quae nox accendit, et illi/parcam eadem lucem dat moduloque parem* (7–8).

[133] Cf. *forsitan hoc prudens voluit natura caveri* (9); *sive usum hunc natura parens seu maluit illum* (13).

[134] Cf. Lucretius, *De Rerum Natura* 3.1–2: *e tenebris tantis tam clarum extollere lumen/qui primus potuisti*; 3.3–4 *inque tuis nunc/ficta pedum pono pressis vestigia signis*. Cf. the praises of Venus as *Natura* at 1.4–5: *per te quoniam genus omne animantum/concipitur visitque exortum lumina solis*; 1.227–228: *unde animale genus generatim in lumina vitae/redducit Venus*. It is interesting to note that Thylesius's *Cicindela* concludes with a hymn to *Natura*—a hymn that is essentially Lucretian in its language. See, for example: *omniparens natura, hominum rerumque creatrix* (20); *nihil est non mirum daedala quod tu/effingis* (25–26). The phrase *rerum natura creatrix* occurs at *De Rerum Natura* 1.629, 2.1117, 5.1362. On *daedala*, cf. 5.233–234: *quando omnibus large/tellus ipsa parit naturaque daedala rerum*.

[135] *quando habet et minimum reptile quod niteat* (16).

mighty (*magni*) to cast aside their pride, and not to spurn the lowly (15).[136]

Such an admonitory tone recurs in Cowper's "The Nightingale and the Glow-Worm," a poem that may be described as essentially Bournian not only in terms of its *dramatis personae*, but also in the shared themes of reciprocity and *aemulatio*. Here in a quasi-*contaminatio* of the *Stradae Philomela*[137] and the *Cicindela*, the warning is voiced by the glowworm itself, whose nocturnal luminosity is strikingly juxtaposed with the nightingale's power of song:

> Did you admire my lamp, quoth he,
> As much as I your minstrelsy,
> You would abhor to do me wrong,
> As much as I to spoil your song;
> For 'twas the self-same pow'r divine
> Taught you to sing, and me to shine;
> That you with music, I with light,
> Might beautify and cheer the night.
>   ("The Nightingale and the Glow-Worm," 15–22)[138]

More specifically, Bourne's presentation of that dual sense of rivalry and respective luminosity shared by both star and glowworm, combined with a concluding admonition about the dangers of pride, is mirrored in Wordsworth's "The Pilgrim's Dream Or The Star and the Glow Worm," perhaps not without a retrospective glance at Bourne's treatment.[139] As the pilgrim of the poem's title halts beneath a tree, he beholds the light of a star above him; the light of a glowworm beneath him:

> Fixed on a Star his upward eye;
> Then, from the tenant of the sky
> He turned, and watch'd with kindred look,
> A glow-worm, in a dusky nook,
> Apparent at his feet. (12–16)[140]

---

[136] *ponite vos fastus, humiles nec spernite, magni* (15).

[137] On Bourne's *Stradae Philomela*, see 60–64 in this chapter.

[138] *Cowper: Poetical Works*, ed. Milford, 301.

[139] On Bourne and Wordsworth, cf. Introduction, 16–17, 19, and chapter 3, 78–79, 85, and 103. It is equally possible that Wordsworth is drawing upon Cowper's verse translation of Bourne's piece, although there are no striking instances of verbal parallels.

[140] Text is that of *William Wordsworth: Shorter Poems, 1807–1820*, ed. C.H. Ketcham (Ithaca and London, 1989), 274–276, at 274.

Enticed to sleep by his nocturnal *locus amoenus*, so to speak, he has a dream in which the Star and the Glowworm engage in a conversation founded upon those concepts of emulation and pride that underlie Bourne's poem: thus the Star taunts the glowworm ("Much did it taunt the humble Light" [25]) scorning the fact that:

> A very Reptile could presume
> To show her token in the gloom,
> As if in rivalship with One
> Who sate a Ruler on his throne
> Erected in the skies. (28–32)

The glowworm replies, however, with a pseudo-Bournian admonition:[141]

> "Exalted Star!" the Worm replied,
> "Abate this unbecoming pride,
> Or with a less uneasy lustre shine" (33–35)

and proceeds to state that he does not aspire "to match the spark of local fire" (42). His radiance, just like that possessed by the star, is essentially transitory,[142] and will disappear at dawn (45–48), a prophetic utterance fulfilled in the ensuing lines as "that Star, so proud of late, looked wan" (53), cast, like Lucifer himself, into the pit (55–56). The whole reaches a stunningly apocalyptic conclusion as new heavens succeed the ancient ether, and the former "Glow-worms of the earth!" (64) are transfigured into heavenly Souls themselves. While Bourne's *cicindela* does not achieve the apotheosis of its Wordsworthian successor, it too mirrors a celestial pattern, and possesses a nobility and worth of its own.

Where the Bournian glowworm can to some degree mirror the celestial, so can the bee reflect an idealized human existence. Three of

---

[141] For the attribution of an admonitory speech to the glowworm, cf. Blake, "A Dream," 13–20: "Pitying I drop'd a tear:/But I saw a glow-worm near,/Who replied: 'What wailing wight/Calls the watchman of the night?/I am set to light the ground,/While the beetle goes his round:/Follow not the beetles hum;/Little wanderer hie thee home.'" Text is that of *The Complete Works of William Blake*, ed. Geoffrey Keynes (London and New York, 1939).

[142] The transience of the glowworm is mirrored to some degree by that of the silkworm in Bourne's *Bombyx*. In this piece, first published in 1743, the silkworm is depicted as maximizing its essentially brief life span in such a way that it comes to function as an example of supreme utility. Cf. lines 13–14: *quotquot in hac nostra spirant animalia terra/nulli est vel brevior vita vel utilior.* For a full-scale neo-Latin treatment of the silkworm, cf. the two-book didactic poem *Bombyx* of Marco Girolamo Vida (1485–1566).

Bourne's Latin poems take as their subject the bee community of Virgil's *Georgics*, whereby this highly organized breed of insect comes to represent a quasi-looking glass, so to speak, a symbol of industry, collaboration, and commitment toward which humans might aspire. Bourne's short piece entitled *Apes*, first published in 1743,[143] depicts bees as a symbol of the well-organized community: frugal, prudent, hard-working, and provident: *gens frugi et prudens, operosa et provida* (1). This sense of prudence and foresight is reminiscent of the bees of *Georgics* 4, who look ahead to winter even in the midst of summer,[144] with Bourne's adjective *provida* aptly encapsulating Servius's comment on *Georg.* 4.219: *colligunt flores, provident pluvias*.[145] They possess shared dwellings (*urbis habent inter sese consortia* [3]) just as Virgil's bees *solae communis natos, consortia tecta/urbis habent* (*Georg.* 4.153–154),[146] and they are highly organized when it comes to the allocation of labor (*cuique/stat sua pars operum, munia cuique sua* [3–4]), an allocation conveyed, as in Virgil, by that distinctive use of *pars*.[147] In the poem's closing lines Bourne posits this as the ideal republic (*res esto haec publica* [7]) just as Virgil had described the bees as the essentially Roman *parvosque Quirites* (*Georg.* 4.201), but this is also seen as the type of republic recommended by Plato (*hic esto populus, res esto haec publica, discat/unde suos cives instituisse Plato* [7–8]). In terms of the latter reference Bourne is making explicit that association between Virgil and Plato highlighted by such commentators as Servius, who,

---

[143] *Poematia* (1743), 211.

[144] *venturaeque hiemis memores aestate laborem/experiuntur et in medium quaesita reponunt* (*Georg.* 4.156–157).

[145] *Servii Grammatici Qui Feruntur in Vergilii Carmina Commentarii*, eds. George Thilo and Herman Hagen (Leipzig, 1887), 337.

[146] R.A.B. Mynors, ed., *Virgil Georgics* (Oxford, 1990), 279, notes that *consors* "a legal term originally for those who shared, for example, an inheritance in common, is used of the thing shared in Lucr 3.332."

[147] Cf. *Georgics* 4.158–161: *namque aliae victu invigilant et foedere pacto/exercentur agris; pars intra saepta domorum/narcissi lacrimam et lentum de cortice gluten/prima favis ponunt fundamina*. Cf. *Georgics* 4.162–163: *aliae spem gentis adultos/educunt fetus; aliae purissima mella stipant*, echoed in Bourne's depiction of Cambridge sparrows in *Passeres Indigenae Coll. Trin. Cant. Commensales*, 7: *ut coram educat teneros ad pabula foetus*. The whole is replicated to describe the highly organized work of the Carthaginians at *Aeneid* 1. 423ff: *pars ducere muros* (423), *pars optare locum tecto* (425), *hic portus alii effodiunt* (427), aptly conveyed in a bee simile commencing at 430.

commenting on the phrase *solae communes natos* (*Georg.* 4.153), had stated:

> Plato, in libris quos περὶ πολιτείας scripsit, dicit amori rei publicae esse nihil praeponendum. Omnes praeterea et uxores et liberos ita nos tamquam communes habere debere, ut caritas sit, non libido confusa, quod praeceptum nullum dicit praeter apes servare potuisse.[148]

Central to the ideal republic of this bee community is the industry of it members. Bourne's *Innocens Praedatrix*, first published in 1743,[149] takes as its subject the bee as an "innocent plunderer." Described as *sedula* (1),[150] it presses together (*stipat* [2]) the honey that it collects.[151] Like its Virgilian and Ovidian equivalents, it wanders (*vagatur* [2])[152] amid purple flowers (*purpureum ... florem* [3]),[153] and is an *opifex* (3),[154] who accumulates a metaphorical treasure upon earth (5–6),[155] flitting from flower to flower and tasting the delights in store, as emphasized by the repetition of *delibat* in lines 8–9.[156] Indeed instead of functioning as a predator, this *praedatrix* is the very antithesis of caterpillars, birds, and

---

[148] *Commentarii*, eds. Thilo and Hagen, 332.

[149] *Poematia* (1743), 233.

[150] Cf. Ovid, *Met.* 13.928: *non apes, inde tulit collectos sedula flores*; Tibullus 2.149–150: *rure levis verno flores apis ingerit alveo,/compleat ut dulci sedula melle flavos.*

[151] On the choice of the verb *stipo* in line 2 (*in cella ut stipet mella*), cf. *Georg.* 4. 163–164: *aliae purissima mella/stipant*; *Aen.* 1.432–433: *aut cum liquentia mella/stipant et dulci distendunt nectare cellas.* Cf. Jacobo Balde, *Lyricorum*, Ode 16: *ut delibatas rore flavo/stipet avis reditura cellas.*

[152] Cf. *vagantur apes* (Ovid, *Fasti* 3.556). Cf. also *peragrant* (*Georg.* 4.53).

[153] Cf. *Georgics* 4.54: *purpureos metunt flores*; cf. *Aen.* 5.79; 6.584; 9.435; 12.413–414.

[154] Cf. Ovid, *Ibis* 541–542: *inque tuis opifex, vati quod fecit Achaeo,/noxia luminibus spicula condat apis.*

[155] *herbula gramineis vix una innascitur agris,/thesauri unde aliquid non studiosa legit* (5–6). Cf. *Georg,* 4.228–229: *si quando sedem augustam servataque mella/ thesauris relines.*

[156] *delibat tactu suave quod intus habent./omnia delibat* (8–9). Cf. Lucretius, *De Rerum Natura* 3.11: *floriferis ut apes in saltibus omnia libant.*

crows (13–16), in that it compensates for its so-called "theft" by producing wax and honey (19–20).[157]

Just as Virgilian bees represent the idealized community, so too are they depicted as a breed meticulous in taking care of their own. Hence they will not hesitate to ward off the drone, the sponger, who lives on the produce of others. Virgil makes this point clearly in *Georgics* 4 as *ignavum fucos a praesepibus arcent*,[158] and the theme recurs in *Aeneid* 1.435ff. As Aeneas and his crew behold the industrious Carthaginians laying the foundations of their city, Virgil introduces a bee simile in which the highly organized Carthaginians are compared to bees building their hive and warding off the lazy drone.[159] The whole is not without irony in view of the fact that Aeneas, a refugee from Troy, is himself an onlooker beholding a Carthaginian hive upon whose resources he too, like the drone, will sponge.

But if an ancient Carthaginian people can be equated with bees, so too can an eighteenth-century Dutch community, in Bourne's short epigrammatic poem entitled *Ignavum fucos pecus a praesepibus*. First published in the *Lusus Westmonasterienses*,[160] this piece depicts a society in which no one is a drone because all play an important part. As is typical of Bourne's poetic methodology, he turns to marginalized communities: the beggar, the blind man,[161] the lame man. Yet this is a world in which *mendicus nemo, nemo vagatur iners* (2).[162] Instead, the lame man is afforded eyes; the blind man hands, whereby each can make a meaningful contribution toward the society in which he lives.[163] Indeed,

---

[157] *vix furtum est illud dicive iniuria debet/quod cera et multo melle rependit apis* (19–20).

[158] *Georgics* 4. 168. Cf. Servius, ad loc: *fucus est similis apibus, dictus eo quo sit apibus nocens, quod cum ipse nihil gignat aliena consumit.*

[159] Cf. Servius ad loc: *ignavum inutile, non aptum industriae; nam industrios navos dicimus.*

[160] *Lusus Westmonasterienses*, 50.

[161] Cf. *Epitaphium in Canem*, and 54–56 in this chapter.

[162] On *vagatur* (of bees), cf. Bourne, *Innocens Praedatrix*, 2; Ovid, *Fasti* 3.336.

[163] *non caecus, non claudus iners; modo sint tibi, claude,/qui prosint, oculi; sint tibi, caece, manus* (3–4). Bourne's sentiment finds an interesting parallel in Caelius Calcaginus, *Caecus et Claudus Iuncti*: *non potis est certo caecus procedere passu:/nec mirum est; oculos non habet ille duces./non potis est claudus recto procedere cursu:/nec mirum est; firmos non habet ille pedes./at caecus claudusque ineunt commercia, et aegre/unius possunt munus obire duo./claudus umeris caecus;*

every child, every old man has his share of duty. In short, the whole constitutes a quasi-Utopia:

> o prudens hominum respublica! natio vestra
> in terris usquam si siet, Utopia est (7–8).

But this somewhat idealized vision of a Dutch society is very different from the grim reality of eighteenth-century England as exemplified by Bourne's depiction of a series of metropolitan identities: the identities of marginalized communities.

---

claudus per devia caecum/dirigit: hic oculos commodat, ille pedes (Carmina Illustrium Poetarum Italorum, 3, 79).

CHAPTER 3

Metropolitan Identities: Perspectives on London

As argued previously, Bourne's depiction of the human and animal worlds foregrounds the concepts of identity and the reflection of identity, and the complexities that ensue when the self faces or strives to mimic the other.[1] Paradoxically such concepts are rarely, if ever, applied on a personal level.[2] For the most part Bourne seems content *not* to look into that mirror, *not* to be self-reflexive, *not* to gaze at himself as other, but instead to function as the observer rather than the observed, as a spectator on life, and as a meticulous one at that. While several of his poems have been seen to take their place within a neo-Latin tradition that was rooted in a felicitous ability to reinvent the classics, others necessarily both embrace and transcend that tradition by affording a window on the contemporary world and on the behavior of humankind. And they do so in language that moves beyond a grandiloquent classical formality to reflect sensibilities that are, as it were, more romantic in their conception. In this sense Bourne was a romantic before his time or, as Charles Lamb would later exclaim: "His diction all Latin, and his thoughts all English. Bless him! Latin was not good enough for him."[3] Moreover, it is this synthesis of, or shifting between, the classical and the romantic, the Latin and the English, so to speak, that makes his poetry strikingly original, and enables it to assume a hitherto unacknowledged place alongside an eighteenth-century vernacular tradition. It is hardly surprising then that it should have appealed to both Augustan and romantic sensibilities, as is attested by its hugely successful publication history extending over the "long eighteenth century" and beyond.[4]

---

[1] See chapters 1 and 2 in this volume.

[2] The only exception to this general rule is *Anus Saecularis*, discussed at chapter 4, 122–129, which conveys the speaker's sense of disillusionment in life, and his express wish to live no longer than fifty years of age. The tone of the whole finds a rather grim parallel in Bourne's letters to a young lady and to his wife, on which see Introduction, 1–2, 12–13, and chapter 4, 113.

[3] See Introduction, 17.

[4] See Introduction, 14–19.

At the heart of this romanticism and indeed at the center of Bourne's life and poetry is the fact that he was a metropolitan through and through, a pupil who would leave Westminster School only to return there as schoolmaster,[5] a man who made London his home in every sense of the word. As Charles Lamb proclaims:

> He is so Latin and yet so English all the while. In diction worthy of the Augustan age, he presents us with no images that are not familiar to his countrymen. His topics are even closelier drawn; they are not so properly English, as Londonish. From the streets and from the alleys of his beloved metropolis he culled his objects which he has invested with an Hogarthian richness of colouring. No town picture by that artist can go beyond his Ballad-singers; Gay's Trivia alone, in verse, comes up to the life and humour of it.[6]

And it is in his depiction of London, and of the Westminster area in particular, that Bourne recreated a series of metropolitan identities. In so doing he found a neo-Latin voice that was both familiar and new. For his is the world of the Westminster nightwatchman, faithfully doing his rounds before dawn breaks over London,[7] or of gossiping fishwives at Billingsgate,[8] or of two ballad-singers at Seven Dials,[9] or of a metropolitan conjuror.[10] And the poet is there among them, watching, commenting wryly on situation or circumstance, and using language to paint pictures of his own. In this regard his methodology would seem to anticipate on a neo-Latin level those famous words of Wordsworth as outlined in his "Preface" to the "Lyrical Ballads":

---

[5] See Introduction, 4–8.

[6] Charles Lamb, "The Latin Poems of Vincent Bourne," *The Works of Charles and Mary Lamb*, ed. Lucas, I, 337. Cf. Bradner, *Musae Anglicanae*, 269: "The sights and sounds and smells of London were dear to him, and he has recorded them for us as lovingly as did *The Tatler* or the *Spectator*." At 270 Bradner suggests that Bourne's "true parallel in painting is Wheatley's *Cries of London*, where there is the same sympathetic attention to humble life."

[7] See *Ad Davidem Cook Westmonasterii Custodem Nocturnum et Vigilantissimum*, discussed at 80–85 in this chapter.

[8] See *Schola Rhetorices*, discussed at 85–90 in this chapter.

[9] See *Cantatrices*, discussed at 90–94 in this chapter.

[10] See *Artis Est Celare Artem*, discussed at 94–99 in this chapter.

> The principal object, then, which I proposed to myself in these Poems was to choose incidents and situations from common life, and to relate or describe them throughout, as far as was possible, in a selection of language really used by men; and, at the same time, to throw over them a certain colouring of imagination, whereby ordinary things should be presented to the mind in an unusual way.[11]

Like Wordsworth, Bourne turns to the world of everyman perhaps "because in that condition the essential passions of the heart find a better soil in which they can attain their maturity, are less under restraint, and speak a plainer and more emphatic language."[12] It is a metropolitan world that has particular meaning because it is the world to which he belongs. He too conveys something of the language used by men; he too presents ordinary things in an unusual way as he replicates everyday experience in a Latin that is unpretentious, superficially simplistic, and frequently reflective of the colloquialisms and repetition of informal discourse.

And if he pauses to paint word pictures of individuals, so too does he take the reader on a guided tour of aspects of the capital itself. Like the romantic poets, who were his successors in more than a chronological sense, Bourne describes the rhythmic tolling of bells, in this instance as a musical competition, whose participants are two different church towers across the Thames,[13] while on another occasion he listens to such tolling with a quasi-romantic sense of enraptured wonderment, acknowledging the enhanced pleasure afforded by the perspective of distance.[14] Almost one hundred years before Wordsworth, Bourne composes a poem on Westminster Bridge, gazing with awe upon its symmetrical perfection;[15] on another occasion, he conveys the "bliss of solitude,"[16] as it were, and the quasi-monastic virtue of silence afforded by a London royal retreat.[17]

---

[11] Text is that of *Wordsworth: Lyrical Ballads*, ed. Michael Mason (London and New York, 1992), 59.

[12] *Wordsworth: Lyrical Ballads*, ed. Mason, 60.

[13] See *Certamen Musicum*, discussed at 100–101 in this chapter.

[14] See *Si Propius Stes, Te Capiet Minus*, discussed at 101–102 in this chapter.

[15] See *Pons Westmonasteriensis*, discussed at 103 in this chapter.

[16] Wordsworth, *Daffodils*, 22.

[17] See *Solitudo Regia Richmondiensis*, discussed at 104–112 in this chapter.

3.1 Watching a Westminster Nightwatchman

In 1716 Bourne addressed a Latin elegiac poem to a certain David Cook, nightwatchman of the parish of St Margaret's, Westminster. Elaborately entitled *Ad Davidem Cook Westmonasterii Custodem Nocturnum et Vigilantissimum Anno 1716*,[18] the piece takes as its subject the watchman's predawn patrol of the Westminster area and its environs, and in so doing follows him on his London itinerary, conveying his dedication to his job as he rises early, patrols the streets without trepidation, braves the inclement weather, and bids good morning to those whom he encounters on his rounds. The poem thus takes us on a metropolitan journey of sorts, details of which are presented with homely intimacy and affection, whereby we not only watch the watchman himself, but we also catch a glimpse of certain moments in urban time. These are provided via a series of kaleidoscopic vignettes appropriately immortalized in the rather free verse-translation of Charles Lamb.[19] But it is also both a literary and linguistic itinerary, so to speak, as the piece uses genre and language to convey the heroism (and at times the mock heroism) of a now-forgotten member of eighteenth-century society.

While evidence of the precise identity of David Cook has not yet been uncovered,[20] his job as Westminster nightwatchman was far from insignificant.[21] In eighteenth-century London it was the responsibility of the nightwatchman to patrol the streets in an attempt to preserve law and order. He would do so by undertaking regularly time-tabled beats, in the course of which he was expected to prevent crime and arrest any suspects. As a profession it was not without its dangers.[22] While the majority of

---

[18] The poem first appeared in *Poematia* (1734), 99.

[19] See Appendix 3 in this volume.

[20] Cook is not included in the *ODNB*. His name does not occur in the Parish records of St Margaret's: *The Register of St Margaret's, Westminster*, ed. L.E. Tanner (London: Harleian Society 64 [1935] and 88 [1968]).

[21] Stephen Inwood, *A History of London* (London, 1998), 375, notes the gradual development of the role of the metropolitan nightwatchman in eighteenth-century London: "In Westminster the Court of Burgesses presided over a system similar to the City one, with householders generally paying others to perform their duties as watchmen and constables.... From the 1730's parishes began to introduce a more effective system, in which communal duties were replaced by a rate-funded body of paid nightwatchmen."

[22] See Elaine Reynolds, *Before the Bobbies: The Night Watch and Police Reform in Metropolitan London 1720–1830* (Stanford, 1998); J.M. Beattie, *Policing and*

nightwatchmen were "drunken and cowardly buffoons 'fuddling in the watch-house or sleeping in their stands,'"[23] Cook by contrast is presented as good at his job,[24] counting the hours and summoning the day more assuredly than the cockerel, bravely going about his business, relying upon his knotty staff,[25] unperturbed by drunkards evicted from the pubs at closing time,[26] or by those who are planning thefts in the silence of their hearts,[27] and signaling his arrival by ringing a bell.[28] He is also portrayed as genial and friendly, always ready to bid good morning to the city's early risers. But the job of nightwatchman was both low in status and poorly paid. Something of this comes across in the content of one of the

---

Punishment in London 1600–1750: Urban Crime and the Limits of Terror (Oxford, 2001); A.T. Harris, *Policing the City: Crime and Legal Authority in London 1780–1840* (Ohio, 2004).

[23] Inwood, *A History of London*, 375–376.

[24] As Inwood, *A History of London*, 375, remarks: "the effectiveness of London's policing depended largely on how well these men did their job."

[25] *nodoso stipite fretum* (11). For the phrase, cf. Ovid, *Heroides* 10.101–102: *nec tua mactasset nodoso stipite, Theseu,/ardua parte virum dextera, parte bovem.*

[26] *quos serae emittunt post vina popinae* (9).

[27] *subdola qui tacito pectore furta parant* (12). Inwood, *A History of London*, 376, notes that "the Old Bailey and Southwark court records suggest that they [nightwatchmen] were sometimes active men, questioning suspects, chasing off muggers and working together to make arrests."

[28] *tinnitus adventum signans* (17). Cf. Charles Lamb, "To David Cook," "Announcing your approach by formal bell" (19). See Appendix 3 in this volume. A certain F.W.T. in *Notes and Queries* 3 [78] (26 April 1851), 324–325, has some interesting discussion of Bourne's poem in the context of "The Bellman, and His History": "I have often read Vincent Bourne's poem 'Ad Davidem Cook, Westmonasterii Custodem Nocturnum et Vigilantissimum, Anno 1716.' ... This nightly guardian, it appears, was accompanied by a dog,... was armed with a stout staff, or knotty club, ... and carried a bell.... To the last-mentioned part of his equipment, he owed the title of 'Bellman.' The Bellman's duty, however, was not confined to crying the rising of the stars, or the shining of the moon, but he cheered his nightly round with many a chant.... The next lines are descriptive of the Bellman's poetry, and tell us the subjects of it." The contributor proceeds to seek explanation concerning the nature of this bellman's song, and wonders: "when did the Bellman lay aside his bell, and assume the rattle; and, with this change (I presume) drop the name of Bellman for that of Watchman, to whom the silent policeman has succeeded? Was the dog the usual aide-de-camp of the Bellman? Are there any other instances in which the dog is mentioned as assisting the Bellman in his nocturnal guardianship?"

poems recited by the patrolling Cook, warning that death makes no distinction between rank or class,[29] and more explicitly in Bourne's concluding wish that the watchman receive proper tips from householders.[30]

In several respects this piece can be seen to be typical of Bourne's methodology already noted. Here again are the themes of reciprocity and reflection, achieved in this instance by the fact that both Cook and the speaker were poets, and that they exchanged verses as well as greetings.[31] In the opening lines the speaker presents his poem in return for the many poems that Cook has given him. This reciprocity is aptly conveyed through syntactical balance and repetition (*indicium ... carmen amoris* [1]; *reddo tibi indicium carmen amoris ego* [2]). The theme recurs later in the poem in two rhetorical questions, wondering how affection may repay affection (47–48).[32] And just as Cook bids good morning to the speaker (3),[33] so the speaker likewise reciprocates and redoubles that greeting

---

[29] *ut imis/summa etiam exaequet mortis amica manus* (45–46).

[30] *mille domus adeas, et non ignobile munus/(nulla minus solido) dent tibi mille domus* (51–52).

[31]   On the bellman as poet, cf. F.W.T., "The Bellman and His History," *Notes and Queries* 3 [78] (26 April 1851), 324–325: "As to the Bellman's poetry, Milton will occur to every one: 'Or the bellman's drowsy charm/To bless the door from nightly harm.' (*Il Penseroso*). 1. Herrick's *Hesperides*, p. 169, is a Bellman's song, a blessing, concluding: 'Past one o'clock, and almost two,/My masters all, good-day to you.' 2. *Ibid.* p. 251 is another song; a warning to remember the judgment-day, and ending – 'Ponder this when I am gone,/By the clock 'tis almost one.' See *The Tatler*, No. 111, for the Bellman's salutation: 'Good morrow, Mr Bickerstaff, good morrow, my masters all.' 'It was the owl that shriek'd, the fatal bellman,/Which gives the stern'st good night.' (Shakespeare, *Macbeth*, Act II. Sc. 2.) Gay refers to the Bellman's song in the following lines: 'Behold that narrow street which steep descends,/Whose building to the slimy shore extends;/Here Arundel's fam'd structure rear'd its frame,/The street alone retains the empty name;/Where Titian's glowing pain the canvass warm'd,/And Raphael's fair design, with judgment, charm'd/Now hangs the bellman's song, and pasted here/The colour'd prints of Overton appear.' (*Trivia*, book ii. 482). In the *Archaic and Provincial Dictionary*, the duty of the Bellman in his poetic character seems to be limited to blessing the sleepers. It appears from the poem by Vincent Bourne, that his Muse took a much more extensive range."

[32] *quid tibi pro totidem meritis speremus? amori/quisve tuo aequalis retribuatur amor?* (47–48).

[33] *qui faustum et felix multum mihi mane precaris* (3). Cf. *faustum felixque* (Livy 1.17.10; 1.28.7; 3.34.2).

(4).[34] Similarly, in the poem's concluding couplet Cook is wished the blessings of the Christmas season that he wishes upon the poet himself (53–54),[35] and again this is conveyed by carefully balanced syntax.

But if there is some degree of mirror-imaging in this piece, so too are there also striking points of contrast between the speaker and the watchman. Thus it is precisely while the speaker is fast asleep in the warmth of his bed with no fear of cold or rain (19–20)[36] that Cook is patrolling the streets amid icy winds and showers and the raging wintry weather (21–22).[37] And there are differences too in terms of the content and quality of their poetic output. The watchman beguiles his patrol by means of many poems (*multo carmine* [24]), and yet the nature of such is conceded to be inelegant and lacking in erudition (*culta minus docta vacet arte poesis* [25]). In short his poetry is simple, his rhythms unsophisticated (*si simplex versus sit numerique rudes* [26]). But this is inconsequential, implies the speaker in a series of affectionately homely *quid si* clauses (25–26) since potential critics are asleep (28–29). Unlike Bourne, Cook writes poems celebrating the saints, and in particular St Crispin, the patron saint of cobblers (31–32),[38] while among his other verses are some that are apparently royalist (33–36), didactic (37–44), and peppered with moral truisms (45–46). Nonetheless, given the importance of reciprocity to the piece as a whole, one might wonder to what extent Cook's *simplex versus* and *numeri ... rudes* are mirrored in Bourne's own elegiacs.

The apparent "simplicity" of Bourne's verses shines through in terms of content and style: in the homely depiction of a watchman accompanied by his dog, as conveyed in the alliterative line *tu comite assuetum cum cane carpis iter* (8); in the threefold, almost childlike, repetition of *nec te* (lines 9–11); in the way in which fairies, the subject of old wives' tales (10),[39] are surprisingly yet neatly sandwiched between

---

[34] *dico atque ingemino nunc tibi rursus: "ave"* (4).

[35] *quemque bonum exoptas nobis laetumque Decembrem,/esto tibi pariter laetus, et esto bonus* (53–54).

[36] *dumque quies nos alta manet, nec frigoris ullus/securos pluviae nec metus ullus habet* (19–20).

[37] *tu gelidos inter ventos versaris et imbres,/cum mala tempestas et nigra saevit hiems* (21–22).

[38] The reference to St Crispin is particularly appropriate, it is implied, in view of the sheer amount of walking undertaken by this patrolling hymnist.

[39] *quos lemures plurima videt anus* (10).

the essentially real terrors (of drunkards [9] and thieves [11–12]), which the watchman may encounter;[40] in the sympathetic portrait of the early morning vegetable monger bringing to the city the produce yielded by his tiny garden (*exiguus ... hortus* [14]); in the oxymoronic juxtaposition of "cobblers" and "noble glory" (31–32),[41] and especially in the use of Latin to replicate the repetitions and lilting colloquialisms of vernacular speech. This is evident in rounded elegiac couplets that end as they began: *tuque tuusque canis ... tuque tuusque canis* (49–50) *mille domos adeas ... dent tibi mille domus* (51–52).

At the same time the poem's syntactical parallelism and carefully balanced structure are strikingly sophisticated, not only mirroring the theme of reciprocity, but also offering the tantalizing possibility of a series of clever puns: between, for example, the salutation *ave* (4) and *avis* (bird) (as the following line describes the *gallus* [5], the cockerel, and its summoning of the morn);[42] or between *serus–a–um* (late) and *sera–ae* (a bar placed across a door for fastening) as London pubs evict late-night drinkers (*quos serae emittunt post vina popinae* [9])[43] or between *canis* (dog) (*cum cane carpis iter* [9]) and *canis* ("you sing") (*utile tu pueris virginibusque canis* [38]). Noteworthy too is the frequently complex way in which the poem interacts with the genre of love elegy in which it is ironically cast. Both the speaker and nightwatchman exchange a *carmen* that is a proof of "love" (*indicium ... carmen amoris* [1; 2]), a love that is to be reciprocated (*amori/...aequalis retribuatur amor* [47–48]), while the portrayal of the nightwatchman himself is not without reminiscences of the paraclausithyron or *exclusus amator* motif.[44] Like the shut-out lover, he is the victim of inclement

---

[40] On the Bellman's possession of both secular and quasi-supernatural powers whereby he could supposedly protect Londoners against goblins, cf. Robert Herrick, "The Bell-man": "From noise of Scarce-fires rest ye free,/From Murders Benedicitie./From all mischances, that may fright/Your pleasing slumbers in the night:/Mercie secure ye all, and keep/The Goblin from ye, while ye sleep." Text is that of Robert Herrick, *Poetical Works*, ed. L.C. Martin (Oxford, 1965), 121.

[41] *nec enim sine carmine fas est/nobile sutorum praeteriise decus* (31–32).

[42] *te neque dinumerat gallus constantius horas* (5).

[43] If a pun was intended this is particularly felicitous in view of the *exclusus amator* subtext, on which see 85 in this chapter. Cf. Ovid, *Amores* 1.6.24: *tempora noctis eunt; excute poste seram!* Tibullus 1.2.6: *clauditur et dura ianua firma sera*; Propertius 1.16.19: *cur numquam reserata meos admittis amores?*

[44] See Horace, *Odes* 1.25; Propertius, *Elegies* 1.16; Ovid, *Amores* 1.6; Tibullus 1.2, and Horace's parody of the tradition in *Epode* 2. See in general F.O. Copley, *Exclusus Amator: A Study in Latin Love Poetry* (Baltimore, 1956).

weather (21–22),[45] an experience that is contrasted with the good fortune of those indoors sleeping in the warmth of their beds (19–20). More specifically, the description of the watchman's lack of fear of nighttime dangers (including drunkards, fairies, and thieves [9–12])[46] seems to echo and invert the *exclusus amator* of Ovid, *Amores* 1.6, who proclaimed that he used to be afraid of the night and of its ghosts (9–10),[47] but that having now experienced love, he has been freed from such fears (14).[48] Indeed the subject of Bourne's poem may be viewed as an *exclusus amator* several times over since he voices by night a whole series of *carmina* before a multitude of dwellings (34–46).

As is frequently true of Bourne's methodology, beneath the poem's superficially simplistic tone (*simplex versus* [26]) there lie a *culta ... poesis* (25) and a *docta ... ars* (25) or to put this in Wordsworthian terms, a methodology whereby "ordinary things [can] be presented to the mind in an unusual way."[49]

3.2   Viewing Metropolitan "Performers"

Where the verses to Cook focus on a largely masculine world, that of a Westminster nightwatchman and his metropolitan itinerary, two of Bourne's other Latin poems recreate essentially female identities, those of London fishwives and ballad singers respectively. His *Schola Rhetorices*, first published in 1734,[50] treats of gossiping fishwives of Billingsgate,

---

[45] For the *exclusus amator* as suffering the cold elements, cf. Propertius 1.16.25–26: *me mediae noctes, me sidera prona iacentem/frigidaque Eoo me dolet aura gelu.* Contrast Tibullus 1.2.31–32: *non mihi pigra nocent hibernae frigora noctis,/non mihi, cum multa decidit imber aqua.*

[46] *nec te, quos serae emittunt post vina popinae,/nec te, quos lemures plurima videt anus,/nec te perterrent nodoso stipite fretum/subdola qui tacito pectore furta parant* (9–12).

[47] *at quondam noctem simulacraque vana timebam/mirabar, tenebris quisquis iturus erat* (Ovid, *Am.* 1.6.9–10).

[48] *non umbras nocte volantes,/non timeo strictas in mea fata manus* (Ovid, *Am.* 1.6.13–14).

[49] Wordsworth, Preface to *Lyrical Ballads*. See 79 in this chapter.

[50] The poem first appeared in *Poematia* (London, 1734), 132.

but, as its title suggests, the poem is in fact a burlesque founded upon the oxymoronic concept of the pseudo-eloquence enshrouding such gossip.

3.2.1   *Schola Rhetorices*

Located just below London Bridge, or as Bourne puts it: *Londini ad pontem Billingi nomine porta est* (1), Billingsgate was inextricably associated with ribaldry and cursing. It was here that fishwives established their trade of oyster-selling from early morning until late.[51] Thus John Gay in his *Trivia or the Art of Walking the Streets of London* proclaims:

> For ease and for Dispatch, the Morning's best
> No Tides of Passengers the Street molest.
> You'll see a draggled Damsel, here and there,
> From *Billingsgate* her fishy Traffic bear.
> *(Trivia, 2.7–11).*[52]

Clad in white aprons, hoods, and broad hats, the Billingsgate fishwives became notorious for indulging in gossip and foul language, with the result that the term "billingsgate" became synonymous with verbal abuse and swearing.[53] But the linguistic vulgarity of the area was also appropriated on a metaphorical level to epitomize what was perceived by

---

[51] Cf. in general Pamela Allen Brown, "Jonson among the Fishwives," *Ben Jonson Journal* 6 (1999), 89–108.

[52] John Gay, *Trivia, Or The Art of Walking the Streets of London* in *John Gay: Poetry and Prose*, ed. V.A. Dearing with C.E. Beckwith (Oxford, 1974), I, 143.

[53] The first *OED* references to Billingsgate in the sense of verbal abuse are dated to 1672. Cf. Samuel Johnson's comments in his *Life of John Philips* that "The style of Billingsgate would not make a very agreeable figure at St James's. A gentleman would take but little pleasure in language, which he would think it hard to be accosted in, or in reading words which he could not pronounce without blushing. The lofty burlesque is the more to be admired, because, to write it, the author must be master of two of the most different talents in nature. A talent to find out and expose what is ridiculous, is very different from that which is to raise and elevate." Text is that of *Johnson's Lives of the Poets*, ed. Arthur Waugh (London, 1896), II, 95–113, at 107. Cf. a Ballad entitled "The Bowes Tragedy" (c. 1714–15): "And being asked the reason why,/Such base objections she did make,/She answered thus scornfully,/In words not fit for Billingsgate." Cf. William Hazlitt, *The Spirit of the Age*, concerning Sir Walter Scott: "deluging, nauseating the public mind with the offal and garbage of Billingsgate abuse and vulgar slang." Text is that of William Hazlitt, *The Spirit of The Age* (Menston, 1971), 131–156, at 155.

several eighteenth-century writers to be a decline in literary standards. John Dryden, lamenting the debasement of literary form and content that proceeded hand in hand with the birth of the burlesque, states:

> In all you write, be neither low nor vile:
> The meanest theme may have a proper style.
>   The dull burlesque appeared with impudence,
> And pleased by novelty, in spite of sense;
> All except trivial points grew out of date,
> *Parnassus spoke the cant of Billingsgate*:
> Boundless and mad disordered rhyme was seen,
> Disguised Apollo changed to harlequin
> (The Art of Poetry 1.79–86)[54]

while Pope exclaims:

> There, stript, fair Rhet'ric languish'd on the ground;
> His blunted Arms by sophistry are born,
> And shameless *Billingsgate* her Robes adorn.
> (The Dunciad, 4.24–26)[55]

But Billingsgate itself could be presented in a burlesque form, and it is in this context that Bourne's poem merits prime consideration. In particular the vulgar colloquialisms, raucous language, swearing and general scurrility associated with the fishwives were frequently satirized by eighteenth-century writers as possessing a pseudorhetoric or eloquence of their own. But whereas Dryden bewails a Parnassus that speaks "the cant of Billingsgate," and Pope laments the languishing of rhetoric, Bourne proclaims a Billingsgate that can, as it were, speak the cant of Parnassus. He does so by appropriating the technical language of rhetoric to a nonrhetorical context whereby the fishwives and their trade assume the identity of performing Roman orators, possessing an eloquence evocative of the ideal rhetorician as delineated by Cicero, Quintilian, and others.

The poem's grandiloquent title, *Schola Rhetorices*, or "School of Rhetoric" aptly encapsulates the element of burlesque that colors the piece as a whole. The term *Schola*, denoting among other things "a place or establishment in which a teacher expounds his views,"[56] possesses

---

[54] *The Poems of John Dryden*, ed. Paul Hammond (London and New York, 1995), II, 155–156. Italics are mine.

[55] Text is that of *Alexander Pope: The Dunciad*, ed. James Sutherland in *The Poems of Alexander Pope* (London and New Haven, 1965), V, 342.

[56] Cf. *OLD* 2 b (of rhetoric).

particular significance when applied to the world of the rhetorician. Thus Quintilian depicts the young would-be orator engaging in a forensic battle and witnessing victory in the *schola* itself.[57] Likewise the formality enshrouding the Grecism *Rhetorices* appropriately suggests "the systemised art of public speaking."[58] But the title is also evocative of the academic context that will become apparent in the poem's closing reference to an Oxbridge community, and the titles of which it boasts (11).[59] It is tempting too to see in *schola* a possible pun on "school" as the collective name for a group of fish,[60] the latter particularly pertinent given the poem's context of fishwives and their wares.[61]

   This methodology continues in the course of the poem proper. The oyster-bearing fishwives themselves are pompously described as "green Sea-Nymphs" (*virides ... Nereides* [2]),[62] engaging in forensic disputation, for it is here that eloquence has chosen for herself a permanent seat (*hic sibi perpetuam legit facundia sedem* [3]). And it is here that these gossiping females seem to fulfill the very prerequisites of the ideal classical orator.

   Throughout the poem Bourne avails of the potential for double entendre provided by the manifold meanings of individual Latin words. It is this that lies at the heart of the piece's sardonic wit. Thus the language

---

[57] Quintilian, *Inst. Orat.* 5.12.22: (*adulescens*) ... *initurus ... forensium certaminum pugnam iam in schola victoriam spectet*. Cf. 12.8.6: *themata in scholis posita*.

[58] *OLD*, s.v. Cf. Quintilian, *Inst. Orat.* 2.17.5: *quidem naturalem esse rhetoricen volunt, et tamen adiuvari exercitatione non diffitentur*. Cf. 5.10.54: *id aut universum verbis complectimur, ut "rhetorice est bene dicendi scientia."*

[59] *utraque quos malit titulos academia iactet* (11).

[60] The use of "school" in the sense of "a shoal or large group of fish" is attested by *OED* from c. 1400.

[61] For a similar pun, cf. Andrew Marvell, *Parodia*, 9: *cum scholae latis genus haesit agris*, in which the scholarly community or "school" of Cambridge is implicitly equated with the *piscium ... genus* (9) of the poem's model (Horace, *Odes* 1.2). See Estelle Haan, *Andrew Marvell's Latin Poetry*, 37–38.

[62] Cf. Tobias Smollett, *The Adventures of Peregrine Pickle*, chapter 87: "She set him at defiance, and held forth with such a flow of eloquence, as would have entitled her to a considerable share of reputation, even among the *nymphs of Billingsgate*; for this young lady, over and above a natural genius for altercation, had her talents cultivated among the venerable society of weeders, podders, and hoppers, with whom she had associated from her tender years." Text is that of *The Adventures of Peregrine Pickle*, (Oxford, 1925), IV, 23. Italics are mine. On metropolitan females as nymphs, cf. *Cantatrices*, discussed at 90–94 in this chapter.

spoken by these fishwives is depicted as lacking neither limit (*modus* [4]) nor shape (*figura* [4]), terms that assume a rather different meaning when read in a specifically oratorical context. In the classical world language that possessed *modus* was characterized by "a rhythmic pattern, measure, beat or rhythm,"[63] that *quodam oratorio numero et modo* hailed by Cicero as pertaining to prose.[64] Likewise in a rhetorical sense *figura* denoted "a form of speech, departing from the straightforward and obvious, figure of speech"[65] or in the words of Quintilian: *figura sit arte aliqua novata forma dicendi.*[66] Certainly the cursing and swearing at Billingsgate constitute a departure from the normal method of speech, but in this instance such is ironically presented as the novelty of forensic embellishment. As the fishwife asks passersby to purchase her wares, she is appropriately described as a "female suppliant," an *oratrix* (5) adorning her conversation with an abundance of flowers (*sermonem densis oratrix floribus ornat* [5]). Read on a rhetorical level, the noun assumes additional force since the Greek term *ῥητορική* itself when translated into Latin was described as possessing characteristics of both the orator and the *oratrix*. Quintilian makes the point very clearly: *rhetoricen in Latinum transferentes tum oratoriam tum oratricem nominaverunt,*[67] while *flos* means both "flower" and a "rhetorical or poetical ornamentation or an instance of it."[68] And this florid language is accompanied by the pouring and redoubling of various figures of speech (*et fundit varios ingeminatque tropos* [6]) whereby the substitution of curses for normal language is depicted as the recourse to rhetorical "tropes."[69] The oratorical subtext becomes more prominent as the poem proceeds, for among the characteristics of the language used by these

---

[63] Cf. *OLD* s.v: meaning no. 7.

[64] Cicero, *De Oratore* 1.151; 3.184. Cf. Cicero, *Brut.* 32: *intellexit enim in soluta oratione, dum versum effugeres, modum tamen et numerum oportere servari.*

[65] Cf. *OLD* s.v: meaning no. 11.

[66] Quintilian, *Inst. Orat.* 9.1.14. Cf. *Laus Pisonis: exornata figuris ... sententia.*

[67] Quintilian, *Inst. Orat.* 2.14.1.

[68] Cf. *OLD* s.v: meaning 11. Cf. Cicero, *Brut.*, 233: *in huius oratione ... erat ... nullus flos ... neque lumen ullum*; Col. 9.2.1: *veterum auctorum placita ... Virgilius poeticis floribus illuminavit.*

[69] Cf. *OLD* s.v. *tropus.* Cf. Quintilian, *Inst. Orat.* 9.1.5: *quare in tropis ponuntur verba alia pro aliis.* Cf. in general, *Inst. Orat.* 8.6; 9.1.

women are further prerequisites of the ideal classical orator including
"stylistic vigour" (*nervi* [7]),[70] abundance (*copia fandi* [7]),[71] and gravity
(*pondus* 8]).[72] The whole culminates in its own rhetorical celebration of
Billingsgate, a seat that is seen as surpassing the very symbols of classical
oratory itself, namely, the *rostrum* and the *forum* (10).[73] But if the poem
heralds a victory over the world of classical Rome, so too does it come
full circle by ending as it had begun—in the world of eighteenth-century
England. Now with succinct epigrammatic irony the speaker predicts that
Billingsgate will be awarded the honorary title of *linguarum Ianua*, and
as such will surpass those titles of which Oxford and Cambridge boast.

Once again Bourne reveals himself as the wry observer of
contemporary Londoners, but here he shows a particular sensitivity to the
verbal and linguistic nuances afforded by the Latin language itself.
Elevating the whole to a realm that transcends the bathetic, the speaker
bestows upon metropolitan fishwives a pseudoclassical identity. He does
so, moreover, in a piece that possesses an embellished oratory of its own:
hic sibi perpetuam legit facundia sedem (3). Now as the language of the
curse is transformed into that of the accomplished orator in performance,
Billingsgate becomes a Parnassus of sorts.

3.2.2   *Cantatrices*

If cursing fishwives can be presented as oratorical Sea-Nymphs, so
too can eighteenth-century ballad-singers assume the role of another
category of classical nymphs, namely, the Sirens themselves. Bourne's
Cantatrices, first published in 1734,[74] takes as its subject two female
ballad-singers selling their wares at London's Seven Dials in St Giles in

---

[70] Cf. *OLD* s.v.: meaning 9: "stylistic vigour." Cf. Cicero, *De Orat.* 3.80: *neque sine forensibus nervis satis vehemens esse orator potest.*

[71] Cf. *OLD* s.v.: meaning 6 "rhet.: The ability to express oneself well and fully, command of the resources of oratory." Cf. Cicero, *De Orat.* 2.151: *orationis copia, videmus ut abundant philosophi.*

[72] Cf. *OLD* s.v.: meaning 7: "gravity (of demeanor or language), dignity, solemnity." Cf. Cicero, *De Orat.* 2.73: *omnium sententiarum gravitate, omnium verborum ponderibus est utendum*; *Brut.* 265: *quantum pondus in verbis.*

[73] *o sedes, totidem multum celebrata per annos!/omne tibi rostrum cedit et omne forum* (9–10).

[74] *Poematia* (1734), 143.

the Fields, a printing district for broadsheets and popular literature, in front of whose presses operated the street vendors themselves. The Broadside ballad, an essentially ephemeral genre, traces its origins back to the end of the fifteenth century.[75] Indeed for several centuries before Bourne's day it had contributed to the mass culture of London's street literature.[76] Printed on only one side of thin paper, the Broadside ballad comprised a narrative song or a poem, usually on such topical themes as love and betrayal in love, sex, religion, social satire, fantasy, and crime. For the most part actual musical notation was not included on the sheet (which was generally of poor printing quality), but there might be a sentence indicating that the words were to be sung to a familiar tune. An essentially cheap product, it was sold at street corners (usually for a penny) by peddlers, for whom such sales proved a vital source of income. While the rate of success depended largely on content and on the vicissitudes of common taste, that the genre generally transcended typical age and class distinctions is attested by its popularity over the centuries. Indeed the more enthusiastic purchaser might even paste such ballads to his or her walls perhaps as an *aide memoire* for learning the piece in question.

And several of these details are captured in Bourne's poem. It is hardly surprising then that this piece in its fusion of realism and classical idealism appealed to eighteenth-century sensibilities. After its initial printings in the 1734 and 1735 editions of Bourne's poems, it reappeared three years later in *The Gentleman's Magazine* of 1738, accompanied on this occasion by a verse translation by a certain S.P.[77] Later it would of course be famously translated by Charles Lamb.[78] Like *Schola Rhetorices* this poem, through the use of grandiloquent language, bestows a mock-heroic identity upon a profession that confined itself largely to an impoverished London class. In so doing it provides a window into eighteenth-century metropolitan habits, customs, and indeed performance.

---

[75] See Leslie Shepard, *The Broadside Ballad: A Study in Origins and Meaning* (London, 1942).

[76] See Leslie Shepard, *The History of Street Literature: The Story of Broadside Ballads, Chapbooks, Proclamations, News-Sheets, Election Bills, Tracts, Pamphlets, Cocks, Catchpennies, and Other Ephemera* (Michigan, 1973), passim. As Shepard, 13, states: "Street literature is concerned with the cheap ballad sheets, pamphlets and other ephemera of the masses, which circulated from the dawn of printing right up to the end of the nineteenth century."

[77] *The Gentleman's Magazine* 8 (July 1738), 371–372.

[78] Cf. Charles Lamb, "The Ballad Singers," and Appendix 3 in this volume.

In the opening lines the speaker zooms in on the physical appearance of the two ballad-singers, whose performance lies at the heart of the whole, conveying in homely detail such aspects of their gypsy attire as a straw hat (3),[79] a huge beaded necklace (3–4),[80] and ankle-length mud-encrusted clothing (4–6).[81] And the portrait painted is a sympathetic one. In a daringly oxymoronic juxtaposition of the maternal and the materialistic, this meticulous observer of London life describes one of the singers with a small infant hanging from her breast (7),[82] and the other holding the broadside "for sale" (8).[83] Later we learn something of the broadside's content and the sequential performance of the same. Thus (i) one of the singers narrates the plot or argumentum (32–33)[84]—a plot concerning betrayed love as a nymph is deceived by the treachery of a perfidious sailor (33–34);[85] (ii) she sings this *flebile carmen* (34) in rhythms that match its subject (35);[86] (iii) the second singer then picks this up and sings alternately (35–36).[87] As we will see, the performers reap the rewards of success.

Indeed despite their impoverished status there is something of the heroic in these particular performers, whose very depiction as two nymphs (*nymphae ... binae* [2]) and more specifically as Sirens (2, 33)[88] recalls those mythological creatures who by the power of their melodious music attempted to lure men to their death on the rocks surrounding the

---

[79] *stramineum capiti tegimen* (3).

[80] *collumque per omne/ingentes electri orbes* (3–4).

[81] *utrique pependit/crustato vestis coeno, limoque rigescens/crure usque a medio calcem defluxit ad imum* (4–6).

[82] *exiguam secum pendentem ex ubere natam* (7). Cf. William Hogarth's *The Enraged Musician* (1741), which includes a depiction of a ballad-singer cradling a baby and holding a broadside in her hand.

[83] *venales dextra tulit altera chartas* (8).

[84] *canticulae interea narraverat argumentum/altera Sirenum* (32–33).

[85] *infidi periuria nautae/deceptamque dolo nympham* (33–34).

[86] *flebilibus ... numeris* (35).

[87] *quos altera versu/alterno excepit* (35–36).

[88] Ovid likewise depicts the Sirens as Nymphs at *Metamorphoses* 5.552.

island they inhabited.[89] It is music that is captured by the poet in this, the traditional meter of epic. But these eighteenth-century Sirens are also portrayed as possessing essentially Orphic powers. Thus it is in response to their song and the attraction of a possible purchase that men and women from all walks of life abandon what they are doing and gather round in a fever of excitement. And Bourne conveys with the ever-watchful eye of the observer something of the whole spectrum of eighteenth-century London society, represented in a mock-epic catalogue of potential buyers: youths and unmarried girls (9–10); a cobbler, who might find in the ballad a means of beguiling the tedium of a winter's night (10–15); a bare-armed maid eagerly running forth (17); a blacksmith, his face still covered in dirt (18–19) but who has abandoned a forge rather reminiscent of that of Vulcan, the divine manufacturer of a hero's amour as depicted in *Aeneid* 8.[90] And the epic undertones continue. Next comes the passing traveler, his back stooped from his knapsack, yet forgetful of his burden as he lingers to listen (21–23). His stupefied reaction is compared to that of Sisyphus in the underworld upon hearing the charming music of Orpheus (24–27).[91] According to Ovid, so spellbound was he by Orpheus's music that he actually sat upon the perpetually rolling rock that served as his infernal punishment.[92] But if a traveler can be Sisyphus, so too does he possess something of the forgetfulness of Orpheus himself. Virgil states that it was because he was forgetful (*immemor heu! victusque animi* [*Georgics* 4.491]) that Orpheus looked back at Eurydice, and hence all his effort was wasted (*ibi omnis/ effusus labor* [491–492]). Something of the Virgilian Orpheus is appropriated by Bourne in his description of Sisyphus as *laboris/ immemor* (25–26) except that here the *labor* has become the physical infernal punishment of rolling a rock up a hill, a labor from which Orpheus's music affords respite. Thus the traveler, like Sisyphus, does not feel the weight upon his shoulders (*umeris nec pondera sentit* [23]), enraptured as he is by the power of music. We catch a glimpse too of London traffic as carts divide the audience, which then reassembles (28–31) like waves that have been divided by a ship—a particularly

---

[89] See, for example, Homer, *Odyssey* 12.39; Virgil, *Aeneid* 5. 846; Ovid, *Met.* 14.88.

[90] Cf. *Aeneid* 8. 449–453.

[91] *sic ubi Tartareum regem Rhodopeius Orpheus/Threiciis studuit fidibus mulcere, laboris/immemor Aeolides stupuit modulamina plectri,/nec sensit funesti onera incumbentia saxi* (23–26).

[92] Cf. Ovid, *Met.* 10.44: *inque tuo sedisti, Sisyphe, saxo.*

appropriate simile in view of the Sirens analogy. And the stupefaction of those infernal characters is mirrored in the gaping, open-mouthed reaction of this audience (36–38) listening to the performance in profound anticipation. It is a performance that ultimately proves successful as a whole host of potential purchasers stretch out their hands to buy a copy, which is distributed to them by the ballad-singers even while they are still performing (40–42). Even a beggar and a grudging old woman give in, the latter eventually demanding the sheet and announcing that she intends to paste it up on the walls of her house (48–53). Such is the force of the ballad's *argumentum*; such is the power of these alluring songstresses, these eighteenth-century *cantatrices*.

3.2.3   *Artis Est Celare Artem*

It has been seen that Bourne's depiction of the fishwives of Billingsgate and the ballad-singers of the Seven Dials exemplifies differing types of metropolitan "performance" by members of largely impoverished feminine communities, that are nonetheless endowed by the speaker with an essentially mock-heroic identity. Such performances were staged, as it were, for the practical purpose of eking a living. But metropolitan performance worked on another, more formal and much more lucrative level.

Eighteenth-century London, especially the London of the 1720s, was home to the illusionist Isaac Fawkes (1675–1731),[93] who sought to disassociate himself from street performers by marketing himself as a professional master of the stage, resulting in a career that was so successful that by the time of his death in May 1731 he had allegedly accumulated a fortune of some ten thousand pounds.[94] Where the fishwives and ballad-singers operated at street corners in the hope of winning the attention (and the money) of the passerby, Fawkes worked not only at London fairs, themselves possessing the potential for disorder and rioting,[95] but also and especially in a number of fixed locations

---

[93] On Isaac Fawkes, see Simon During's excellent study: *Modern Enchantments: The Cultural Power of Secular Magic* (Harvard and London, 2002), 79–85.

[94] Cf. *The Gentleman's Magazine*, I (May 1731), 221, which, in recording his death on 25 May, proclaims him as "Mr Fawkes noted for his Dexterity of Hand, said to die worth 10,000*l*."

[95] During, *Modern Enchantments*, 82, notes that while the London fairs at which Fawkes performed were generally viewed with suspicion by the authorities and could also prove to be the occasions for rioting, they were, however, more orderly than their predecessors.

including the Opera House, Haymarket (now Her Majesty's Theatre), and the Old Tennis Court in James Street (known as Whitcom Street since 1905).[96] Moreover, as will be noted, instead of relying upon the whim of the passerby, he actively ran an advertising campaign that was highly sophisticated for its day.[97] The conjuring shows that he staged charged an admission fee of two shillings, one shilling and sixpence, with prices varying according to the status and rank of his audience members, which, as Simon During notes, "indicates demand from various social sectors."[98] Eager to distinguish himself from the potentially dangerous reputation that attended upon supernatural magic,[99] this shrewd businessman achieved his fame largely as a consequence of his sleight of hand and the frequently surprising tricks that came to characterize his shows. In short, it was in the skillful art of conjuring that Fawkes made his mark in early eighteenth-century London.

Central to the conjuror's art is, of course, the ability to conceal that art. Bourne's short Latin poem entitled *Artis Est Celare Artem* takes Fawkes as its subject, and presents the conjuror in terms that describe not only the variety of tricks for which he became famous, but also, it will be argued, aspects of that marketing campaign mentioned previously. According to Mitford, the piece first appeared in the 1743 edition of Bourne's poetry.[100] While it is certainly true that the poem was included in that edition, an earlier version, unnoticed by Mitford, perhaps because of its different heading (*Ignoti Multa Cupido*), occurs in the *Lusus Westmonasteriensis* of 1730.[101] Apart from the different title and some significant textual variants in the closing couplet,[102] the version does not

---

[96] Cf. During, *Modern Enchantments*, 82.

[97] See 96–97 in this chapter.

[98] Cf. During, *Modern Enchantments*, 82.

[99] Cf. During, *Modern Enchantments*, 81.

[100] Mitford, ed. *Poematia*, 233.

[101] *Lusus Westmonasterienses*, 165,

[102] Lines 15–16 of the *Lusus Westmonasterienses* version read: *sic ignota iuvant, sic abdita poscimus omnes;/Fawksi, artem retegas, et nihil artis habes.* In the 1743 version this has become: *multum habet ingenii, multum delusor et artis;/qui, simul ac aperit se, nihil artis habet.* The change may reflect Bourne's wish to convey more precisely in the poem's closing couplet the essence of his new heading *Artis Est Celare Artem.*

differ very substantially from the *Artis est Celare Artem*.[103] First
published then in a Westminster collection of 1730, and thus composed
during Fawkes's lifetime, this elegiac piece reveals once more Bourne as
meticulous observer, or in this instance, "spectator" of contemporary
metropolitan life.

Inherent in the poem's title is the proverbial notion that true art is
to be equated with concealed art. It is a sentiment that traces its origins
back to the classical world. Thus Ovid proclaims of the would-be
seducer: *si latet, ars prodest* (*Ars Amat.* 2.313) or of the statue of
Pygmalion: *ars adeo latet arte sua* (*Met.* 10.252), while Quintilian
expounds on the subject on two occasions, applying the proverb to the art
of oratorical declamation: *nam si qua in his ars est dicentium ea prima
est ne ars esse videatur* (1.11.3); *ubicumque ars ostendatur, veritas
abesse videatur* (9.3.102). Perhaps Bourne's *ars poetica*, so to speak, at
least as manifested in the Fawkes poem, is, like that of the conjuror
whom it celebrates, enshrouded in clever "concealment," and thus
possessed of tricks and dexterity of its own?[104] Perhaps some attempt to
understand such tricks, and to uncover or to discover that art is integral to
the respective responses of reader to poem or of spectator to show. The
meaning, if not the answer, must lie in that attempt.

In the opening lines, the speaker takes pains to emphasize that
Fawkes actively "invites" his potential audience to his show, and that
they come not unwillingly (*pulchra nec invitos vocat ad spectacula
cives/Fauxius* [1–2]). He also highlights the skills possessed by the
conjuror: thus he is a man of excellent "dexterity" (*egregiae dexteritatis
homo* [2]), than whom no other is more skilled in deluding his spectators
(*fallere spectantes* [3]) whether in terms of verbal trickery (*vel linguae
insidiis* [4]) or sleight of hand (*vel levitate manus* [4]). In issuing an
invitation (*vocat* [1]) highlighting "dexterity" and "sleight of hand" (as
opposed to traditional magical or demonic skills) these opening lines read
rather like those advertisements that lay at the very heart of Fawkes's
self-marketing. As During notes, this conjuror in particular exploited the
potential for self-advertisement provided by the medium of print, with the
result that he "was the first to produce what would nowadays be called a

---

[103] Further textual variants in the 1730 *Lusus* version include *rara* (1), *deceptor* (5),
speciosus (5), *hunc* (6), *tum* (9), *invertens* (9), *fallacem orditur* (9), *sponte sua* (11),
summa (11), *laetus spectator* (13).

[104] If so, then its methodology might be seen to resemble that of Bourne's poems
celebrating musical harmony, themes that are mirrored in the poems' internal
linguistic and syntactical harmonies. See 100–103 in this chapter.

'campaign.'"[105] Central to that campaign was his placing of adverts in such popular "newspapers" of the day as *The Daily Post, Mist's Journal, Pasquin, London Journal, Weekly Journal, Daily Courant*, and *The Grub Street Journal*,[106] in all of which he "invited" his spectators to a conjuring feast of dexterity and sleight of hand. These were the tricks that took the place of the traditional role of necromancy. And if such advertisements happened to refer to magic, they did so with heavy-handed irony:

> By an Express from the Haymarket we are informed that the conjuring Fawkes is lately arrived from the lower Regions, where, we suppose, he has been consulting his Daemons, because they tell us, he has got a whole Budget full of new fashion'd Tricks, which he designs shortly to show out of hand.[107]

Indeed, as During perceptively remarks, "Fawkes carefully marketed himself as an artist in 'dexterity of hand' and openly advertised his diversions as 'tricks' whose attractions lay in their capacity to cause 'surprise.'"[108] It is in this context that Bourne's opening "advertisement," as it were, should be read.[109] For the speaker of *Artis Est Celare Artem*, just like the conjuror it celebrates, "invites" (*vocat* [1]) its readers, its willing audience, to a literary spectacle, while simultaneously proclaiming Fawkes not as magician, but as a man of *egregiae dexteritatis* (2), possessed of tricks (*insidiis* [4]) and sleight of hand (*levitate manus* [4]), in terms strikingly reminiscent of his own advertising campaign.

---

[105] During, *Modern Enchantments*, 83.

[106] Cf. During, *Modern Enchantments*, 83.

[107] *Mist's Journal*, Jan. 20, 1728. Cf. During, *Modern Enchantments*, 81 and 297. It is interesting to note in this regard the highly fanciful and certainly exaggerated report of Fawkes's so-called magical skills as described in *The Gentleman's Magazine* I (Feb. 1731), 79: "The Algerine embassadors went to see Mr. Fawkes, who, at their request, shew'd them a prospect of Algier, and rais'd up an apple-tree which bore ripe apples in less than a minute's time, which most of the company tasted of." During, *Modern Enchantments*, 81, is probably correct in assuming that such a contradiction represents "two sides of the media's magic primitivism."

[108] During, *Modern Enchantments*, 81. Cf. Advertisements collected in the Harry Price Collection, Scrapbook 3, University of London, and During, *Modern Enchantments* 297.

[109] During appears to be unaware of Bourne's poem and hence of the way in which it seemingly mirrors the advertising campaign itself.

Dressed in an elegant wig and a conventional jacket,[110] Fawkes won contemporary and posthumous acclaim for his immense versatility and for the range and surprising novelty of the tricks he performed. In 1746, some fifteen years after the conjuror's death, a Christmas Book entitled *Round About Our Coal Fire, or Christmas Entertainments*, would offer a succinct summary of such versatility:

> These are the old Heroes in Magick; and next to them I place Mr. Fawkes, one of our modern Conjurers, who, after having anointed himself with the Sense of the People, became so great a Conjurer, that he amassed several Thousand Pounds to himself. He was so great a Magician, that either by the Force of his Hocus-Pocus Power, or by the Influence of his Conjuring Wand, he could presently assemble a multitude of People together, to admire the Phantoms he raised before them, viz. Trees to bear Fruit in an instant, Fowls of all sorts, change Cards into Birds, give us Prospects of fine Places out of nothing, and a merry Jig without either a Fiddler or a Piper; and moreover, to show that Money was but a Trifle to him, with a Conjuring Bag that he had, would every now and then shower down a Peck or two of Gold and Silver upon his Table; and that this Money should not die with him, he has conjured up a Son who can do the same things; so that one may say his Conjuration is hereditary.[111]

Bourne's poem progresses from the self-proclaimed advertisement to the content of the show itself, and does so in a tone of heightened excitement. This is conveyed by means of rhetorical exclamation as the conjuror produces a little ball (*orbiculum* [6]), which he then causes to disappear and reappear. And this is replicated in the staccato language and syntax of the Latin lines: in the daring macaronic pun on "Hey Presto": *en! vobis (aperitque manum deceptor utramque)/orbiculum! hei praesto!—fugit, abivit—adest* [5–6]); in the excitedly breathless *est hic, est illic* (7); in the contrast between *nusquam* (7) and *ubique* (7), and in the threefold repetition of *in* (*in mensa—in loculis huius—in ore tuo* [8]). There follows a second trick as Fawkes turns a bag upside down, producing from it an egg followed by a flock of hens and birds (*tunc peram invertit, fraudemque exorsus ab ovo/gallinam profert aligerumque gregem* [9–10]). This is a reference to probably one of Fawkes's most celebrated tricks, the "egg-bag trick," which involved the repeated turning inside and out of an empty bag, from which the conjuror would produce

---

[110] See During, *Modern Enchantments*, 83. For iconographical depictions of Fawkes in performance, see the print by William Hogarth, *The Bad Taste of the Town* (1724).

[111] *Round About Our Coal Fire, or Christmas Entertainments* (London, 1746), 30–31. Cf. During, *Modern Enchantments*, 84.

eggs, gold, silver, and sometimes even hens.[112] Another trick for which Fawkes had won acclaim largely because of its essential novelty and element of surprise is that of a pack of cards thrown up into the air and suddenly transformed into a flock of birds.[113] Or, as Bourne describes it: *chartula (pro monstrum!) summi ad laquearia tecti/subvolat et formam iussa capessit avis* (11–12). As During notes, this trick is not to be found in seventeenth-century trick books.[114] Hardly surprising, then, that Bourne should proclaim this act of skilful conjuring as a *monstrum*. Indeed Alexander Pope seems to allude to this and to other Fawksian tricks in his "Epistle to Bathurst" (1733):

> Blest paper-credit! last and best supply!
> That lends Corruption lighter wings to fly!
> Gold imp'd by thee, can compass hardest things,
> Can pocket states, or fetch or carry Kings.
> ("Epistle to Bathurst," 69–72)[115]

The result is one of both pleasure (*spectator laetus videt* [13]) and stupefaction (*stupet* [14]) as the spectator watches these "miracles" (*miracula rerum* [13]) and is captivated by the hidden trickery (*occulti captus amore doli* [14]). If earlier in the poem the conjuror was depicted as opening each of his two hands (*aperitque manum deceptor utramque* [5]), now in a witty tour de force the closing lines emphasize that if he were to "open up" his very self this would prove detrimental to his art (*qui simul ac aperit se, nihil artis habet* [16]). In short, the essence of the conjuror's art is precisely that concealment celebrated in the piece as a whole.

---

[112] The trick is described in Henry Dean's *The Whole Art of Legerdemain: or Hocus Pocus in Perfection. By which the meanest Capacity may perform the Whole Art without a Teacher. Together with the Use of all the Instruments belonging thereto. To which is now added, Abundance of New and Rare Inventions, the like never before in Print but much desired by many* (London, 1763), 26–27. Cf. During, *Modern Enchantments*, 83 and 298.

[113] Cf. During, *Modern Enchantments*, 84.

[114] Cf. During, *Modern Enchantments*, 84.

[115] Text is that of *The Poems of Alexander Pope*, ed. John Butt (London, 1940), III.ii, 90.

3.3   Sensing Metropolitan Harmonies

Bourne's depiction of contemporary London is colored by his acknowledgement of the harmony that is achievable through the reconciliation of seemingly disparate elements. And this works on the levels of sound, sight, and architecture. His *Certamen Musicum*, first published in 1734,[116] takes as its subject two different types of tolling produced by the bells of two Thames-side churches: St Mary-le-Bow and St Bride's (i.e., Wren's church on Fleet Street), which possess eight and twelve bells, respectively. The tolling produced by the latter is light and swifter; that produced by the former is weighty and slower. Such a disparity is replicated both syntactically and rhythmically in a poem whose language mirrors the sounds themselves: syntactically through the use of the contrasting adjectives *tenues* (3) and *grandes* (4), the diminutive *modulos* (3) as opposed to *modos* (4), and the comparative adverbs *properantius* (3) as opposed to *lentius* (4); rhythmically in the largely dactylic *haec tenues urget modulos properantius aedes* (3) versus the heavier spondaic *alternat grandes lentius illa modos* (4). As its title suggests, the whole is presented in terms of a musical contest, whose judge (*iudex* [5]) would in fact be unable to distinguish (*distinguat* [5]) whether the former or the latter is more captivating to the ear. For the effect of this *contentio musica* (7) is one not of dissonance, but of great harmony (*tantae ... est harmoniae* [7]), a harmony achieved precisely by the alternation between rhythm (*numeros* [8]) and weight (*pondus* [8]), and in poetic terms by the echo of the verb *alternat* (4) in the closing line's balancing of *altera ... altera* (8). In a sense then the poem, like the sounds it celebrates, achieves a self-referential *harmonia* through the reconciliation of both the aural and the linguistic.

In singing the praises of tolling church bells Bourne's piece takes its place within a neo-Latin and vernacular tradition. Worthy of comparison, for example, is William Dillingham's captivating *Campanae Undellenses*, anthologized by Bourne in his edition of the *Musae Anglicanae*[117] or Thomas Hood's effusive salutation of "Dear Bells! how sweet the sound of village bells/When on the undulating air they swim!"[118] Dating to the early eighteenth century of course is that anonymous though now all-too-familiar piece "Oranges and lemons,/Say

---

[116] *Poematia* (1734), 140.

[117] *Musae Anglicanae*, I, 244–248.

[118] Thomas Hood, "Ode to Rae Wilson," 159–160. Text is that of The *Complete Poetical Works of Thomas Hood*, ed. Walter Jerrold (London, 1906), 511.

the bells of St Clements," a rhyme doubtlessly familiar to most children, but not without interest in portraying as virtual *dramatis personae* a whole range of bells from a variety of churches (including Whitechapel, Aldgate, St Catherine's, St Clement's).

For the most part eighteenth-century and romantic poems treating of church bells tend to focus upon the listener rather than the bells themselves, emphasizing both aural and emotional sensibilities, and interrogating more closely the effect of such tolling as it gradually wafts upon the breeze, or as George Orwell would later proclaim:

> All the while that they were talking the half-remembered rhyme kept running through Winston's head. Oranges and lemons, say the bells of St Clement's, You owe me three farthings say the bells of St Martin's! It was curious, but when you said it to yourself you had the illusion of actually hearing bells, the bells of lost London that still existed somewhere or other, disguised and forgotten. From one ghostly steeple after another he seemed to hear them pealing forth. Yet so far as he could remember he had never in real life heard church bells ringing.[119]

For Bourne, harmony, and in particular the harmony produced by London church bells, can be enhanced by the perspective of distance. This is the theme of his short Latin epigram on the theme *Si Propius Stes, Te Capiet Minus*, a title that inverts Horace's famous dictum comparing reader response to poetry with the respective advantages afforded by closer and more distant perspectives of a painting:

> ut pictura, poesis: erit quae, si propius stes,
> te capiat magis, et quaedam, si longius abstes;
> haec amat obscurum, volet haec sub luce videri,
> iudicis argutum quae non formidat acumen;
> haec placuit semel, haec deciens repetita placebit
> (Horace, *Ars Poetica* 361–365)[120]

Bourne's poem, first published in 1743,[121] transforms the Horatian positive (*te capiat magis*) into a negative (*te capiet minus*), while adapting the whole to describe aural rather than visual perspective. The piece conveys the sense of enraptured awe awakened in the listener by the distant church bells of St Mary Overie, an awe that is aptly recreated on a

---

[119] George Orwell, *Nineteen Eighty-Four*, ed. Bernard Crick (Oxford, 1984), 242.

[120] Text is that of *Horace, Epistles Book II and Epistle to the Pisones (Ars Poetica)*, ed. Niall Rudd (Cambridge, 1989), 70.

[121] *Poematia* (1743), 231.

poetic level through the use of rhetorical exclamation, proclaiming in turn the sweetness of the music produced by the church tower (*quam tua dat turris dulce, Maria, melos!* [2]), the uniformity of tone maintained by the bells themselves (*ut servat iustum quaevis campana tenorem!* [3]), and the way in which the variety of sounds reverberates on the breeze (*pulsata ut variis contremit aura sonis!* [4]). They also evoke emotions of cheerfulness and joy (*hilares ... vices* [6]; *laetantur corda* [8]), and central to that joy is the very pleasure that arises from distant harmony (*talis ab harmonia surgit distante voluptas* [9]). For, as the speaker proceeds to state, if one were to enter the actual church tower all would be a din (*clangor* [10]).[122]

The theme recurs in the poetry of William Cowper, who, like his teacher before him, conveys something of the cheerful joy (*laetantur corda*) evoked by such music: "Tall spire, from which the sound of cheerful bells/Just undulates upon the listening ear."[123] Indeed Bourne's insightful acknowledgement of the contrastingly complex nature of the tolling itself and of the pleasure afforded by distant harmony as carried upon the breezes is perhaps most aptly describable as Cowperian in essence:

> There is in souls a sympathy with sounds;
> And, as the mind is pitch'd, the ear is pleas'd
> With melting airs, or martial, brisk, or grave:
> Some chord in unison with what we hear
> Is touch'd within us, and the heart replies.
> How soft the music of those village bells,
> Falling at intervals upon the ear
> In cadence sweet, now dying all away,

---

[122] Shelley translates the poem as follows: "Down the river's gentle tide,/As to London bridge we glide,/Hark! The bells of Mary's tower/Sweetly warbled music pour!/With what harmony and grace/Each preserves its stated place!/While the air, above, around/trembles with the various sound!/Merry changes ceaseless glide/To old Thames's willow'd side:/Still recede; and sweeter still,/Through the raptured breast they thrill./Such the pleasure to our hearts,/Distant melody imparts—/Enter once within the tower/All the harmony is o'er" (*The Complete Poetical Works of Percy Bysse Shelley*, ed. Neville Rogers [Oxford, 1972]), I, 7–8). Cf. the contribution of a certain "Rufus" to *Notes and Queries* 1.16 (16 Feb. 1850), 253: "Glide down the Thames by London Bridge, what time/St. Saviour's bells strike out their evening chime;/Forth leaps the impetuous cataract of sound,/Dash'd into noise by countless echoes round./Pass on—it follows—all the jarring notes/Blend in celestial harmony, that floats/Above, below, around: the ravish'd ear/Finds all the fault its own—it was too near." "St. Saviour's" church and that of St Mary Overie are one and the same (present day Southwark Cathedral). On Bourne's nineteenth-century reputation, see Introduction, 11, 13–14, and 17–18.

[123] "The Task," 1.174–175.

> Now pealing loud again, and louder still,
> Clear and sonorous, as the gale comes on.
> (The Task 6.1–10)

But harmony can work on an architectural level also. In *Pons Westmonasteriensis*, first published in 1743,[124] Bourne, in anticipation of Wordsworth, produced his own "Compos'd Upon Westminster Bridge," so to speak. Constructed at the shallowest point of the Thames to connect Westminster and Waterloo, the bridge described in Bourne's piece was commenced in 1739 and would eventually see completion some three years after his death.[125] But whereas Wordsworth's bridge would be used as a vantage point from which to view and celebrate London at dawn, Bourne focuses on the structure itself. In this instance the reconciliation or harmony achieved is between architectural and structural components: *qua partes haerent partibus harmonia!* (6).

Once again we sense that predilection for symmetry and balance that has come to characterize much of Bourne's Latin verse. This is conveyed through verbs and phrases denoting union (*coalescunt* [3]) as boulders are joined to boulders; balance (*ardua ... iusto pendet libramine moles* [5]) as the steep structure hangs in perfect balance, an archway sustaining the weight (4), and equidistance (*pontis aperturae ... distant legibus aequis* [9]). But the symmetry that lies at the heart of the poem is replicated in its own syntax and structure, most noticeably in the seven successive rhetorical exclamations upon which the whole is balanced: *quam* (2), *quanto* (3), *quo* (4), *quam* (5), *qua* (6), *quos* (7), *quam* (9). Such exuberant anaphora is for the most part matched by respective line-endings proclaiming individual aspects of the bridge's physical structure: its *opus* (2), *saxa* (3), *onus* (4), *moles* (5), *harmonia* (6). And the speaker celebrates the consequences of such harmony. Now nothing can impede the placid and silent course of the river itself (*nihil impedit undas/quove minus placidus vel taciturnus eas* [11–12]). It is a *lenissimus amnis* (15) that, like its Wordsworthian successor, can meander at will (*flexu idem, reflexu idem* [15]):

> Ne'er saw I, never felt, a calm so deep!
> The river glideth at his own sweet will:
> Dear God! The very houses seem asleep;
> And all that mighty heart is lying still.
> ("Compos'd Upon Westminster Bridge," 11–14)

---

[124] *Poematia* (1743), 196.

[125] For an eighteenth-century iconographical perspective of the bridge, cf. Antonio Canaletto's *Westminster Bridge, London on Lord Mayor's Day* (1747).

3.4   A Metropolitan Retreat: *Solitudo Regia Richmondiensis*

Bourne's London can also offer its own "calm so deep." The *Solitudo Regia Richmondiensis* first appeared, as Mitford notes, in the 1734 collection of Bourne's *Poematia*.[126] The piece celebrates not the White Lodge, as Mitford suggests,[127] but in fact The Hermitage at Richmond Park, which had been built by William Kent at the instruction of Queen Caroline. Located to the northeast of the present-day Azalea Garden (in Kew Gardens), this building constituted a stunning blend of the grand and the simple, the ancient and the modern. It possessed a triple façade that emerged from a mount, while its interior consisted of a domed octagon, a "grotto," which was surrounded on three sides by cells containing busts of Locke, Boyle, Newton, Clarke, and Wollaston.[128] The Hermitage provided King George and, in particular, his Queen with a quasi-rural retreat from the cares and burdens of state affairs.

Unnoticed by Mitford and by subsequent editors is the fact that the piece is one of several Westminster poems on the subject compiled in 1732 and appended to the 1740 edition of the *Lusus Westmonasterienses*. The supplement is highlighted in the title page of the *Lusus* as a whole (*Quibus Adiicitur Nunc Primum Edita Solitudo Regia*),[129] while, in the main body of the collection, it is furnished with a title page proclaiming: *Solitudo Regia a Musis Westmonasteriensibus Adumbrata 1732*. The collection comprises fourteen poems[130] (including Bourne's),[131] thirteen

---

[126] *Poematia* (1734), p. 95.

[127] Mitford, ed. *Poematia*, 125, glossing the poem's title, states: "George the Second built 'the White Lodge' in Richmond Park, where he occasionally resided. See Horace Walpole's Reminiscences." White Lodge was likewise in Richmond Park, and is now the Royal Ballet School. There is no evidence as to what led Mitford astray. See Judith Cotto, "Kent's Hermitage for Queen Caroline at Richmond," *Architecture* 2 (1974), 181–191.

[128] See *The Gentleman's Magazine*, III (1733), 208: "On the Five Bustoes in her Majesty's Hermitage"; "On the Bust of the Hon. Robert Boyle Esq; being set up in her Majesty's Hermitage at Richmond; concerning which we have some Verses in the foregoing Page."

[129] *Lusus Westmonasterienses, sive Epigrammatum et Poematum Minorum Delectus: Quibus Adiicitur Nunc Primum Edita Solitudo Regia* (London, 1740).

[130] The poems occur on pages 273–292.

[131] Bourne's piece occurs on page 279.

of which are in Latin and one in English.[132] In all but one instance the Latin poems are followed by English verse-translations,[133] in all probability composed by the individual authors themselves as an accompaniment to their Latin originals. If this is the case, as is suggested by significant metrical and stylistic variations between the respective translations,[134] the collection is of particular value in its inclusion of a hitherto unnoticed vernacular translation possibly by Bourne himself,[135] whose Latin poems were of course famously translated by Cowper[136] and Lamb.[137] Thus the *Solitudo Regia Richmondiensis* and its English verse equivalent take their place within a specific eighteenth-century, Westminster context, but, as will be argued, they would also seem to move beyond that in a number of ways.

That the collection was compiled in 1732 is particularly interesting in view of the fact that in 1732 and 1733 *The Gentleman's Magazine* held a poetry competition, advertising a prize for the best verses acclaiming "Her majesty's Grotto at Richmond."[138] There seems to have been a very

---

[132] Cf. *Lusus*, 276, in which the English poem beginning "This Roof etc." has no parallel Latin original. This would seem to suggest that it is not a translation of an original Latin piece but rather the only example in the collection of an original English verse treatment of the theme in question.

[133] Cf. *Lusus*, 287–288. The neo-Horatian piece *O sacra condis* has no English translation.

[134] While all are cast in rhyming couplets, as was highly typical of eighteenth-century English verse, there is no singularly definitive style that would seem to unite the translations.

[135] The verse-translation of Bourne's Latin poem occurs at *Lusus*, 280. Because of the possibility that this is Bourne's own version, I cite it in full: "If in Garden, or in Grove,/For a while be some Remove,/From the gay Fatigues of State,/Peaceful Ease and Rest be there,/Let the Shade be sacred, where/Princes chuse to meditate./Who to Palaces resort,/Who for Favours croud to Court,/Never, here are never seen;/Here no Cringings insincere,/Here no Bows, no Fawnings here,/All is silent, all serene./Gilded Pomp and gaudy Show/No felicity bestow,/Can no real lustre be;/But the Mind that's wise and great,/Can within itself retreat,/That alone is Majesty./Lordly Grandeur you that love,/Seek the Pleasures you approve,/Interrupt not this Recess;/They, that for a Kingdom's Peace/Sacrifice the Sweets of Ease,/Justly claim this Happiness."

[136] See Appendix 2 in this volume.

[137] See Appendix 3 in this volume.

[138] The following advertisement appeared in *The Gentleman's Magazine*, III (April, 1733), 208: "We propose, agreeably to a Hint given us in a Letter about a Year ago, that the copy of Verses on this Subject which shall be adjudg'd to excel the rest, be

positive response as is attested by the series of poems that the magazine published over those two years,[139] even if such verses were of variable quality.[140] Indeed such was the proliferation of poems on the subject that Alexander Pope would complain "Every man, and every boy, is writing verses on the Royal Hermitage."[141] The majority of these never really attained the standard of even the less accomplished of the *Lusus* Richmond poems, none of which, incidentally, appeared in the magazine. Indeed most of the verses published in *The Gentleman's Magazine* differ from the poems in the *Lusus* collection in that their emphasis is upon the busts included in the "Grotto"[142] rather than on The Hermitage itself or on

---

rewarded with a Volume of our Magazine for the present Year on Royal Paper, finely bound in Morocco, and properly Letter'd; with the Name of the Author if he pleases. The Gentleman or Lady whose piece shall be judged to merit the second Place shall be entitled to a Volume in Common Paper, handsomely bound, and letter'd also in a proper manner." The advertisement proceeds to announce that five gentlemen will be selected to adjudicate. After some delay, the winner was eventually announced in *The Gentleman's Magazine* IV (March 1734), 158: "the Majority of Opinions for the first prize, are in favour of No. VIII" (i.e. "To her Majesty, on her Grotto" published in *The Gentleman's Magazine*, III [August 1733], 430), "and for the Second in favour of No. I" (i.e. "On the Five Bustos in the Queen's Grotto" published in *The Gentleman's Magazine*, III [June 1733], 317).

[139] See *The Gentleman's Magazine*, II (1732), 922, 923, 1121; *The Gentleman's Magazine*, III (1733), 41, 96, 207, 208. The Prize-Verses are listed at III, 217, 429–431.

[140] See, for example, the verses included in *The Gentleman's Magazine*, III (April 1733), 207, which have virtually no literary merit, and were indeed followed (208) by an apologetic note: "these lines thus mark'd are inserted instead of better, which the Reader would have met with, had not the Undertaker, since he saw this Instance of her Majesty's great and just Discernment, been too much indisposed to apply to his Poetical Friends. We are satisfy'd this Hint would be sufficient to bring us a Supply." Contrast, however, the winning contributions (see notes 138 and 139 above), which are not without merit.

[141] Alexander Pope, Letter to John Gay (2 October 1732). Pope continues: "I hear the Queen is at a loss which to prefer, but for my own part I like none so well as Mr. Poyntz's in Latin." Text is that of *The Correspondence of Alexander Pope*, ed. George Sherburn, III, 1729–1735 (Oxford, 1956), 318.

[142] See, for example, *The Gentleman's Magazine*, II (August 1732), 922: "On her Majesty's setting up the Bustoes of Mr Locke, Sir Isaac Newton, Mr Wollaston, and Dr Clarke, in the Hermitage at Richmond": "With Honour, thus by Carolina lac'd/How are these venerable Bustoes grac'd/O Queen! With more than regal Title crown'd,/For Love of Arts and Piety renown'd!" or III (Feb. 1733), 96: "Of the Queen's Hermitage": "Not more by Ensigns than select Abodes,/Distinguish'd are the Goddesses and Gods./In Paphos Isle, fair Cytherea dwells;/Neptune and Thetis in their

the retreat that it afforded the royal couple. This doubtlessly reflects the terms and conditions of the competition itself. But the verses are important since it was partly by means of this highly public and publicized competition that The Hermitage achieved contemporary acclaim and fame. Thus just over one year after the competition had closed, a poem entitled "Richmond Park," which likewise appeared in *The Gentleman's Magazine*, contrasts the present-day fame which the park has attained with its previous anonymity ("When yet its beauties were unknown to fame,/Unsung by bards, nay e'en without a name")[143] and proceeds to assert:

> But Caroline has most advanced its pride,
> And added new delights on ev'ry side:
> Woods, hills and lawns, diversify the view:
> And, ev'ry way we look, the scene is new.[144]

To what extent is Bourne's Richmond scene new? In what ways does he partake of, yet transcend, a contemporary literary vogue? As will be argued, his Latin poem merits close analysis in the context of a collection that emphasized the seclusion which The Hermitage provided for the royal couple. And this works on a number of levels. Several of the pieces are colored by the quasi-monastic subtext inherent in the very concept of "hermitage";[145] others allude explicitly to The Hermitage itself,[146] and to the busts included therein.[147] Some expand the theme of retreat to depict an essentially pastoral world of shade and *otium*,[148] in

---

wat'ry Cells;/High on Olympus Top sits Sceptr'd Jove,/And Britain's Pallas, in her green Alcove" or III (April 1733), 208: "On the Five Bustoes in Her Majesty's Hermitage": "How are these venerable sages grac'd/To have their Busto's in this temple plac'd/And with what nice discernment has the Queen/Chose out fit worthies to adorn her scene!"

[143] "Richmond Park," lines 11–12, *The Gentleman's Magazine*, IV (September 1734), 505.

[144] "Richmond Park," lines 27–30, *The Gentleman's Magazine*, IV (September 1734), 505.

[145] On hermitage and the language of seclusion, see 109–112 in this chapter.

[146] See 109–110 in this chapter.

[147] See 109–110 in this chapter.

[148] See 109–110 in this chapter.

which the troubles and worries of state affairs can either be forgotten or
else transformed when regarded from a quasi-rural perspective. Others
emphasize rustic simplicity as opposed to wealth.[149] In short, the
collection provides a hitherto neglected neo-Latin and vernacular context
that affords much insight into Bourne's methodology. It is a methodology
that both mirrors and moves beyond that tradition.

Bourne's piece begins by expressing the wish that if any "corner"
(*angulus* [1]) in either a woodland or garden "retreat" (*in recessu* [2]) has
room for "solitude" (*solitudini vacet* [3]) then let there exist beneath an
hospitable shade (*hospita sub umbra* [4]) a welcome repose for royalty.
The phraseology appropriately suggests hermitage, a theme much more
explicitly stated later in the poem as the speaker urges that those who
delight in arrogant tumult should not begrudge the king and queen this
"little cell" (*nec his, superbi quos iuvant tumultus,/invidete cellulam* [20–
21]). Several pieces in the collection likewise emphasize the quasi-
religious atmosphere of the setting by describing it as a "cell."[150] Others
depict it as a virtual shrine or temple (*aediculam*,[151] *templum*,[152]
sacellum,[153] *sacra ... penetralia*),[154] while the Queen herself is presented
as "meditating" or "praying."[155] Moreover, as the person responsible for

---

[149] See 110–111 in this chapter.

[150] Hence "Britons, approach with Awe the Cell" (273); "Carolina's rural Cell" (274);
"What to this humble Cell alone they owe" (275); *felicius Carolina cella
temperat/palatium* (275); "Observe her in the Cell, or Royal Seat" (276); "within the
silence of this mossy cell" (289). For the theme as exemplified by the "prize-verses"
in *The Gentleman's Magazine*, cf. III (August 1733), 429, lines 29–34: "From
splendid scenes which females most admire,/Behold the solitary Queen retire!/She
seeks her humble Cell, and turns her eyes/Where the five venerable Bustoes
rise;/Then feeds on thoughts, sublime which raise the mind/Above the trifling cares of
humankind." Cf. the prize-winning entry in *The Gentleman's Magazine*, III, (August
1733), 430, lines 13–16: "Not with more awe the pious chief essay'd/To view the
wonders of that hallow'd shade;/Than we thy venerable Cell survey,/And to its
honour'd guests our solemn visit pay."

[151] *Lusus*, 273.

[152] *Lusus*, 274.

[153] *Lusus*, 277.

[154] *Lusus*, 287.

[155] "To read, or pray, or meditate" (273); *interea meditans colit hoc Carolina sacellum*
(277); "And often here, at this poor gloomy shrine/With due Devotion meets the
Pow'r divine" (277).

the construction of this shrine, so to speak,[156] she comes to function as a second Augustus figure, builder of temples, but also as a quasi-priestess herself, as one who can unite town and country, the worlds of state and rustic or, in the words of one of the contributors (with a punning allusion to The Hermitage itself):

> The two Extremes are here united seen
> The Cave and Court, the Hermit and the Queen.[157]

Further aspects of Bourne's treatment are likewise mirrored in the neo-Latin and vernacular companion-pieces: 1) the allusion to retreat (*recessu silvulae* [2]), which finds a parallel in the collection's recurring leitmotif of *secessus, recessus,* "withdrawal," or "retirement;"[158] 2) the emphasis upon the theme of quiet (*quies* [5]) and silence (*in silentio casae* [19]; *hac brevi quiete* [22]);[159] the quasi pastoral subtext inherent in Bourne's focus on both shade (*hospita sub umbra* [4]; *sub hac ... sub hac* [6–8]) and *otium* (*otioque simplici* [23]),[160] which represents on a microcosmic level a theme that permeates several of the pieces in question.[161] Indeed the pastoral potential of the whole is most fully expanded in one accomplished contribution, in which Naiads, Pan, Fauns, and Dryads approach the solitary Queen, to whom they deliver a lengthy

---

[156] Cf. Plac'd here by a Royal Hand" (273); "This Roof, that rose by Caroline's Command" (276); *tuo/regna iussu structa* (278); *o sacra condis quae penetralia* (287).

[157] *Lusus,* 275.

[158] Cf. *in hac [sc. Aedicula] secessum quaerit* (273); "withdraws from Court and State" (273); *hoc in recessu* (275); "She found Retirement" (275); "Here in the Mid-day Silence she retir'd" (276); *sublustri gaudens Carolina recessu* (283).

[159] Cf. "the thoughtful Silence of Recess" (277); "within this silent Cavern's Gate" (282); "She tastes of private Quiet here" (282); *in luco silenti* (287).

[160] Contrast Storey, "The Latin Poetry of Vincent Bourne," 143, who sees in the poem "the determination to avoid pastoral affectations." I would argue, however, that one of hallmarks of Bourne's achievement is the initial tension between, and ultimate reconciliation of, a pastoral subtext and more courtly affectations.

[161] Cf. *huius sub umbra tegminis* (274); "Oft to these Shades the Royal Pair resort" (275); *in otium .../Christina se summovit* (275); *lucos opacos et nemorum silentia* (278); *hic experitur quale dat otium/fortuna privato* (281); *sacra sub umbra* (281); *per tilias, spatiisque sitas aequalibus ulmos* (283); *quercus inter et ilices* (287). Cf. *The Gentleman's Magazine,* III (June 1733), 317, lines 23–24: "Amid surrounding glooms her Grot she founds,/Deep silence reigns thro' all the solemn bounds."

speech of consolation,[162] or in another in which the shepherds Myrtalus and Lycidas weave garlands in her honor.[163]

But the ability to enjoy this pastoral world can be afforded only if there is the opportunity to forget the cares and accoutrements of state. This sense of escapism (*refugerint* [10]) is a major theme of Bourne's poem. The Hermitage provides for the royal couple an ability to shun the queues of courtiers (*agmen aulicorum/usque et usque supplicum* [6–7]), the hosts of flatterers (*molestas gratulationes/confluentium undique* [8–9]) the tedium of rule (*taedium imperi* [11]), and the burden of rank (*onusque dignitatis* [12]). Likewise other contributors proclaim the dwelling as *alma curarum requies, superbis/principum tectis nimis ingruentum*,[164] emphasize the sense of escape that it affords from the tumult of the kingdom,[165] and from the associated tedium,[166] while conceding (like Bourne's *parumper* [6]) that such an escape is only temporary.[167]

Several of the contributors stress the rustic simplicity and virtual primitivism of The Hermitage,[168] which they contrast with the pomp and adorned splendor of courtly life.[169] Or in the words of Stephen Duck as expressed in a poem on the subject, which he contributed to *The Gentleman's Magazine* in 1732:

---

[162] Cf. *Lusus*, 283–284, and the accompanying English verse-translation at 284–286.

[163] Cf. *Lusus*, 291, and the accompanying English verse-translation at 291–292.

[164] *Lusus*, 274. Cf. "Relief of Cares,/That haunt the troubled Monarch's Breast" (274).

[165] Cf. *regni tumultus et fugiens opes/fastidiosas* (281).

[166] Cf. *oblita curae taedia splendidae* (281); "Forgetting Toil and splendid Care" (282).

[167] Cf. "Or cares, for some short interval, suspend" (285), *assiduas inter curas durosque labores* (289), "Here for a while from Toils of state released" (290).

[168] Cf. "A rude and lonely Hut I stand" (273); "This rustick Grott, where Art is scarce perceiv'd" (276); *agrestem quicunque domum, congestaque saxa/saxa vides* (288); "Whoe'er this rude, this homely Mansion views" (289); "See how the broken Rocks, unrought around,/Spread pleasing Terror o'er the sacred Ground!/See how the humble Turf and hanging Wood,/Conspire to form the blissful Solitude" (289). Cf. *The Gentleman's Magazine*, III (Jan., 1733), 41: "On the Queen's Grotto," lines 1–4: "This indigested pile appears/The relict of a thousand years;/As if the rock, in savage dance,/Amphion hither brought by chance."

[169] Cf. *felicius Carolina Cella temperat/Palatium* (275); *ut vicissim/Pauperies simulata reges/delectet ipsos* (281); "From haughty Wealth and noisy State" (282); "Aside the pomp of Grandeur throws" (282).

> Now blush, Calypso; 'tis but just to yield,
> That all your Mossy Caves are here excell'd.
> See how the Walls in Humble Form advance.
> With careless Pride and simple Elegance;
> See Art and Nature strive with equal Grace,
> And Fancy charm'd with what she can't surpass.[170]

Bourne, however, moves beyond the other contributors in his fusion of the classical makarismos with a proclaimed beatitude that functions on both a moral and a spiritual level. Twice in the poem he alludes to happiness or blessedness: first, in depicting the royal couple's rustic disassociation from the tedium of rule (*tum verius beati/quando taedium imperi/semoverint* [10–12]);[171] and second, in a quasi-didactic "beatitude" of his own. And it is this latter point that affords a rather different reading of the whole. Perhaps (as though reflecting the potential tensions inherent in the oxymoronic juxtaposition of *solitudo* and *regia* in the poem's title and that of the collection as a whole) the royal couple can be viewed as following an essentially eremitic tradition, whereby they inhabit in "The Hermitage" a desert (*solitudo*)[172] of their own. After all, the call of the desert constituted a vocation to pursue a life of solitude (*siquis uspiam angulus ... solitudini vacet* [1–3]) and silence (*quies* [5]; *in silentio casae* [19]; *brevi quiete* [22]), a place where the hermit or blessed man could be at one with God. In so doing this "blessed" couple (*beati* [10]) can likewise escape from the band of "supplicating" royal pilgrims, so to speak (*agmen aulicorum/usque et usque supplicum* [6–7]).

---

[170] "On the Queen's Grotto," lines 1–6, *The Gentleman's Magazine* II (Dec. 1732), 1121. Later in the poem Duck interestingly alludes to poems composed on this precise subject by members of both Westminster and Eton Schools, and presents the whole as a virtual competition in itself: "But cease, my Muse, and cast thy wand'ring Eyes/Where Phoebus' lofty Domes majestick rise;/Whose tuneful Train have sung this Grotto's Praise;/Contending each, 'till each deserves the Rays" (21–24). An explanatory footnote to line 22 states: "Westminster and Eaton Schools." On Bourne's links with Duck, see his Latin poem *Ad Stephanum Duck*.

[171] Cf. Horace, *Epode* 2, who describes as *beatus* the rustic who is a recluse from civilization: *beatus ille qui procul negotiis,/ut prisca gens mortalium,/paterna rura bobus exercet suis/solutus omni faenore* (*Epode* 2.1–4). Likewise Virgil proclaims as *fortunatus* the rustic who knows the country deities: *fortunatus et ille deos qui novit agrestes* (*Georgics* 2.493) and is immune to the attractions of civic support or wealth: *illum non populi fasces, non purpura regum/flexit* (*Georgics* 2.495–496).

[172] *Solitudo* occurs as a metonym for desert. See *OLD*, 4 "uninhabited country or a tract of it, desert, waste."

Where some of the other contributors had described the Queen in terms suggestive of a second Augustus,[173] Bourne through the appropriation of the adjective *augustus* on a spiritual level suggests where true wealth and happiness may dwell. The poem contrasts literal and spiritual treasures in a way unparalleled in the collection as a whole. Posing a rather surprising question to the reader: *grande quid vel aureum/conspexeris?* (13–14), the speaker voices a "beatitude" of his own. It is not wealth that "augments" royalty (*nec illud est, nec illud/principes quod augeat* [14–15]). Rather only those who possess prudence (*prudentia* [16]), a moderate heart (*rite temperatum/pectus* [16–17]) and an august mind in control of itself (*et sui potens/augusta mens* [17–18]) can attain happiness "in abundance" (*felix, abunde felix* [18]). Such a contrast between literal and spiritual wealth lies at the very heart of the eremitic tradition. Read in this light the poem's closing lines, asserting that peace and repose are only fitting for those *salute qui pro civium laborant* (24), may assume additional significance. Now a royal couple's endeavors on behalf of the *salus*, the well-being, the safety, even the "salvation" of citizens are rewarded by the *vita beata* of a metropolitan retreat. It is hardly a coincidence that hermitage, withdrawal, and silence were the very ideals toward which Bourne would aspire in his twilight years, and beyond the grave itself.

---

[173] Cf. *Lusus*, 275: *hoc in recessu Augusta secum cogitat/super salute gentium.*

CHAPTER 4

Recreating Identity? Death and Art

Every monument has its instruction, and every hillock has its lesson of mortality. 'Tis not ... without great compassion, I see the kind endeavour of the survivor to preserve the memory of a departed friend so soon frustrated and disappointed.[1]

Thus proclaims Vincent Bourne in his "Letter to a Young Lady." It is a statement that conveys his sense of the well-intentioned yet ultimately futile attempt to perpetuate or indeed to recreate the identity of the deceased by means of elaborate memorials or inscriptions. As he surveys the headstones in an unnamed "country churchyard" his perspective appears to be diametrically opposed to that of, say, Thomas Gray, in whose "Country Churchyard" "dumb Forgetfulness" (85) can be countered by the notion of remembrance after death as the self is recreated through the power of memory:

> On some fond breast the parting soul relies,
> Some pious drops the closing eye requires;
> Ev'n from the tomb the voice of nature cries,
> Ev'n in our ashes live their wonted fires.
> (Gray, *Elegy Written in a Country Churchyard*, 89–92)

Ultimately for Gray memory and poetry combine in the saving power of voice, and in tears, the physical emblem of sensibility. Bourne, while assuming his own melancholic place within the graveyard school of poetry,[2] focuses solely on the physical memorial, observing that "here, by the injury of time and weather, the register begins to be interrupted, and the letters are generally so defaced, that if an inscription can be made out, it is not without much difficulty and conjecture."[3] Such comments are not without irony. Where Bourne the man finds himself oddly at home in the company of the dead ("I am just come from indulging a very pleasing

---

[1] Bourne, "Letter to a Young Lady." Cf. Mitford, ed. *Poematia*, x.

[2] Cf. Bradner, *Musae Anglicanae*, 270.

[3] Bourne, "Letter to a Young Lady." Cf. Mitford, ed. *Poematia*, x.

melancholy in a country churchyard"),[4] Bourne the poet in methodological defiance of his own dictum inscribes and immortalizes the deceased through the power of the written word. And he does so most notably perhaps in two Latin elegies on unidentified individuals: (i) a Cambridge bed attendant and oarsman;[5] (ii) an old woman who died on her one hundredth birthday.[6] Such elegies serve to recreate the identities of their deceased subjects through subtle intertextual links with the Latin poetry of Virgil and Horace. Moreover, despite his professed comments above, Bourne reveals an awareness of the power of art to immortalize its subject.[7] This can be seen in *Lacrimae Pictoris*[8] as a painter depicts his deceased son. But it is a power that is contrasted with another type of memorial. It emerges that "the injury of time and weather" can in fact be outlasted by moral integrity, a pyramid, which in the poem of that title (*Pyramis*),[9] replaces and ultimately displaces its Horatian equivalent.

4.1   Identity and Death: A Cambridge Charon

That predilection for parallelism, mirror-imaging, and subtle contrast evident in Bourne's Latin poetry as a whole[10] recurs in his *In Obitum Roussaei*, a Latin elegiac poem on the death by drowning (in the river Cam) of a certain Rouse in 1721. Printed separately in 1726, and proclaimed as an *editio altera*,[11] the piece would seem to take its place

---

[4] Bourne, "Letter to a Young Lady." Cf. Mitford, ed. *Poematia*, x.

[5] *In Obitum Roussaei*, discussed at 114–121 in this chapter.

[6] *Anus Saecularis*, discussed at 122–129 in this chapter.

[7] On a more formel level Bourne was the composer of several Latin inscriptions (on named and unnamed contemporaries). These are rather self-consciously grouped together under the title *Epitaphia* in the 1743 edition of his poetry. See Bourne, *Poematia* (1743), 236–240.

[8] See 129–131 in this chapter.

[9] See 131–133 in this chapter.

[10] See, in particular, chapters 1 and 2 in this volume.

[11] *In Obitum Roussaei Collegio Trinitatis Servi a Cubiculis Anno 1721 Editio Altera* (London, 1726). Mitford, ed. *Poematia*, xxxiv, remarks that the poem appears "to have been printed and sold separately" but that he has not seen the first edition (p. 132). No copies of the first edition are known to survive.

alongside other such Cambridge *epicedia*. This emerges from a reading of the poem proper, in which the speaker indicates that Cambridge undergraduates (here denoted by the phrase *Grantae moesta iuventa* [20]) have mourned Rouse's death in many poems (*carmine multo* [19]). From this it is evident that the event certainly affected the Cambridge academic community, while obviously spurring Bourne into print in more than one edition. But if these "many poems," these *carmina multa*, ever did exist, they must have done so in manuscript form only (there is no evidence of their ever having been printed), and have long since faded into oblivion. For this reason, and in the absence of a published collection, it would probably be naïve to presume that Rouse's drowning evoked in the university a reaction on a scale that was in any way comparable to that prompted almost a century earlier by the tragic drowning of Edward King off the coast of Anglesey. King, unlike Rouse, was the subject of an entire volume of published Cambridge laments,[12] including most famously Milton's *Lycidas*.[13] Perhaps this apparent disparity reflects a striking contrast between the comparative age and status of the deceased in each instance. King drowned tragically young, but even in his short life, he had already achieved something of a reputation as a Cambridge Latin poet,[14] as one who "knew/himself to sing, and build the lofty rhyme" (*Lycidas*, 10–11).[15] Scarcely comparable perhaps is the drowning of an old man (*senex* [12]), a bed attendant at Trinity College, Cambridge (the latter role is denoted by the title of the piece [*In Obitum Roussaei Collegio Trinitatis Servi a Cubiculis Anno 1721*],[16] as printed in the 1734 edition of Bourne's poetry).

---

[12] See the bipartite *Iusta Edovardo King* (Cambridge, 1638). Part 1 consists of twenty Latin and three Greek poems; Part 2 consists of thirteen English poems.

[13] Milton's *Lycidas* is the last and the longest poem in the *Iusta*.

[14] See Nigel Postlethwaite and Gordon Campbell, eds. "Edward King, Milton's *Lycidas*: Poems and Documents," *Milton Quarterly* 28.4 (1994), 77–111.

[15] Cf. Milton's comment in the headnote to *Lycidas* that King was "a learned Friend."

[16] The Bursar's accounts of Trinity College, Cambridge make reference to the *Cubicularius*. It is evident that he was one of the three servants whose specific duty, according to the Statutes (1560, cap. 1), was to attend upon the Master (*Sint quattuor famuli praeterea, quorum tres magistro inserviant, unus pro cubiculo, alter qui eum comitetur, et tertius qui equos custodiat; quartus vero equos Collegii servet*). According to Statute 43 each of these servants was to receive a shilling a week for his commons while in College (*Cubicularius magistri, alter famulus qui eum comitetur, custos equorum magistri, custos equorum Collegii, quorum singuli habeant pro commeatu hebdomadatim cum domi sint, xii d*). However, the Senior Bursar's book for 1721 records that by this time the *Cubicularius* was in receipt of a regular payment

Several biographical details about Rouse[17] may be deduced from Bourne's poem itself. Thus it is evident that he lived in Cambridge (*nostri accola Cami* [11]), and that he did so for a substantial part of his life, since the river Cam is depicted as knowing him both as a boy and as an old man (12).[18] Twice in the poem (lines 5–6 and 27) Bourne remarks on his vast physical bulk. But most significant for the purposes of the whole and of central importance to Bourne's methodology in the poem is the fact that Rouse was a "boatman," (*nauta* [24]), who surpassed his peers whether in rowing or punting (14). He is also described as a talented fisherman (16) and as someone who had hardly two pennies to rub together (25–26).

Such then is the sparse biographical information provided by Bourne's poem. It will be argued, however, that the Latin lines move far beyond this to create a series of essentially literary "lives" through points of contact and contrast between Rouse and several characters from Virgil's underworld. Thus through intertextual links with *Aeneid* 6, the elegy in quasi-kaleidoscopic fashion sets up a whole spectrum of other pseudobiographical identities, so to speak: between Rouse and Charon; between Rouse and Palinurus; between Rouse and the mighty, massive Hercules himself. And the biographical and mythological coalesce, as one series of parallels neatly dovetails into its successor. To some degree then the soul of the poem's deceased subject is envisaged as undergoing a literary journey of sorts through an underworld that is both familiar and unfamiliar, both Virgilian and new.

Read on the simplest of levels, Bourne's poem constitutes an address to Charon, the mythological ferryman of Virgil's underworld, whose role it was to transport buried souls across the river Styx.[19] Substituting the supplicatory adjective *almus* (1; 20) for the Virgilian epithet *horrendus*,[20] the speaker asks the ferryman to cast his eye over the

---

of 13s. 4d a quarter. For the preceding information I am indebted to Adam Green, Assistant Archivist and Manuscript Collector, Trinity College Library.

[17] The Senior Bursar's book of Trinity College Cambridge records only the servant's title. Adam Green informs me that Rouse's name does not seem to appear elsewhere in the Trinity College Records.

[18] *quem puerum novit, novit et unda senem* (12).

[19] For an excellent study of Charon and his reception, see R.H. Terpening, *Charon and the Crossing: Ancient, Medieval and Renaissance Transformations of a Myth* (Lewisburg, 1985).

[20] Cf. *Aeneid* 6. 298.

souls flocking about the river bank, urging that if he happens to see a soul that is larger than the rest elbowing his way through their midst, he should draw his boat to the shore and take him on board, despite his physical bulk. Charon, though generally averse to ferrying larger passengers,[21] is envisaged as reaping the reward of receiving a fellow boatman. For Rouse can ultimately become a collaborator in his infernal duties since Charon will be enabled to divide his labor, which will thereby be rendered all the easier. In fact the two boatmen will be so indistinguishable that there will be some doubt as to which of them is the other's twin.

Bourne's poem is founded upon a witty conceit, which manifests itself in a series of parallels between two *nautae*, Charon and Rouse. Like Charon, Rouse is a boatman, and an exceptionally talented one at that. In a miniature flashback of Rouse's past life, the speaker proclaims that there was no better boatman than he (*navita non illo melior fuit* [13]) whether as oarsman or as punter (*seu remis conto seu subigenda ratis* [14]). The language employed in this retrospective compliment, especially in terms of the *seu ... seu* construction, is appropriately reminiscent of the boasting boat (*phasellus*) of Catullus 4, which confidently claims to have been the swiftest of ships (*ait fuisse navium celerrimus* [2]), one that could not be overtaken by any other, whether by rowing or by sailing (*sive palmulis/opus foret volare sive linteo* [4–5]). But whereas Catullus's boat, having experienced many travels, has already withdrawn into retirement, this will not be the eventual fate of Rouse's ghost. For central to the bargaining with Charon is the precise notion that even in the underworld Rouse will be able to employ (or redeploy) his nautical talents as a means of providing very practical assistance to the mythological ferryman. The implication of the whole is that surely this in itself should merit his transportation across the Styx.

But until that bargaining point is reached, in death itself Rouse is bereft of identity: a sailor without a boat, a soul just like the others in the sense that he is in urgent need of ferrying by the poem's other boatman, Charon himself. The latter is urged to survey all the souls flocking before the Styx (*omnesque recense/manes ad Stygias qui glomerantur aquas* [3–4]). The use of the verb *glomerantur* recalls perhaps Virgil's bird simile in *Aeneid* 6, a simile employed (of congregating souls) in an identical Stygian context: *quam multae glomerantur aves, ubi frigidus annus/trans pontum fugat et terris immitit apricis* (6. 311–312). But as Charon is asked to review (*recense* [3]) such souls, he would also seem to assume, temporarily at least, the role of a second Anchises, who reviewed

---

[21] See 120–121 in this chapter.

(*recensebat*) the line of his and of Rome's descendants (*omnemque suorum/forte recensebat numerum* (6. 681–682) with the additional irony, of course, that Anchises was surveying Elysian souls, who were awaiting not a crossing of the Styx, but rebirth itself (*inclusas animas superumque ad lumen ituras* [6. 680]). Such a glorious fate is hardly envisaged for this eighteenth-century bed maker, who, despite the supplications of a Cambridge community (*hunc nostro ut reddas caelo* [19]), must remain subject to the laws of an inexorable underworld.[22]

Now with the second imperative (*prospice* [5]) traditional roles are reestablished. Thus Charon resumes his role as the ferryman who looked forth from the Stygian waters and beheld the approach of Aeneas and the Sibyl (*navita quos iam inde ut Stygia prospexit ab unda* [6. 385]); likewise Rouse becomes the typical supplicatory shade, stretching out his hands in his need to be transported to the Elysian shore (*tibi navita dextram/tendet ad Elysii traiiciendus agros* [9–10]) just like those flocking souls at *Aeneid* 6, who stood before the river and the ferryman for precisely the same purpose (*stabant orantes primi transmittere cursum,/tendebantque manus ripae ulterioris amore* [6. 313–314]). But not for long: for in Bourne's poem the soul beheld by Charon is in many ways a reflection, an *imago*,[23] of Charon himself. As is typical of Bourne's poetic methodology, even in the world of the dead the self in quasi-narcissistic fashion,[24] unwittingly sees the other in a face-to-face encounter,[25] an "other" who by the end of the poem will in several respects become that self, indistinguishable and, in this instance, "twinned" (32).

In terms of the poem's language and of its intertextual links with the Virgilian scenes in question, Rouse, in a sort of cross-comparison, is depicted as *squalidus et pinguis totus* (9).[26] But in Virgil, it was Charon himself who was a figure of terrible squalor (*terribili squalore Charon* [6. 299]), his unkempt beard upon his chin,[27] his eyes full of flame, with a

---

[22] *sin parcae prohibent et inexorabilis Orci/quem petimus, reditum lux inimica vetat* ... (21–22).

[23] On the theme of the *imago* in Bourne's Latin poetry, see chapters 1 and 2 passim.

[24] Cf. Narcissus at Ovid, *Metamorphoses* 3. 504–505, who even in the underworld gazed upon his own reflection in the waters of the Styx. See also chapter 1, 23–24.

[25] See in general chapter 1.

[26] Worthy of comparison perhaps is William Cowper's description of the physical slovenliness of Bourne himself, on which see Introduction, 14.

[27] *cui plurima mento/canities inculta iacet* (6. 299–230).

filthy cloak hanging down from his shoulders (*sordidus ex umeris nodo dependet amictus* [301]). Something of the latter detail may underlie the brief flashback provided of Rouse's past skills as a fisherman, when in life he cast a fishing net from his left shoulder (*nec quisquam ex umero contorsit rete sinistro/certius* [15–16]). The whole conveys a surreal sense of mirror-imaging as the reader recognizes (even if Charon may not) an *imago* that is in several respects the ferryman's second self.[28]

But once again identities shift as Rouse assumes characteristics of a further inhabitant of Virgil's underworld: Palinurus, Aeneas's helmsman (*gubernator* [6. 337]), another boatman who, like Rouse, met his death by drowning. At the end of *Aeneid* 5 Virgil describes Palinurus's tragic death at the hands of the beguiling god of sleep, *Somnus*, who sprinkles his temples with Lethean dew (854–856),[29] and hurls him along with his helm headlong into the sea.[30] Throughout the episode Palinurus is presented as a passive, innocent victim.[31] And some sense of that victimhood and passivity is inherent in the question that Aeneas puts to his shade in the underworld (*quis te, Palinure, deorum/eripuit nobis medioque sub aequore mersit?* [6. 341–342]). This concept of a treacherous deity plunging (*mersit*) an innocent victim into the sea recurs in Bourne as the god Somnus is now replaced by Camus, the river deity of Cambridge, who has plunged an innocent victim into his *own* waters, no less! (*Camus cum perfidus idem/Roussaeum inviso merserit amne suum!* [17–18]). Common to both also is the posing of alternative requests for rescue—requests that cannot be granted, and as such are presented as unreasonable. Palinurus begs Aeneas either to snatch him from his misfortunes (*eripe me his, invicte, malis* [365]) or to give him his hand and carry him across the waves (*da dextram misero et tecum me tolle per undas* [370–371]), and is subsequently rebuked by the Sibyl for his *tam dira cupido* (373) as she reprimands him for hoping that the

---

[28] Contrast Anchises's words of recognition as expressed to Aeneas upon their meeting in the underworld at *Aeneid* 6.687–694, and Aeneas's reciprocal comment: *tua me, genitor, tua tristis imago/saepius occurrens haec limina tendere adegit* (*Aen.* 6.695–696).

[29] *ecce deus ramum Lethaeo rore madentem/vique soporatum Stygia super utraque quassat/tempora* (*Aen.* 5.854–856).

[30] *cumque gubernaclo liquidas proiecit in undas/praecipitem* (*Aen.* 5.859–860). On the discrepancies between this version of his death and that provided by Palinurus to Aeneas in the underworld of book 6, see *Virgil: Aeneidos Liber Quintus*, ed. R.D. Williams (Oxford, 1960), xxv–xxviii.

[31] Cf. *Aen.* 5.840–841: *te, Palinure, petens, tibi somnia tristia portans/insonti*.

decrees of the gods can be changed through supplication (*desine fata deum flecti sperare precando* [376]). This is paralleled in Bourne's poem by a plea uttered not by the ghost himself, but by the speakers of those Cambridge laments – a plea that Charon either restore Rouse to the upper air (*hunc nostro ut reddas coelo, te carmine multo,/alme Charon, Grantae moesta iuventa petit* [19–20]), or if (as Virgil's Sibyl had implied) this is forbidden by the Fates and by the hated law of an inexorable underworld (*sin Parcae prohibent et inexorabilis Orci/quem petimus, reditum lex inimica vetat* [21–22]), then that at least he transport him across the Stygian waters. And it is in this envisaged transportation that Rouse would seem to assume one further and final identity.

For if Rouse is a second Charon; if Rouse is a second Palinurus, so too is he depicted as a second Hercules. The identification is achieved in a number of ways. In *Aeneid* 6 a somewhat churlish and querulous Charon, upon encountering Aeneas and the Sibyl, remarks that this is a place of shades (*umbrarum hic locus est* [6. 390]), and that the laws of the underworld forbid him from transporting mortals in his boat (*corpora viva nefas Stygia vectare carina* [6. 391]). He continues by conveying his regret in having "received" Hercules upon his lake (*nec vero Alciden me sum laetatus euntem/accepisse lacu* [392–393]). However, upon seeing the golden bough, which functions as Aeneas's passport, as it were, he admires the gift, his anger subsides, and he dislodges other souls from his boat (*inde alias animas, quae per iuga longa sedebant,/deturbat* [6. 411–412]), into which he now "receives" Aeneas (*simul accipit alveo/ingentem Aeneas* [412–413]). At this juncture Aeneas is ironically depicted in quasi-Herculean terms, as a "huge" Aeneas.[32] Significantly his reception on board by the becalmed Charon is mirrored by the fracturing of the boat, which groans under his weight and "receives" marsh water (*gemuit sub pondere cumba/sutilis et multam accepit rimosa paludem* [413–414]).

Bourne picks up this Herculean theme of size and applies it to the hefty Rouse himself. Upon his first appearance in the poem he is depicted as a large shade (*crassa ... umbra* [5]), in fact, as a shade that is larger

---

[32] For a further equation between the "huge" Aeneas and Hercules, cf. the description of his entering the abode of Evander in *Aeneid* 8.366–367: *dixit, et angusti subter fastigia tecti/ingentem Aenean duxit*, occurring appropriately during a feast in honor of Hercules. Evander has just narrated to Aeneas the story of Hercules and Cacus (8. 184–275), which in several respects functions as a proleptic allegory of Aeneas's forthcoming victory over Turnus. See G.K. Galinsky, "The Hercules-Cacus Episode in *Aeneid* VIII," *American Journal of Philology* 87 (1966), 18–51; J.G.A.M. José, "*Hercules exempli gratia*: de Hercules-Cacus-episode in Vergilius *Aeneis* 8. 185–305," *Lampas* 23 (1990), 50–73. Indeed, earlier, Evander himself was described in terms rather reminiscent of Charon as he "receives" Aeneas (*accipit Aenean* [8. 178]).

than all the others (*non est in toto crassior umbra loco* [6]). And as if usurping the prerogative of Virgil's Charon, who would ultimately "disturb" or dislodge the other shades (*alias animas ... deturbat* [6.411–412]) in order to receive the Herculean Aeneas, Rouse is already "disturbing" smaller shades as he elbows his way through their midst (*animasque hinc inde minores/turbantem ut cubito pandat utroque viam* [7–8]).[33] Later in an echo of the Sibyl's plea to Charon to receive the mortal Aeneas on board, and in quasi-acknowledgement of the ferryman's initial obstinacy in this regard, the poem's speaker apologetically considers the possibility that Charon may not wish to transport such large shades (*quod si tam crebras transmittere te piget umbras* [27]) and may in fact shun such a task (*et longum refugis, portitor unus, opus* [28]). Upon seeing the golden bough, Virgil's Charon had dramatically turned his boat toward the shore (*caeruleam advertit puppim ripaeque propinquat* [6. 410]). This is precisely what Bourne's Charon is asked to do (*admota ad littora cymba,/per Stygium nautam transvehe nauta lacum* [23–24]).[34] The Virgilian *accipere* motif recurs as Charon is exhorted to receive (*accipe* [29]) this unusually large shade, for in so doing his work will be alleviated by having Rouse as his fellow companion in "labor" (29–30). In the poem's concluding lines Charon and Rouse are depicted as *gemini*,[35] as virtually indistinguishable twin boatmen (*adde quod (ut similes estis) dubitabitur utrum/Roussaeus geminus sit geminusve Charon* [31–32]), sharing a pseudoHerculean "labor" (*accipe divisi socium comitemque laboris;/divisus levior fiet utrique labor* [29–30]). Here the motif of mirroring is once again central to an understanding of Bourne's methodology. These *imagines* are literary and mythological. Perhaps even in the world of the dead the self can become the other.

---

[33] For the theme of physical vastness, cf. the short piece *Consule quid valeant umeri* (on Atlas) at *Lusus Westmonasterienses*, 12–13, especially lines 3–4: *quos nervos, quam cervicem, quae bracchia, crurum/quam validos nexus tam grave poscit onus!*

[34] For a neo-Latin parallel, cf. Philip Albertus, *In Obitum P. Ghisceri*, 17–22: *quippe Charon longo auditos post tempore cantus,/pulsantemque stupens pectine fila lyrae,/advortet ripae proram, dulcedine captus,/caerulea accipiens corpora viva rate,/trans Styga et incolumes exponet, nullo aere petito,/exigat ille avidus portitor aera licet.* Text is that of *Carmina Illustrium Poetarum Italorum*, 1, 464.

[35] The theme of twinning is likewise associated with Virgil's golden-bough episode. Cf. *primo avulso non deficit alter/aureus et simili frondescit virga metallo* (6.143–144); *vix ea fatus erat geminae cum forte columbae/ipso sub ore viri caelo venere volantes* (6.190–191); *liquidumque per aera lapsae/sedibus optatis geminae super arbore sidunt* (6.202–203).

4.2   Death and the Old Woman: *Anus Saecularis*

But if the self can become the other, so too is the other contrasted with the self. Some seven years later there occurred the death of a further unidentifiable individual, who, like Rouse, would nonetheless be immortalized in Bourne's poetry. *Anus Saecularis*, Bourne's "chief lyric effort,"[36] takes as its subject an old woman,[37] who died on her one hundredth birthday, or as the piece's title elaborately puts it: *Anus Saecularis quae iustam centum annorum aetatem ipso die natali explevit et clausit anno 1728.* While congratulating the old woman on her longevity, the piece laments the afflictions associated with old age, culminating in the speaker's very personal wish to be released from this fate (at the age of fifty) by death itself. As such the poem would seem to take its place alongside several shorter pieces in the *Lusus Westmonasterienses*. One contributor, for example, describes an old man oppressed by afflictions and wretched old age, who calls upon death to visit him, and whose wish is granted.[38] Another, expounding the Horatian

---

[36] Money, *The English Horace*, 223.

[37] On the old woman as a recurring theme in Bourne's Latin poetry, cf. in particular *Denneri Anus*. This ekphrastic piece, which first appeared in the 1734 edition of Bourne's poems, takes as its subject one of Balthasar Denner's paintings of an old woman. Denner (1685–1749) was invited to England in 1720 by a group of English lords and ladies whom he met in Hanover. He stayed in London from 1721 to 1728. One of his many portraits of old women was painted in London in 1724. Appended to the Latin poem is the following footnote indicating that the painting described in the piece was put on display for a long time in the Palace-Yard next to Westminster Cathedral: *diu publico fuit spectaculo egregia haec Tabula in Area-Palatina exteriori, iuxta Fanum Westmonasteriense.* Cf. Mitford, ed. *Poematia*, 139. Bourne's poem ironically depicts the old woman in terms reminiscent of Ovid's represention of young Roman girls in *Ars Amatoria*. The description of the old woman's white hair peeping out from under her headdress (*apparent nivei vittae sub margine cani,/fila colorati qualia Seres habent* [7–8]) seems to fuse Ovid's injunction at *Ars Amatoria* 1.31: *este procul, vittae tenues, insigne pudoris*, with his account in *Amores* 1.13–14 of the dye with which Roman women color their hair (*quid, quod erant tenues, et quos ornare timeres?/vela colorati qualia Seres habent*). Later, as spectators flock to see the painting (*spectatum veniunt* 13]), they recall Ovid's females flocking to the Roman games (*spectatum veniunt, veniunt spectentur ut ipsae* [*Ars Amatoria* 1.99]).

[38] *Lusus Westmonasteriensis*, 2: *Aerumnis graviter pressus miseraque senecta/"sola," inquit, "mea sunt morte levanda mala./exoptata veni mihi mors gratissima rerum."/Mors venit, et tremulo sic ait ore senex./"debemur, fateor, tibi nos et nostra, sed, o mors,/si placet, ulterius debitor esse velim."*

dictum *nemo vitae satur, ut conviva, recedit*,[39] describes the paradox of a sick old woman who calls upon death, yet whose home is crammed with abundant medicines.[40] But Bourne's piece moves far beyond such commonplaces, and does so in a number of ways. Like the poem on Rouse, it interacts in a rather complex way with classical Latin literature, in this instance, with Horace[41] (and to some degree with Catullus)—an interaction highlighted not only by the choice of Horatian meter, but also and most notably by a series of intertextual links with, and inversions of, aspects of Horace's celebratory *Carmen Saeculare*. As will be argued, these not only lend several levels of irony to the whole, but also serve to intensify what would seem to be a very personal sense of despondency and despair[42] that characterizes this subtly skillful poem.

Horace's *Carmen Saeculare*, commissioned by Augustus to celebrate the *Ludi Saeculares*, is in effect a hymn to Apollo and Diana for their blessing upon the Roman people in general and upon Augustus in particular.[43] As is suggested by the title and indeed by details in the poem proper, the speaker draws upon the Sibylline tradition of computing time by *saecula* (usually of 110 years each). In this computation the year was supposed to attain completion when all the heavenly bodies had returned to the same position in which they had been at the beginning of the world. It was believed that once this happened, then every part of the universe would replicate its past history. In short, the tradition promulgates an essentially cyclical view of history and of life itself on both a macrocosmic and a microcosmic level. This is mirrored in, for example, Virgil's fourth *Eclogue*, which hails the arrival of the last age of Sibylline

---

[39] Cf. Horace, *Satires* 1.1.117–119: *inde fit ut raro, qui se vixisse beatum/dicat et exacto contentus tempore vita/cedat uti conviva satur reperire queamus.*

[40] *Lusus Westmonasterienses*, 71: *"Mors, ades," inquit anus, "maturamque accipe praedam,"/ilia dum miserae tussis anhela quatit./at phialas, vetulae ingreditur conclavia siquis,/omnia dispositas per tabulata videt,/nam quamvis mortem votis vel millibus optet,/ne tamen eveniat, quod petit, illa cavet.*

[41] For a very general assessment, see Money, *The English Horace*, 223–225.

[42] For similar expressions of seeming despondency, see Bourne's "Letter to a Young Lady," discussed at Introduction, 1–2, and his "Letter to His Wife," discussed at Introduction, 12–13.

[43] On the *Carmen Saeculare*, see, among others, Alessandro Barchiesi, "The Uniqueness of the *Carmen Saeculare* and its Tradition," in *Traditions and Contexts in the Poetry of Horace*, eds. Tony Woodman and Denis Feeney (Cambridge, 2002), 107–123; M.C.J. Putnam, *Horace's Carmen Saeculare: Ritual Magic and the Poet's Art* (New Haven and London, 2002).

prophecy, and the birth of the mighty line of *saecula*.[44] Where Virgil sees the birth of an unidentified *puer* as inaugurating the return of the Golden Age, and all that that *aetas* comes to represent,[45] Horace conveys the cyclical process whereby nature herself is continuously renewed. This process is mirrored in the "return" to earth and to the Roman state of those virtues traditionally associated with the Golden Age. It is a renewal made possible by the very presence and actions of Augustus himself. The speaker utters separate prayers to Apollo and Diana, each of whom is identified with certain aspects of those unceasing cycles: Apollo, as exemplified in the continuous settings and risings of the sun; Diana, as symbolized by the birth of new generations, fertility and abundance. Central to life (and to the hymn itself) is the preservation of nature's cyclical order. The speaker prays for constant crops and showers to nourish the plants. In the second half of the poem this cyclical patterning, as it were, is applied to the context of Rome, with the all-important subtext that the golden *saecula* have in fact returned. But even this cannot be the end. Apollo and Diana are now invoked as preservers of the Roman state, and the prayer moves beyond this in its express hope that that state be preserved for an even longer and better age. Such is the process of continuity celebrated in Horace's hymn.

Unlike contemporary poets, who tended to adapt Horace's poem to suit an essentially public context,[46] Bourne applies it to a more private realm: the actual life span of an old woman and the envisaged life span of the speaker himself. The theme of revolving and recurring *saecula* so central to Horace's *Carmen Saeculare* is conveyed in Bourne's grandiloquent title *Anus Saecularis*. In terms of the old woman in question, it is a *saeculum* that has come full circle in virtue of the fact that she has died on her one hundredth birthday.[47] The cyclical notion and indeed motion underlying the whole are suggested in a number of ways: 1) in the felicitous similarity between the words *anus* (*anus saecularis*) and *annus* (*centum annorum aetatem anno*) in the title, and indeed as a

---

[44] *ultima Cumaei venit iam carminis aetas/magnus ab integro saeclorum nascitur ordo* (Virgil, *Ecl.* 4.4–5).

[45] See in particular *Ecl.* 4.21–30.

[46] In 1699, for example, Matthew Prior entitled his celebration of William's reign *Carmen Saeculare*.

[47] It is interesting to note that according to Valerias Antias the Sibylline *saeculum* was of one hundred years' duration.

punning subtext of the poem proper (*annorum series* [3],[48] *imbecillibus annis* [19–20]); 2) in the possible pun between *anus* (f.) (old woman) and *anus* (m.) (a ring or circle),[49] as in a sense the old woman and the ring are synonymous; 3) in the use of nouns (*orbem* [4]; *circulus* [40]) and verbs (*volvi et revolvi* [39]) denoting a circle or circular movement, and 4) in the striking statement concerning the movement of the *saecula* themselves whereby past, present, and future events are depicted as part of a never-ceasing cyclical pattern (33–36).[50] This motion is reflected in the very structure of a poem that achieves some form of ring-composition. Beginning by proclaiming the old woman as a marvel of a unique old age, whose sequence of years has come to an end in a "full circle" (*cuius annorum series in amplum/desinit orbem* [3–4]), the poem ends (*desinit*) by congratulating the old woman upon her "full age" (*integram aetatem tibi gratulamur* [41]). But such a neat resolution is suddenly shattered in the final lines, which somewhat self-consciously turn the whole upon its head. The speaker announces his opinion that the attainment of only half of that circle, so to speak, would be enough for him (*si ... dimidiemus* [43–44]). As will be noted, Bourne's poem ultimately serves to deconstruct the very computation of *saecula* that lies at its core, and indeed at the heart of Horace's *Carmen Saeculare*.

This process of deconstructing Horace, as it were, manifests itself in a quasi-parodic sequence whereby the essentially positive imagery of fertility and birth is replaced, and in fact displaced, by images of death and decay. Horace depicts as part of nature's cycle the continuous setting and rising of the sun. Thus, invoking Apollo as sun-god, the speaker conveys how the sun draws forth and hides the day, and is then born (9–11);[51] likewise Diana is called upon as Lucina, goddess of childbirth, or as Genitalis, and asked to rear the young to ripeness (17), and to enhance the laws of matrimony, which in turn will enable the birth of a new

---

[48] This is an ironic echo of Horace, *Odes* 3.30.5: *annorum series et fuga temporum* (3. 30.5). For links between this Ode and Bourne's *Pyramis*, cf. chapter 4, 131–133. On the possible wordplay between *anus* and *annus*, cf. Ovid, *Ars Amatoria* 1.765–766: *nec tibi conveniet cunctos modus unus ad annos;/longius insidias cerva videbit anus*; *Ars Amatoria* 2.677–678: *illae munditiis annorum damna rependunt,/et faciunt cura, ne videantur anus*.

[49] Cf. Varro, *De Lingua Latina* 6.8: *vocatur annus, quod ut parvi circuli anuli, sic magni dicebantur circites ani, unde annus*.

[50] *id quod/saeculum praesens videt illud ipsum/vidit elapsum prius, et videbit/omne futurum* (33–36).

[51] *curru nitido diem qui/promis et celas aliusque et idem/nasceris* (9–11).

generation (19). It is this continuous pattern of birth and rebirth that will allow the *saecula* to rotate (*certus undenos deciens per annos/orbis* [21–22]). Even the Fates seem to participate in this process in that they are asked to add propitious destinies to those already accomplished (25–28).[52] Hence the prayer that the earth, which is *fertilis frugum* (29), may present Ceres with corn, and that showers and breezes may nurture (*nutriant* [31]) the growing plants.

In Bourne, however, birth imagery is displaced by imagery of death. After all, the old woman's cycle of life has come to an end (*desinit* [4]), an end that contrasts sharply with the emphasis on beginnings in Horace. And where Horace conveyed the fruitfulness and abundance of nature and the health-giving products of earth, Bourne ironically applies such imagery of sustenance and abundance to the context of death itself, describing humankind in the strikingly oxymoronic phrase as *pabulum nos luxuriesque leti* (9). Now that Horatian list of life-bringing and sustaining forces is transmuted into the destructive violence of fever (*rapidaeve febris/vim repentinam* [14–15]), while the only seeds that are sown here are those of disease (*aut male pertinacis/semina morbi* [15–16]),[53] matched by the grim sequence of human ailments (*morbidi questus gemitusque anheli* [22]) that impair life itself.[54] Likewise the Horatian series of virtues symptomatic of the return of a new Golden Age (*fides, pax, honos, pudor* [57], *virtus* [58], *copia* [60]) is transformed into a list of the evils attendant upon a long span of life (*iniuria, vis, furta, dolus* [29] *insolentia* [29–30]).[55] And if in Horace Diana is seen as fostering life

---

[52] Cf. in particular lines 27–28: *bona iam peractis/iungite fata*. Cf. Horace, *Odes* 4.7.17: *quis scit an adiciant hodiernae crastina summae/tempora di superi.*

[53] Money, *The English Horace*, 225, notes links between Bourne's phrase *male pertinacis* (15) and Horace, *Odes* 1.9.24, stating: "He takes a famous phrase about the amorous games of the young, and applies it to insidious disease. The shock is probably deliberate, the bad taste purposeful." Money, however, does not note the subtle points of contact and contrast between Bourne's poem and Horace's *Carmen Saeculare.*

[54] On Bourne's list of ailments (21–24), cf. his "Letter to a Young Lady," at Mitford, ed. *Poematia*, xi: "the jealousies and fears, the discontents and suspicions, the animosities and misunderstandings ... here end all resentments and contentions." See also Introduction, 1–2.

[55] Money, *The English Horace*, 225, interestingly compares Gray's "Ode on a Distant Prospect of Eton College," a poem composed only eight years after Bourne's piece. Cf. lines 81–90: "Lo! In the vale of years beneath/A grisly troop are seen,/The painful family of Death,/More hideous than their Queen:/This racks the joints, this fires the veins,/That every labouring sinew strains,/These in the deeper vitals rage:/Lo! Poverty, to fill the band,/That numbs the soul with icy hand,/And slow-consuming

from its earliest stages, now death is depicted as a process that is ironically seen as incipient from the time of birth itself: from the cradle to the grave (*nos statim a cunis cita destinamur/praeda sepulchro* [11–12]).[56] Furthermore where in Horace the Parcae could predict *quod ... stabilisque rerum/terminus servet* (26–27), Bourne in a quasi-inversion of that statement, moralizes that even if life itself could transcend its own brief *terminus* (17–18),[57] whatever remains, far from being stable, would in fact be beset by weakness (18–20).[58] Horace's speaker had asked for repose for quiet old age (46), a request replicated on a macrocosmic level in a prayer for the continuity of the Roman state and for its prolongation by Apollo himself (66–68).[59] The speaker of Bourne's poem concludes with a wish that turns this whole concept of continuity upon its head. Focusing on the self as opposed to the other, he "estimates" that he will have enough if he can "halve" the number of years lived by the old woman (*et dari nobis satis aestimamus/si tuam, saltem vacuam querelis/dimidiemus* [42–44]).[60]

That juxtaposition of *satis* and *aestimamus*, and the overall numerological context may lend a further and final level of irony to the whole. The phrase interacts perhaps with two other statements addressed not to an old woman, but paradoxically to a vibrantly active (and sexually active) young mistress. In Catullus's fifth poem, the speaker addressing his beloved Lesbia, had urged that they should live and love (*vivamus, mea Lesbia, atque amemus* [1]), and regard (*aestimemus* [3]) the rumors

---

Age." As Money, 226, states: "While the sight of youth brings these thoughts to Gray, Bourne gets the same idea, less surprisingly, from age."

[56] For the expression of a rather similar sentiment in an eighteenth-century neo-Latin "Horatian" poem, cf. *The Gentleman's Magazine*, 5 (February 1735), 96: *Ad Sylvanum Urban Gen. Per Varios Casus*, lines 5–8: *heu! Quam caduco sydere nascimur,/vitaeque mortem protinus additam/lugemus, emissique cunis/ad tacitam properamus urnam.* The author is designated merely as *Cambro-Christicola*, and the poem is dated 16 February.

[57] *sin brevem posset superare vita/terminum* (17–18).

[58] For the expression of a similar sentiment, see in general *Lusus Westmonasterienses*, 58: *Longa Senectus Plena Malis.* See in particular lines 5–6: *bis quamvis redeant renovato in corpore firmae/vires, bis miserum curva senecta premet.*

[59] *remque Romanam Latiumque felix/alterum in lustrum meliusque semper/prorogat aevum* (66–68).

[60] Contrast Horace, *Odes* 3.30.6–7: *non omnis moriar multaque pars mei/vitabit Libitinam.*

of stern old men as worthless.[61] The choice of verb is significant, given the fact that the primary meaning of *aestimare* is "to estimate the money value of, price, value."[62] And he had proceeded to count out (not, as in Bourne, one hundred years), but the hundreds and thousands of kisses to be given by his beloved.[63] Catullus's poem itself is set out in terms rather reminiscent of an itemized monetary account. This is reflected in the use of repetition at the beginnings (*dein ... deinde ... dein* [8–10]) and endings (*centum ... centum ... centum* [8–10]) of lines. The motif of giving, denoted in the Catullian imperative *da mi basia mille* (7), and the associated exhortation to "estimate" (*aestimemus*) are transmuted in Bourne's lines into a rather banal and quasi-prosaic statement of fact (*et dari nobis satis aestimamus* [42]) as an imperative becomes a passive infinitive, kisses become years, and a jussive subjunctive becomes an indicative.

And that *satis* is not without significance. Catullus's poem 5 finds a companion piece in poem 7, in which the speaker, in a reply to his beloved's question as to how many kisses may be enough and more than enough for him (*quaeris, quot mihi basiationes/tuae, Lesbia, sint satis superque* [7.1–2]), employs traditional images of infinity (grains of sand or stars in the sky) to create an answer that transcends numerology. In fact both poems 5 and 7 conclude by deconstructing the accounting metaphor upon which they are founded. In 5, the speaker predicts that in order to prevent the envious from knowing the amount of their kisses, they will in fact put the account into disarray (*conturbabimus illa* [11]).[64] In 7 the speaker and his beloved will indulge in so many kisses that the inquisitive (*curiosi* [11]) will *not* be able to keep count of them (*nec pernumerare .../possint* [11–12]). Perhaps Bourne's poem likewise deconstructs its accounting metaphor.

In fact, as in Catullus, computation and accounting function as a recurring leitmotif of the *Anus Saecularis*. In a series of rhetorical exclamations the speaker remarks on the difference between the computation employed by ordinary human beings and that which is applicable to the old woman's life (*vulgus infelix hominum dies*

---

[61] *rumoresque senum severiorum/omnes unius aestimemus assis!* (2–3).

[62] Cf. *OLD*, s.v. 1.

[63] *da mi basia mille, deinde centum,/dein mille altera, dein secunda centum,/deinde usque altera mille, deinde centum* (7–9).

[64] It is noteworthy that *conturbare* has a further monetary meaning: "to go bankrupt, default." See *OLD* s.v. 3.

en/computo quam dispare computamus! [5–6]). He comments on how very far removed from her sum is our little sum (*quam tua a summa procul est remota/summula nostra!* [7–8]). And the accounting metaphor is developed in the course of the poem. Thus complaints of infection and breathless groans greatly detract (or subtract) from (*detrahunt multum* [21]) and lessen (*minuunt* [21]) one's lot. But the minus becomes a plus as days and pains increase to reach an equal number (*ad parem crescunt numerum diesque/atque dolores* [23–24]). Regarded in this light, the closing lines of the poem present a speaker who is content perhaps to do his own counting (and accounting), but instead of citing those images of infinity exemplified by Catullus, he expresses a personal wish for a reduction (by half) in a one-hundred-year life span.[65] In a sense by wishing to halve the whole he too will throw into disarray (*conturbabimus illa*) the computation of *saecula*. For Bourne, it is a wish that almost came true since he was just fifty-three years of age at the time of his own death.

4.3 Recreating Identity: Artistic Replication

Set against the ultimately grim finality of the *Anus Saecularis* are several Latin poems in which the deceased is envisaged as achieving some form of immortality. *Lacrimae Pictoris*[66] takes as its subject a painter's successful attempt to recreate via the power of his own art the identity of his deceased son.[67] Although grief-stricken by the premature death of the infant, he orders the corpse to be brought before him, which he proceeds to paint. The poem merits comparison perhaps with Vasari's account of the reaction of the artist Luca Signorelli to the untimely death of his son in battle:

> It is said that a son of his, most beautiful in countenance and in person, whom he loved dearly, was killed at Cortona; and that Luca, heart-broken as he was,

---

[65] Cf. Bourne, "Letter to a Young Lady," at Mitford, ed. *Poematia*, xiv–xv: "It must be the frequent perusal of gravestones and monuments, and the many walks I have taken in a churchyard, that have given me so great a distaste for life."

[66] The piece was first published in *Poematia* (1734), 124.

[67] Contrast Bourne, *In Statuam Sepulchralem Infantis Dormientis*, 6–8, in which the deceased child is wished a sleep of innocence that cannot be depicted either by the artist or by art itself: *et somno simul,/quem nescit artifex nec ars effingere,/fruaris innocentiae.*

had him stripped naked, and with the greatest firmness of soul, without lamenting or shedding a tear, portrayed him, to the end that, whatever he might wish, he might be able by means of the work of his own hands to see that which nature had given him and adverse fortune had snatched away.[68]

—a tale that would itself be immortalized in the nineteenth century by John Addington Symonds.[69] In Bourne, the painter is identified only by the pseudogeneric term Apelles, the celebrated artist of Augustan Rome,[70] while the *lacrimae pictoris* of the poem's title contrast sharply with the tearlessness of his Italian counterpart.[71] And the tragedy of the whole is intensified by the fact that in this instance the deceased is not a youth but an infant (*infantem ... puerum* [1]).

Demanding his paintbrush and paints (5),[72] the father begins to paint the eyes he has just closed (7),[73] recreating in art the boy's brow, hair, and his lips not yet pale (9–10).[74] Even now he can still see the gentle smile upon his son's lips and the blush upon his cheeks (13–14).[75] And under the impulse of breathless inspiration he swiftly transfers these to his painting (*transtulit in tabulam* [16]).[76] In so doing he replicates the very *imago* of the deceased,[77] an *imago* that will live for a long time

---

[68] *Giorgio Vasari: Lives of the Painters, Sculptors and Architects*, trans. G.C. de Vere with an introduction and notes by David Ekserdjian (London, 1996), I, 612.

[69] See John Addington Symonds, "An Episode," and especially notes 75–77 below.

[70] On the application of Apelles as a generic term for the artist, cf. *Lusus Westmonasterienses*, 101: *pingere equi spumam ter frustra expertus, Apelle.*

[71] Cf. "without lamenting or shedding a tear" (Vasari).

[72] *et calamum et succos poscens* (5).

[73] *dixit, et, ut clausit, clausos depixit ocellos* (7).

[74] *frontemque et crines nec adhuc pallentia formans/oscula, adumbravit lugubre pictor opus* (9–10).

[75] *vidit adhuc molles genitor super oscula risus;/vidit adhuc veneres irrubuisse genis* (13–14). Cf. Symonds, "An Episode," 8–10: "Thy son is dead,/Slain in a duel; but the bloom of life/Yet lingers round red lips and downy cheek."

[76] Cf. Symonds, "An Episode," 21–22: "Then Luca seiz'd his palette: hour by hour/ Silence was in the room; none durst approach."

[77] Cf. Symonds, "An Episode," 24–26: "and saw the painter/Painting his dead son with unerring hand-stroke,/Firm and dry-ey'd before the lordly canvas."

(*filioli longum vivet imago tui* [18]). The poem's closing couplet presents a twofold reward of immortality:

> vivet, et aeterna vives tu laude, nec arte
> vincendus pictor nec pietate pater. (19–20)

The recreated *imago* of the infant is mirrored by the eternal fame that the artist and father will enjoy.

The very nature and essence of the immortalized *imago* is closely interrogated in Bourne's *Pyramis*. First printed in 1734, this short elegiac poem questions the expense involved in building pyramids in memory of the deceased, recommending instead an upright and moral life, which can in effect function as its own figurative pyramid. In that instance a tomb comprising a mere six feet should be enough. The tone of the whole is one of righteous indignation conveyed through the use of rhetorical question (1–2), emotive exclamation (*ah!* [3]), rhetorical statements (5–6) and sardonic repetition (*ergo ... ergo* [5–6]; *tot ... tot* [6]). While the sentiment finds a parallel in, for example, one of the *Lusus Westmonasterienses* pieces entitled *Sepulcri Mitte Supervacuous Honores*,[78] the originality and ingenuity of Bourne's poem emerge through an understanding of the subtle ways in which it interacts with a range of classical Latin intertexts.

The notion of a figurative pyramid is one that occurs in both Horace and Propertius. In *Odes* 3.30 Horace sees his own poetry as a *monumentum* which is more enduring than bronze and loftier than the royal rubble of pyramids (*exegi monumentum aere perennius/regalique situ pyramidum altius* [1–2]),[79] an edifice that will outlast such physical constructions and will remain impervious to the elements and to time itself (3–5). Likewise Propertius, in Elegy 3.2, a poem that seems to interact with Horace,[80] picks up the theme. Celebrating the Muses as his companions, the speaker predicts immortality for his beloved in virtue of the fact that she has been celebrated in his poetry, which will constitute a

---

[78] *Lusus Westmonasterienses*, 113.

[79] On *Odes* 3.30, see, among others, Tony Woodman, "*Exegi monumentum*: Horace, *Odes* 3.30," in Tony Woodman and David West, eds. *Quality and Pleasure in Latin Poetry* (Cambridge, 1974), 115–128; C.A. Rubino, "Monuments and Pyramids: Death and the Poet in Horace's *Carmen* 3.30," *Classical and Modern Literature* 5 (1985), 99–110; C.J. Simpson, "*Exegi Monumentum*: Building Imagery and Metaphor in Horace, *Odes* 1–3," *Latomus* 61 (2002), 57–66.

[80] See, for example, J.F. Miller, "Propertius 3.2 and Horace," *Transactions of the American Philological Association* 113 (1983), 289–299.

monument to her beauty (*carmina erunt formae tot monumenta tuae* [3.2.18]). He proceeds to contrast this with expensive pyramids, which though rising to the stars (*pyramidum sumptus ad sidera ducti* [19]), are among structures that are not impervious to death (22)[81] since they will be impaired either by fire or the elements, or else destroyed by the passage of time (23–24).[82] By contrast, the fame that is attendant upon genius provides immortal glory (25–26).[83]

Bourne's piece begins with a clear echo of Propertius in its rhetorical denunciation of *pyramidum sumptus ad coelum et sidera ducti* (1). But it is a viewpoint that would seem to have a special personal application, and one that is mirrored elsewhere in Bourne's writings. In his "Letter to a Young Lady" he had proclaimed:

> To continue the remembrance of the deceased, though by a mound of earth, a turf of grass, or a rail of wood, is an instance of affection and humanity equal to the most costly monuments of brass and marble, in everything but expense and duration, and yet how preferable are even those! How fruitless is the expense, and how short the duration![84]

The Latin lines move beyond Propertius in conveying a rather gothic sense of morbidity as the speaker focuses on the contents of the pyramids themselves: the black ugly corpse (*nigrum informe cadaver* [3]) and the mummified flesh (*durata in saxum est cui medicata caro* [4]). Again the sentiment finds a parallel in that same letter:

> The sepulchre too may be painted without, but within is full of filthiness and uncleanness; and the corpse may be wrapt in velvet and fine linen, yet in velvet and fine linen it shall rot. The leaden coffin and the arched vault may separate it from vulgar dust; but even here shall the worm find it, nor

---

[81] *[neque] ... mortis ab extrema condicione vacant* (3.2.22).

[82] *aut illis flamma aut imber subducet honores,/annorum aut tacito pondere victa ruent* (3.2.23–24). Cf. Shakespeare, *Sonnet* 55.1–4: "Not marble nor the gilded monuments/Of princes shall outlive this pow'rful rhyme,/But you shall shine more bright in these contents/Than unswept stone besmeared with sluttish time." Text is that of *William Shakespeare: The Complete Sonnets and Poems*, ed. Colin Burrow (Oxford, 2002), 491.

[83] *at non ingenio quaesitum nomen ab aevo/excidet: ingenio stat sine morte decus* (3.2.25–26).

[84] Bourne, "Letter to a Young Lady," Mitford, ed. *Poematia*, x–xi.

shall his hunger be satisfied till he strip it to the bones. In the meantime the laboured epitaph is mocking it with titles, and belying it with praises.[85]

Indeed the grotesque morbidity seems to color Bourne's depiction of the *monumentum* itself, and it does so through Virgilian reminiscence. His comment regarding monuments stretching over acres (*ergone porrigitur monumenta in iugera tota* [5]) is endowed with sardonic irony in its implementation of language evocative of Virgil's description of the infernal torment endured by Tityos, who lay stretched across nine acres (*per tota novem cui iugera corpus/porrigitur* [*Aen.* 6.596–597]) as his liver was eternally cropped by a huge vulture (*immanis vultur* [597]).

Strikingly absent, however, from Bourne's piece is any sense of that literary self-consciousness inherent in both Horace and Propertius whereby the eternal monument becomes poetry itself. Bourne substitutes a morally upright life: *integra sit morum tibi vita; haec pyramis esto* (7) in a line ironically reminiscent of Horace, *Satires* 1.22.1: *integer vitae scelerisque purus.*[86] The moral of this piece is clear. Or, as recast in the words of the poet's epitaph:

> PIETATIS SINCERAE
> SUMMAEQUE HUMILITATIS,
> NEC DEI USQUAM IMMEMOR
> NEC SUI,
> IN SILENTIUM QUOD AMAVIT
> DESCENDIT
> V.B.[87]

A virtuous life can function as its own memorial. As the ultimate *imago* it is this that can transcend silence itself, creating and recreating "another Bourne identity."

---

[85] Bourne, "Letter to a Young Lady," Mitford, ed. *Poematia*, xii. Cf. viii: "though the body be sleeping and mouldering in the grave." The comment regarding the "laboured epitaph" is not without irony in view of the fact that Bourne himself was the composer of a whole series of Latin epitaphs: on a certain J.L.G., Mitford, ed. *Poematia*, 253; William Dickinson, Mitford, ed. *Poematia*, 253; John Woodward, Mitford, ed. *Poematia*, 254; Jonathan Martin, Mitford, ed. *Poematia*, 255; a female E.H., Mitford, ed. *Poematia*, 256; a certain M.R. Mitford, ed. *Poematia*, 256; a young girl, Mitford, ed. *Poematia*, 257; a certain woman F.T. Mitford, ed. *Poematia*, 258, and a "Poor John," Mitford, ed. *Poematia*, 259–260.

[86] Cf. *The Gentleman's Magazine*, II (December, 1732), 1122, "*Integer Vitae, scelerisque purus, Hor.*: Virtue, my Friend, needs no defence,/The surest guard is Innocence." On the poet's celebration of his own moral integrity, cf., for example, Catullus 76.19: *si vitam puriter egi.*

[87] Mitford, ed. *Poematia*, xxv. Cf. Introduction, 1–2.

APPENDIX 1

VINCENT BOURNE'S LATIN POETRY
(SELECTIONS)

LATIN TEXT AND FACING ENGLISH TRANSLATION[1]

BY

ESTELLE HAAN

---

[1] In all instances, Latin text is that of Mitford, ed. *Poematia*. I have modernized spelling and punctuation.

Anus Saecularis
Quae Iustam Centum Annorum Aetatem
Ipso Die Natali Explevit Et Clausit
Anno 1728

Singularis prodigium o senectae
et novum exemplum diuturnitatis,
cuius annorum series in amplum
      desinit orbem!

Vulgus infelix hominum dies en   5
computo quam dispare computamus!
quam tua a summa procul est remota
      summula nostra!

Pabulum nos luxuriesque leti,
nos simul nati incipimus perire,   10
nos statim a cunis cita destinamur
      praeda sepulchro.

Occulit mors insidias ubi vix,
vix opinari est, rapidaeve febris
vim repentinam aut male pertinacis   15
      semina morbi.

Sin brevem posset superare vita
terminum, quicquid superest vacivum
illud ignavis superest et imbe-
      cillibus annis.   20

Detrahunt multum minuuntque sorti
morbidi questus gemitusque anheli;
ad parem crescunt numerum diesque
      atque dolores.

Siquis haec vitet (quotus ille quisque est!)   25
et gradu pergendo laborioso
ad tuum, fortasse tuum, moretur
      reptilis aevum:

At videt moestum tibi saepe visum in-
iurias, vim, furta, dolos, et inso-   30
lentiam quo semper eunt eodem
      ire tenore.

Nil inest rebus novitatis; id quod
saeculum praesens videt, illud ipsum
vidit elapsum prius, et videbit   35
      omne futurum.

An Old Woman of a Century,
Who Brought to Completion and Closed a
Perfected Age of One Hundred Years on Her Very
Birthday in the Year 1728

O marvel of a unique old age, and recent example of longevity, whose sequence of years has come to an end in a full circle!

Behold, with how different a calculation do we, the wretched throng of men, calculate our days! How far removed is our little amount from your total!

We, Death's fodder and indulgence, we, as soon as we are born, begin to perish; from the cradle we are instantly destined to be rapid prey for the tomb.

Death conceals her snares, where one would hardly, hardly imagine: the sudden violence of a rapid fever or the seeds of a wretchedly tenacious disease.

If life could conquer its brief extremity, whatever remains, remains not free from sluggish and feeble years.

The complaints of infection and breathless groans cause great detriment and impair one's lot; days and pains increase to reach an equal number.

If anyone avoids these things (what a rarity is he!) and by proceeding with laboured gait creeps his tardy way to perhaps your age:

Still he sees (a wretched sight frequently beheld by you) injustices, violence, theft, trickery and insolence proceeding in the same course as they always do.

There is nothing new in circumstances; that which the present century beholds, that very thing has the previous seen to elapse, and it is that which every century to come will behold.

Temporum quicquid variatur et quod
uspiam est nugarum et ineptiarum,
unius volvi videt et revolvi
       circulus aevi.   40

Integram aetatem tibi gratulamur,
et dari nobis satis aestimamus
si tuam saltem vacuam querelis
       dimidiemus.

Ad Grillum
Anacreonticum

O qui meae culinae
argutulus choraules
et hospes es canorus,
quacunque commoreris,
felicitatis omen;   5
iucundiore cantu
siquando me salutes,
et ipse te rependam,
et ipse, qua valebo,
remunerabo musa.   10

Diceris innocensque
et gratus inquilinus,
nec victitans rapinis,
ut sorices voraces
muresve curiosi   15
furumque delicatum
vulgus domesticorum,
sed tutus in camini
recessibus quiete
contentus et calore.   20

Beatior cicada,
quae te referre forma,
quae voce te videtur,
et saltitans per herbas,
unius, haud secundae,   25
aestatis est chorista:
tu carmen integratum
reponis ad Decembrem,
laetus per universum
incontinenter annum.   30

Whatever the vicissitudes of time and whatever trifles
and follies exist anywhere, the cycle of a single age
beholds them going round and round again.

We congratulate you upon an unreduced span of life;
and we reckon that enough will be given to us if we
attain at least half your age free from complaints.

To a Cricket
Anacreontic

O you who are the chirping
player of my kitchen, and a
songful guest, an omen of good
luck wherever you linger; if ever
you greet me with your very
delightful song, I myself will
repay you in turn, and I myself,
insofar as I am able, will return
the favour by my muse.

You will be proclaimed a
harmless and a welcome lodger,
and not subsisting on plunder
like ravenous rodents or
inquisitive mice or the frivolous
throng of domestic thieves, but
safe in the hearth's retreat,
content with peace and with
warmth.

Happier than the cicada which
seems to recall you in appearance,
which seems to recall you in
voice; and dancing across the
grass, is the chorister of one
summer, but not a second: you
store away until December a
song that is renewed, joyful and
without rest through the entire
year.

Te nulla lux relinquit,
te nulla nox revisit
non musicae vacantem,
curisve non solutum:
quin amplies canendo,   35
quin amplies fruendo
aetatulam vel omni
quam nos homunciones
absumimus querendo
aetate longiorem.   40

Solitudo Regia Richmondiensis

Siquis uspiam angulus
   vel in recessu silvulae vel horti
   solitudini vacet,
sit, o sit illic hospita sub umbra
   grata regibus quies.   5
sub hac parumper agmen aulicorum
   usque et usque supplicum,
sub hac molestas gratulationes
   confluentium undique
refugerint: tum verius beati   10
   quando taedium imperi
semoverint onusque dignitatis.
   grande quid vel aureum
conspexeris? nec illud est, nec illud,
   principes quod augeat: 15
prudentia sed rite temperatum
   pectus, et sui potens
augusta mens, felix, abunde felix,
   in silentio casae.
nec his, superbi quos iuvant tumultus,   20
   invidete cellulam:
fruantur, aequum est, hac brevi quiete
   otioque simplici,
salute qui pro civium laborant.

Mutua Benevolentia Primaria
Lex Naturae Est

Per Libyae Androcles siccas errabat arenas
   qui vagus iratum fugerat exsul erum.
lassato tandem fractoque labore viarum
   ad scopuli patuit caeca caverna latus.

No day leaves you, no night comes back to see you without your having your fill of music or, freed from anxieties, without you singing more fully, without you enjoying more abundantly a little span of life longer even than every life-time that we little men waste in complaining.

The Regal Solitude of Richmond

If either in a woodland or garden retreat any corner has room for solitude, let there be, o, let there be there, beneath an hospitable shade a welcome repose for kings.

Beneath this may they take refuge for a short time from the ever constant troop of suppliant courtiers; beneath this from the troublesome felicitations of people flocking together from every side; then all the more truly blessed when they have removed the tedium of rule and the burden of rank.

Why do you have regard for what is mighty or made of gold? It is not that, not that which augments princes: but prudence, a heart properly moderated, and an august mind in control of itself, happy, abundantly happy in the silence of a cottage.

And you who delight in arrogant tumult, do not begrudge these their little cell. It is fitting that those who toil for the salvation of citizens should enjoy this brief repose and simple leisure.

Reciprocal Kindness
Is the Primary Law of Nature

Through the deserts of Libya there wandered Androcles, who as a roaming exile had escaped from his angry master. Eventually wearied and broken by the toil of his travelling, there was exposed to him a hidden cave at the side of a cliff.

hanc subit, et placidae dederat vix membra quieti   5
   cum subito immanis rugit ad antra leo:
ille pedem attollens laesum et miserabile murmur
   edens, qua poterat voce precatur opem.
perculsus novitate rei incertusque timore,
   vix tandem tremulas admovet erro manus: 10
et spinam explorans (nam fixa in vulnere spina
   haerebat) cauto molliter ungue trahit.
continuo dolor omnis abit, taeter fluit humor,
   et coit, absterso sanguine, rupta cutis.
nunc iterum silvas dumosque peragrat, et affert   15
   providus assiduas hospes ad antra dapes.
iuxta epulis accumbit homo conviva leonis,
   nec crudos dubitat participare cibos.
quis tamen ista ferat desertae taedia vitae?
   vix furor ultoris tristior esset eri!   20
devotum certis caput obiectare peric'lis
   et patrios statuit rursus adire lares.
traditur hic fera facturus spectacula plebi,
   accipit et miserum tristis arena reum.
irruit e caveis fors idem impastus et acer,   25
   et medicum attonito suspicit ore leo;
suspicit, et veterem agnoscens vetus hospes amicum,
   decumbit notos blandulus ante pedes.
quid vero perculsi animis stupuere Quirites?
   ecquid prodigii, territa Roma, vides?   30
unius naturae opus est: ea sola furorem
   sumere quae iussit ponere sola iubet.

Ad Davidem Cook
Westmonasterii Custodem Nocturnum
Et Vigilantissimum Anno 1716

Indicium qui saepe mihi das carmen amoris
   reddo tibi indicium carmen amoris ego.
qui faustum et felix multum mihi mane precaris
   dico atque ingemino nunc tibi rursus: "ave!"
te neque dinumerat gallus constantius horas   5
   nec magis is certo provocat ore diem.
cum variis implent tenebrae terroribus orbem,
   tu comite assuetum cum cane carpis iter.
nec te, quos serae emittunt post vina popinae,
   nec te, quos lemures plurima vidit anus,   10
nec te perterrent nodoso stipite fretum
   subdola qui tacito pectore furta parant.
sed si cui occurras prima qui portat ad urbem
   sub luce exiguus quas dedit hortus opes,
hunc placidis dictis et voce affaris amica,   15

This he entered, and had hardly given his limbs to peaceful repose when suddenly a savage lion roared before the cave: he, raising up an injured paw, and uttering a pitiful roar, begs for help in whatever tones he could. Struck by the strangeness of the situation and faltering because of fear, at last the fugitive applies with difficulty his trembling hands: and inspecting a thorn (for a thorn was sticking fast in his wound) gently and with careful nail he drags it out. Instantly all the pain departed, the filthy moisture flowed, and the ruptured skin joined together, as the blood was wiped away. Now he traverses once more woods and briars, and the provident guest brings a constant feast to the cave. The man reclines as the lion's fellow guest close to the banquet, and does not hesitate to partake of the raw food. However, who could endure that weariness of the desert life! Hardly would his avenging master's fury be more stern! He decided to expose his doomed life to certain danger and to approach once more his native abode. He is handed over to create a cruel spectacle for the people, and the stern arena receives its wretched charge. By chance there rushed from the cage the same lion, famished and fierce, and with astonished expression he looks up at his doctor; he looks up, and the guest of old, recognizing his old friend, charmingly lies down before the feet that he knew. But why were the citizens astounded, stricken in their minds? Do you see some sort of omen, o terrified Rome? This is the work of one and the same Nature: she alone who has ordered someone to adopt fury, she alone orders him to lay it aside.

To David Cook, Most Vigilant Nightwatchman of Westminster in the Year 1716

I return a poem as a token of affection to you, who often give me a poem as a token of affection. I say and now redouble "Hail" to you, who in the morning wish me good fortune and much good luck. The cockerel does not calculate the hours more consistently than you, nor does he summon the day with a more assured call. When darkness covers the world with its variety of terrors, you press upon your customary journey with your dog as companion. Trusting in your knotty stick, you are not frightened either by those whom the late pubs evict after drinks nor by those fairies whom many an old woman beholds, nor by those who prepare sly thefts in the silence of their hearts. But if you run into anyone who at first light is carrying to the city the produce which his tiny garden has afforded him, you address him with gentle words and a friendly voice,

utque dies fausta luce precaris eat.
tinnitu adventum signans, oriantur an astra
     narras an pure lucida luna micet.
dumque quies nos alta manet, nec frigoris ullus
     securos pluviae nec metus ullus habet,   20
tu gelidos inter ventos versaris et imbres,
     cum mala tempestas et nigra saevit hiems.
seu te praesentem vicus seu viculus audit,
     nocturnum multo carmine fallis iter.
quid si culta minus docta vacet arte poesis,   25
     si simplex versus sit numerique rudes;
invidiam somnus (tanta indulgentia noctis)
     opprimit, et livor, te recitante, silet.
divorum hiberni menses quotcunque celebrant,
     cuique locum et versum dat tua musa suum: 30
Crispino ante omnes; neque enim sine carmine fas est
     nobile sutorum praeteriisse decus.
nec tua te pietas fieri permiserit unquam
     Caesaris immemorem Caesareaeque domus.
officio dominos multo dominasque salutas,   35
     gratia nec fidae sedulitatis abest.
multa docens iuvenes et pulchras multa puellas,
     utile tu pueris virginibusque canis:
coniugium felix monitis utentibus optas,
     cunctaque quae castus gaudia lectus habet.   40
tu monitor famulis sexus utriusque benignus,
     munditias illis praecipis, hisce fidem.
omnibus at votis hoc oras atque peroras
     ut dominis cedant prospera quaeque tuis.
unum hoc prae cunctis meminisse hortaris: ut imis   45
     summa etiam exaequet mortis amica manus.
quid tibi pro totidem meritis speremus? amori
     quisve tuo aequalis retribuatur amor?
tuque tuusque canis si nos visetis, uterque
     grati eritis nobis tuque tuusque canis.   50
mille domos adeas, et non ignobile munus
     (nulla minus solido) dent tibi mille domus;
quemque bonum exoptas nobis laetumque Decembrem,
     esto tibi pariter laetus, et esto bonus.

In Obitum Roussaei
Collegio Trinitatis Servi A Cubiculis Anno 1721

Alme Charon (nam tandem omnes qui nascimur et qui
     nascemur tua nos cymba aliquando manet),
per ripas fer circum oculos omnesque recense
     manes ad Stygias qui glomerantur aquas;

and you pray that his day may proceed with the light of good fortune. Indicating your arrival by the ringing of your bell, you tell whether the stars are rising or whether the bright moon is shining clearly. And while deep repose awaits us and no fear of cold or of rain possesses us, free as we are from care, you come and go amid icy winds and showers when an evil storm and black winter rage. Whether a street or a byway hears your presence, you beguile your nightly journey with many a poem. What if your poetry is inelegant and lacking in learned skill, if the verse is simple and the rhythms unsophisticated! Sleep stifles ill-will (so great is night's indulgence) and as you recite, malice falls silent. As many saints as the months of winter celebrate, your muse gives to each its own setting and verse: to Crispin above all; for it is not right that the honourable glory of cobblers has passed by without a poem. Nor has your dutifulness ever allowed you to become forgetful of Caesar and the house of Caesar. With great courtesy you greet lords and ladies; and the grace of trusty assiduity is not absent. Teaching many things to young men, and many things to beautiful girls, you sing a song useful to boys and to virgins: you wish to those who make use of your advice a happy marriage and all the joys which a chaste bed possesses. You are a kind adviser to servants of both sexes, to these you recommend elegance, to those fidelity. But with every prayer you beg and beseech this: that everything might turn out prosperously for your masters. You encourage them to remember this one thing before all others: that the friendly hand of death equates the loftiest with the lowliest. What hopes may we express for you in return for so many merits? Or what affection may be repaid to match your affection? If you and your dog come to visit us, both of you will be welcome to us, you and your dog. May you approach a thousand homes and may a thousand homes give you a gift that is not mean (nothing less than a shilling); may the good and prosperous December which you wish for us be equally prosperous and good for you.

On the Death of Rouse,
Bed Attendant to Trinity College in the Year 1721

Kindly Charon (for eventually your boat awaits us all at some point—both those of us who are born and those who will be born), direct your gaze along the banks and review all the souls who are swarming together before the Stygian waters;

prospice si crassam fors exploraveris umbram,   5
  non est in toto crassior umbra loco.
luctantem cernes animasque hinc inde minores
  turbantem ut cubito pandat utroque viam.
squalidus et pinguis totus tibi navita dextram
  tendet ad Elysii traiiciendus agros.   10
dum vixit Roussaeus erat, nostri accola Cami,
  quem puerum novit, novit et unda senem.
navita non illo melior fuit, esset agenda
  seu remis conto seu subigenda ratis.
nec quisquam ex umero contorsit rete sinistro   15
  certius incautis piscibus exitium.
quid tamen haec memoro, Camus cum perfidus idem
  Roussaeum inviso merserit amne suum!
hunc nostro ut reddas caelo te carmine multo,
  alme Charon, Grantae moesta iuventa petit.   20
sin Parcae prohibent et inexorabilis Orci
  quem petimus, reditum lex inimica vetat,
hoc saltem concede: admota ad litora cymba,
  per Stygium nautam transvehe nauta lacum.
nec poscas naulum, loculos nam vivus inanes   25
  gessit, et haud obolum quem tibi solvat habet.
quod si tam crebras transmittere te piget umbras
  et longum refugis, portitor unus, opus,
accipe divisi socium comitemque laboris;
  divisus levior fiet utrique labor.   30
adde quod (ut similes estis) dubitabitur utrum
  Roussaeus geminus sit geminusve Charon.

Epitaphium In Canem

Pauperis hic Iri requiesco Lyciscus, erilis
dum vixi tutela vigil columenque senectae,
dux caeco fidus, nec me ducente solebat
praetenso hinc atque hinc baculo per iniqua locorum
incertam explorare viam, sed fila secutus   5
quae dubios regerent passus, vestigia tuta
fixit inoffenso gressu, gelidumque sedile
in nudo nactus saxo, qua praetereuntium
unda frequens confluxit, ibi miserisque tenebras
lamentis noctemque oculis ploravit obortam.   10
ploravit nec frustra; obolum dedit alter et alter,
queis corda et mentem indiderat natura benignam.
ad latus interea iacui sopitus erile
vel mediis vigil in somnis, ad erilia iussa
auresque atque animum arrectus, seu frustula amice   15
porrexit sociasque dapes, seu longa diei
taedia perpessus reditum sub nocte parabat.

look forth if by chance you inspect a large shade; no shade is larger in the whole region. You will see someone struggling and throwing into confusion on this side and on that the smaller souls, so that with each elbow he may open up a pathway. Filthy and utterly fat, the boatman will stretch out his right hand to you in his need to be transported to the Elysian fields. While he lived, this was Rouse, an inhabitant of our Cam, whose waters knew him as a boy and knew him as an old man. There was no better boatman than he, whether a raft had to be driven by oars or propelled by a pole. Nor did anyone twist from his left shoulder a net with greater accuracy—a destruction to fish caught off their guard. However, why do I relate these things when that same perfidious Cam plunged its own Rouse into its hated river! O kindly Charon, the grieving youth of Granta seeks with many a verse that you restore him to our sky. If the Fates do not allow and the hostile law of inexorable Orcus forbids the return which we seek, grant this at least: move your barque to the shore and, boatman yourself, transport a boatman across the Stygian lake. And do not demand a fare; for while alive he carried empty cash-boxes and he doesn't have a coin with which he may pay you. But if it doesn't please you to send across ghosts so large, and if as the only ferryman you shun the lengthy task: receive an ally and companion in a shared toil; the toil will become lighter divided between you both. Add the fact that (as you are alike) there will be doubt as to whether Rousius is the twin or whether Charon is the twin.

Epitaph on a Dog

Here rest I Lyciscus, the watchful guard dog, while I was alive, of my poor master Irus, and crown of his old age, a trusty guide to him in his blindness. Nor, when I lead him, was he accustomed to seek through rough regions his tottering way with staff outstretched on this side and on that; but following the threads which might guide his wavering steps, he planted footsteps safely with gait that did not stumble; and coming upon a cold seat upon bare rock where the tide of passersby flocked in great numbers, there with wretched lamentation he bewailed the darkness and the blindness clouding his eyes. Nor did he bewail in vain; one and then another, upon whom nature bestowed kindness of heart and of mind, gave a coin. Meanwhile I lay asleep at my master's side, vigilant even in the midst of sleep, my ears and mind pricked in response to my master's commands, whether in friendship he held out morsels and his shared feast, or whether having endured to the end the long tedium of the day, he was preparing to return at the approach of night.

Hi mores, haec vita fuit, dum fata sinebant,
dum neque languebam morbis nec inerte senecta
quae tandem obrepsit, veterique satellite caecum   20
orbavit dominum; prisci sed gratia facti
ne tota intereat, longos deleta per annos,
exiguum hunc Irus tumulum de caespite fecit,
etsi inopis, non ingratae, munuscula dextrae;
carmine signavitque brevi dominumque canemque   25
quod memoret: fidumque canem dominumque benignum.

Idem Agit Idem

Felicula ad speculum saltu lascivit erile;
    lascivam saltu feliculamque videt.
nigra videt nigram; bicolor naso, bicolorem;
    glaucaque torquentem lumina, glauca tuens.
et sociam ad lusus lentae incurvamine caudae   5
    provocat et lepidi mobilitate pedis.
utraque utramque lacessit et utraque palpat utramque,
    et molle oppositos explicat unguiculos.
iam tumet in tergum et simulatas exspuit iras;
    et tumet et similes exspuit umbra minas.   10
quaenam haec sit, mima unde sui tam mimica quaerit
    felis, an in speculo post speculumne siet.
te quoque praesentem praesens quam quaeris et illa
    quaerit, an in speculo post speculumne sies.
alterutra alterutram quaeritque et decipit; idque   15
    feliculae facitis quod facis una duae.

Simile Agit in Simile

Cristatus pictisque ad Thaida psittacus alis
    missus ab Eoo munus amante venit.
ancillis mandat primam formare loquelam;
    archididascaliae dat sibi Thais opus.
"Psittace," ait Thais, fingitque sonantia molle   5
    basia, quae docilis molle refingit avis.
iam captat, iam dimidiat tirunculus, et iam
    integrat auditos articulatque sonos.
"Psittace mi pulcher pulchelle," era dicit alumno;
    "Psittace mi pulcher," reddit alumnus erae.   10
iamque canit, ridet, deciesque aegrotat in hora,
    et vocat ancillas nomine quamque suo.
multaque scurratur mendax et multa iocatur,
    et lepido populum detinet augurio.
nunc tremulum illudit fratrem, qui suspicit, et "pol!   15

This was my character, this my life, while the Fates permitted, while I did not languish in disease or in lifeless old age which eventually crept upon me and bereft my blind master of his old bodyguard: but lest his thanks for my former service should totally perish, wiped out across the long years, Irus made this little tomb of turf, the little gift of a right hand albeit impoverished, but not ungrateful, and he marked it out with a brief inscription to recall both master and dog, both faithful dog and kind master.

The Same Behaves in the Same Way

A kitten leaped and frisked before its mistress's mirror, and it sees a kitten frisking and leaping. Black in itself, it sees a black self; its two-toned nose sees a two-toned nose; gazing with grey eyes at one rotating grey eyes. And it summons its companion to play by the curving of its flexible tail and by the movement of its charming paw. Each assails the other, and each humors the other; and gently unfolds little claws in front of the other's. Now its back swells up and it spews forth simulated wrath; and the reflection swells and spews forth similar threats. The cat seeks what this is, whence this actress so mimics iself, or if it exists in the mirror or behind the mirror. That one whom you seek is present and it looks for you who are also present, and asks whether you are in the mirror or behind the mirror. Each seeks and deceives the other; and, two kittens, you perform the action of one!

Like Acts as Like

A crested parrot with colored wings reached Thais, having been sent as a gift from her Eastern lover. Thais instructs her maids to mould its first utterance; to herself she assigns the task of head-teacher. "Parrot," says Thais, and produces gently sounding kisses, which the bird, apt to learn, gently reproduces. The little novice now tries to listen, now halves and now renews and articulates the sounds that it has heard. "My beautiful, beautiful little parrot," the mistress says to her pupil. "My beautiful parrot," replies the pupil to its mistress. And now it sings, it laughs, it is sick ten times an hour, and it calls each of the maids by her own name. Untruthfully it utters many offensive comments and makes many jokes and it holds the populace with its charming predictions. Now it jeers at a trembling brother, who looks up, and says: "Pol,

carnalis, quisque te docet," inquit, "homo est."
argutae nunc stridet anus argutulus instar;
   respicit, et "nebulo es, quisquis es," inquit anus.
quando fuit melior tiro meliorve magistra!
   quando duo ingeniis tam coiere pares!   20
ardua discenti nulla est, res nulla docenti
   ardua, cum doceat femina, discat avis.

Agens Et Patiens Sunt Simul

Duxit Acon Leonillam; haud una atque altera luna
   interiit male cum se nova nupta tulit:
os pallet, languent oculi, stomachoque fit ista
   nausea quae gravidas denotat esse nurus.
esto fides dictis: eadem quoque nausea Aconti est: 5
   pallidus est pariter vultus, ocellus hebes.
nutrix, sedula anus, fomenta utrique ministrat:
   cardiacum uxori cardiacumque viro.
quis novus hic, nutrix, morbus? socii unde dolores?
   quave sumus gravidi condicione viri?   10
nutrix, callida anus, "fuit," inquit, "utrique voluptas;
   aequa satis lex est ut sit utrique dolor."

Lacrimae Pictoris

Infantem audivit puerum, sua gaudia, Apelles
   intempestivo fato obiisse diem.
ille, licet tristi perculsus imagine mortis,
   proferri in medium corpus inane iubet,
et calamum et succos poscens: "hos accipe luctus,   5
   maerorem hunc," dixit, "nate, parentis habe."
dixit, et ut clausit, clausos depinxit ocellos,
   officio pariter fidus utrique pater;
frontemque et crines nec adhuc pallentia formans
   oscula, adumbravit lugubre pictor opus.   10

Perge, parens, maerendo tuos expendere luctus;
   nondum opus absolvit triste suprema manus.

Vidit adhuc molles genitor super oscula risus;
   vidit adhuc veneres irrubuisse genis;
et teneras raptim veneres blandosque lepores,   15
   et tacitos risus transtulit in tabulam.
pingendo desiste tuum signare dolorem,
   filioli longum vivet imago tui;
vivet, et aeterna vives tu laude, nec arte
   vincendus pictor nec pietate pater.   20

whoever is your teacher is a carnal fellow!" Now like a chattering old woman it screeches shrilly; the "old woman" looks round and says: "Whoever you are, you are a scoundrel!" When has there been a better pupil or a better teacher; when have two intellects so equal come together! When a woman teaches and a bird learns there is nothing that is difficult for teacher or for learner.

The Agent and the Sufferer Are One and the Same

Acon married Leonilla; one and another moon had not disappeared when the new bride felt unwell. Her face grows pale, her eyes droop, and in her stomach there occurs that sickness which indicates that young women are pregnant. Trust these words: Acon too has the same sickness; his countenance is equally pale; his eyes weak. The nurse, an attentive old woman, administers remedies to them both: a stomach remedy to the wife, and a stomach remedy to the husband. Nurse, what is this new disease? Whence these shared pains? Or by what condition do we husbands become pregnant? The nurse, a shrewd old woman, said: "Both of you had pleasure; it is a fair enough condition that both of you should have pain."

The Painter's Tears

Apelles heard that his infant child, his own joy, had met with death by an untimely fate. He, although stricken by the sad image of death, orders the lifeless body to be brought forth into his midst. And summoning his paintbrush and paints, he said "Receive this grief, my son, have this mourning of a parent." He spoke, and when he had closed them, he painted the closed eyes, a father equally faithful to each duty: and depicting his brow and his hair and his lips that were not yet pale, the painter sketched a work of gloom.

Proceed, o parent, to expend your grief through mourning; the final touch has not yet brought the sad work to completion.

The father saw smiles still gentle upon his lips; he saw charms still blushing upon his cheeks: and hastily he transferred into his painting the tender charms, the gentle graces, and the silenced laughter. Cease signalling your grief through painting. The image of your little son will live for long. It will live, and you too will live in eternal praise; a painter not to be surpassed in art, a parent not to be surpassed in dutifulness.

Schola Rhetorices

Londini ad pontem Billingi nomine porta est,
    unde ferunt virides ostrea Nereides.
hic sibi perpetuam legit facundia sedem,
    nec modus hic verbis neve figura deest.
sermonem densis oratrix floribus ornat,   5
    et fundit varios ingeminatque tropos.
et nervi et veneres et vis et copia fandi
    insunt, et iustum singula pondus habent.
O sedes, totidem multum celebrata per annos!
    omne tibi rostrum cedit et omne forum.   10
utraque quos malit titulos academia iactet:
    at tibi linguarum Ianua nomen erit.

Canis Et Echo

Puris in coelo radiis argentea luna
    in Tamisis tremula luce refulsit aquis.
improbus hoc vidit catulus, ringensque malignum
    solvit in indignos ora proterva modos:
lunamque in coelo, lunamque aggressus in undis,   5
    in sidus pariter saevus utrumque furit.
sub ripis latuit fors ulterioribus Echo,
    audiit et vanas ludicra nympha minas;
audiit, et rabie rabiem lepidissima vindex
    ulcisci statuit, parque referre pari.   10
ille repercussae deceptus imagine vocis,
    irarum impatiens iam magis estque magis.
reddere latratus pergit latratibus Echo;
    quemque canis statuit servat imago modum.
tandem ubi lassatae fauces et spiritus et vox,   15
    defervet rabies tota siletque canis.
et poterat siluisse prius; furor omnis ineptus,
    omnisque in sese futilis ira redit.

Certamen Musicum

Octo trans Tamisin campanis diva Maria,
    cis Tamisin bis sex diva Brigetta sonat.
haec tenues urget modulos properantius aedes,
    alternat grandes lentius illa modos.
nec quis in alterutro distinguat litore iudex   5
    an magis haec aurem captet an illa magis.
tantae est harmoniae contentio musica, turris
    altera cum numeros, altera pondus habet.

The School of Rhetoric

Near London's bridge there is a gate by the name of Billing whence green Sea-Nymphs carry oysters. Here eloquence has chosen for herself a permanent seat; here words lack neither limit nor shape. Here the female suppliant adorns conversation with florid elaboration, and pours and redoubles various figures of speech. And included are stylistic vigour and charm and force and an abundance of speech, and each individual utterance possesses perfect weight. O seat greatly celebrated so often through the years! To you yields every platform and every forum. Let each of the universities boast of whatever titles it prefers, but you will have the name "Gate of Tongues."

The Dog and Echo

The silver moon with clear rays in the sky shone brightly again with shimmering light in the waters of the Thames. A mischievous pup saw this and spitefully snarling, it violently barked in a shocking manner: accosting both the moon in the sky and the moon in the waves, it rages equally savagely against both planets. It happened that Echo lay hidden beneath the more distant waters, and the sportive Nymph heard the empty threats. She heard, and the most delightful avenger decided to exact retribution for the savageness with savageness of her own and to equal her match. The dog, deceived by the echo of the reverberating sound, is more and more intolerant of anger. Echo proceeds in returning the barking with barking; the echo maintains the behavior which the dog has established. At last when his jaws, his breath, and his voice grew exhausted, the entire savagery cooled down, and the dog becomes silent. He could have been silent long before; all fury is silly and all futile anger returns upon itself.

A Musical Contest

Across the Thames St Mary resounds with eight bells; on this side of the Thames St Bride resounds with twelve. The former church rings out its slight notes more hastily; the latter alternates mighty measures more slowly. And no adjudicator could discriminate on either shore as to whether the former or the latter captivates the ear more. The musical contest is of such harmony; since one turret possesses rhythm; the other weight.

Pyramis

Pyramidum sumptus ad coelum et sidera ducti,
    quid dignum tanta mole, quid intus habent?
ah! nihil intus habent nisi nigrum informe cadaver,
    durata in saxum est cui medicata caro.
ergone porrigitur monumentum in iugera tota!   5
    ergo tot annorum, tot manuumque labor!
integra sit morum tibi vita; haec pyramis esto:
    et poterunt tumulo sex satis esse pedes.

Stradae Philomela

Pastorem audivit calamis philomela canentem,
    et voluit tenues ipsa referre modos;
ipsa retentavit numeros didicitque retentans
    argutum fida reddere voce melos.
pastor inassuetus rivalem ferre, misellam   5
    grandius ad carmen provocat, urget avem.
tuque etiam in modulos surgis, philomela, sed impar
    viribus, heu impar, exanimisque cadis.
durum certamen! tristis victoria! cantum
    maluerit pastor non superasse tuum.   10

Cantatrices

Qua septem vicos conterminat una columna,
consistunt nymphae Sirenum ex agmine binae:
stramineum capiti tegimen, collumque per omne
ingentes electri orbes: utrique pependit
crustato vestis coeno, limoque rigescens   5
crure usque a medio calcem defluxit ad imum.
exiguam secum pendentem ex ubere natam
altera, venales dextra tulit altera chartas.
    His vix dispositis pueri innuptaeque puellae
accurrunt: sutor primus, cui lorea vitta   10
impediit crines, humili quae proxima stabat
proruit e cella, chartas si forte placerent
empturus; namque ille etiam se carmine multo
oblectat, longos solus quo rite labores
diminuit fallitque hibernae taedia noctis.   15
collecti murmur sensim increbrescere vulgi
audit et excurrit nudis ancilla lacertis.
incudem follesque et opus fabrile relinquens,
se densae immiscet plebi niger ora Pyracmon.
it iuxta, depressum ingens cui mantica tergum   20
incurvat tardo passu; simul ille coronam

Pyramid

What do the expenses of pyramids rearing up to the sky and the stars, what do they possess inside that is worthy of a structure so great? Ah! They possess nothing inside except a black ugly corpse, whose flesh has been treated and hardened into stone. Is it for this that a monument is extended over all these acres! For this the toil of so many years, of so many hands! Let your life be morally unblemished; let this be your pyramid: and six feet will be able to suffice for your tomb.

Strada's Nightingale

A nightingale heard a shepherd playing on his reed pipe, and she herself wished to reproduce the fine tones; she herself tried out the rhythms again, and as she tried them out she learnt how to render the shrill song with faithful voice. The shepherd, unaccustomed to admitting of a rival, challenges and provokes the poor little creature to a greater song. You too rise up to the strains, o nightingale, but unequal, alas, unequal to the strength, you fall down lifeless. A cruel contest! A sad victory! The shepherd should have preferred not to have surpassed your song.

The Ballad Singers

Where one column forms the boundary for seven streets there stand two nymphs from the company of the Sirens; upon their head is a straw hat; all around their neck are huge amber necklaces; from both there hangs a garment caked with filth, which, stiffened with mud, flows from the middle of their legs down to their ankles. One carries a tiny daughter hanging from her breast; the other bears in her right hand ballad sheets for sale.

Scarcely have they arranged themselves in order when boys and unmarried girls run up to them: first a cobbler, his hair tucked under a leather cap, rushes out of his lowly hovel, which is located nearby, in order to buy whatever ballads happen to please him; for even he takes delight in many a song by which in solitude he duly lessens his lengthy toils and deceives the tedium of a winter's night. A maidservant hears the murmur of the assembled throng gradually becoming more frequent and rushes out in bare arms. Pyracmon, abandoning the forge, bellows, and his smithy, mingles, his face still black, with the packed crowd. Close by there proceeds with slow step one whose back is weighed down by a huge knapsack; as soon as he beholds the circle of the crowd,

aspectat vulgi, spe carminis arrigit aures;
statque morae patiens, umeris nec pondera sentit.
sic ubi Tartareum regem Rhodopeius Orpheus
Threiciis studuit fidibus mulcere, laboris   25
immemor Aeolides stupuit modulamina plectri,
nec sensit funesti onera incumbentia saxi.
saepe interventus rhedae crepitantis ab illo
vicorum aut illo stipantem hinc inde catervam
dividit; at rursus coeunt, ubi transiit illa,   30
ut coeunt rursus puppis quas dividit undae.
    Canticulae interea narraverat argumentum
altera Sirenum: infidi periuria nautae,
deceptamque dolo nympham; tum flebile carmen
flebilibus movit numeris, quos altera versu   35
alterno excepit. patulis stant rictibus omnes:
dextram ille, acclinat, laevam ille attentius aurem,
promissum carmen captare paratus hiatu.
longa referre mora est, animum qua vicerit arte
virgineum iuvenis. iam poscunt undique chartas   40
protensae emptorum dextrae, quas illa vel illa
distribuit cantatque simul: neque ferreus iste
est usquam auditor, dulcis cui lene camoena
non adhibet tormentum, et furtivum elicit assem.
stat medios inter baculoque innititur Irus,   45
nec tamen hic loculo parcit, sed prodigus aeris
emptor adest, solvit pretium, carmenque requirit.
fors iuxta adstabat vetula iracundior aequo,
quae loculo ex imo invitum longumque latentem
depromens vix tandem obolum: "cedo, femina, chartam,"   50
inquit, "ut aeternum monumentum in pariete figam,
cum laribus mansurum ipsis: quam credula nymphis
pectora sint, fraudis quam plena, et perfida nautis."

Cornicula

Nigras inter aves avis est quae plurima turres
    antiquas aedes celsaque fana colit.
nil tam sublime est quod non audace volatu,
    aeriis spernens inferiora, petit.
quo nemo ascendat cui non vertigo cerebrum   5
    corripiat, certe hunc seligit illa locum.
quo vix a terra tu suspicis absque tremore,
    illa metus expers incolumisque sedet.
lamina delubri supra fastigia, ventus
    qua coeli spiret de regione docet;   10

he pricks his ears in the hope of a song; and he stands enduring the delay, and does not feel the weight upon his shoulders. Thus when Orpheus of Rhodope was eager to soothe with his Thracian lyre the king of Tartarus, the son of Aeolus, forgetful of his toil, was astounded at the modulations of his plectrum, and did not feel the pressing weight of the deadly boulder. Often the disruption of a rattling carriage divides the crowd, milling together on this or on that side of the street; but they reassemble when it has crossed over, just as waves divided by a ship reassemble.

Meanwhile one of the Sirens has narrated the plot of the Ballad: the broken oaths of a faithless sailor and a nymph deceived by trickery: next she sings the lamentable song with mournful rhythms, which the other takes up in alternating verse: all stand open-jawed: this one inclines his right, that one his left ear more attentively, ready with open mouth to hear the promised song. It would take a long time to relate with what craft the young man conquers the virgin's heart. Now from all sides the stretched-out hands of purchasers demand the ballad sheets, which one or the other distributes, while singing at the same time: and no member of the audience is so hard-hearted that the sweet muse does not afflict him with gentle torment, eliciting a furtive halfpenny. In their midst stands Irus, resting upon his stick, and this purchaser does not spare his purse, but is at hand generous with his money, pays the price and asks for the song. By chance there was standing close by an old woman more angry than is fitting; and at last taking out from the bottom of her purse a coin that was reluctant and concealed for long, she said: "Girl, give me the ballad so that I may pin it up on the wall as an eternal memorial that will last with the house itself as to how credulous are the hearts of nymphs, how full of fraud and perfidious are those of sailors!"

The Jackdaw

Among blackbirds there is a bird which frequents towers, ancient churches and lofty temples. No spot is so high that it does not make for it in daring flight, disregarding lower regions by comparison with those of the air. Where no one may climb without dizziness laying hold of his brain, this indeed does he choose for his place. Where you can hardly look up from earth without fear, he sits with no share of fear, and unharmed. On top of the church's heights a plate teaches from which region of the heavens the wind is blowing;

hanc ea prae reliquis mavult, secura pericli,
    nec curat nedum cogitat unde cadat.
res inde humanas sed summa per otia spectat,
    et nihil ad sese quas videt esse videt.
concursus spectat plateaque negotia in omni,   15
    omnia pro nugis at sapienter habet.
clamores quos infra audit, si forsitan audit,
    pro rebus nihili negligit et crocitat.
ille tibi invideat, felix cornicula, pennas,
    qui sic humanis rebus abesse velit.   20

Pons Westmonasteriensis

Tamisi, regales qui praeterlaberis arces,
    quam se magnificum, suspice, tollit opus!
quanto cum saxis coalescunt pondere saxa!
    quo nexu incumbens sustinet arcus onus!
ardua quam iusto pendet libramine moles!   5
    qua partes haerent partibus harmonia!
quos, cerne, ad numeros, ab utrovis litore sensim
    sunt supra acclives alterutrinque viae!
pontis aperturae quam distant legibus aequis,
    exterior quaevis interiore minor!   10
hunc artis splendorem inter nihil impedit undas
    quove minus placidus vel taciturnus eas.
nil tibi descensum accelerat; non vorticis ullus
    impetus in praeceps unde ferantur aquae.
fluxu idem, refluxu idem, lenissimus amnis   15
    incolumem subtus sternis, ut ante, viam:
seris indicium saec'lis quo principe tanta
    haec tibi surrexit gloria liber eris.

Cicindela

Sub saepe exiguum est nec raro in margine ripae
    reptile quod lucet nocte dieque latet;
vermis habet speciem, sed habet de lumine nomen;
    at prisca a fama non liquet unde micet.
plerique a cauda credunt procedere lumen,   5
    nec desunt credunt qui rutilare caput.
nam superas stellas, quae nox accendit, et illi
    parcam eadem lucem dat moduloque parem.
forsitan hoc prudens voluit natura caveri
    ne pede quis duro reptile contereret: 10
exiguam, in tenebris ne gressum offenderet ullus,
    praetendi voluit forsitan illa facem.
sive usum hunc natura parens seu maluit illum,

this he prefers above the rest, free of danger, and has no concern, let alone thought, as to whence he might fall. From there but in supreme leisure he watches human affairs, and sees that the things that he sees are of no concern to him. He watches gatherings of people, business negotiations in every street, but wisely he regards them all as trifles. If by chance he listens to the shouting which he hears below, he disregards it as worth nothing, and he caws. O happy jackdaw, may the man envy you who would thus wish to be absent from human affairs.

Westminster Bridge

O Thames, who flow past regal citadels, look how magnificent a structure rears itself up. With what weight do rocks join with rocks! With what a formation does the inclining arch sustain its weight! With what an appropriate balance does the steep structure hang. With what harmony do parts adhere to parts! To what numbers from either shore, behold, do the sloping paths respond on either side! How equidistant are the bridge's openings! How smaller the outer one in comparison to the inner! Amid this wonder of art nothing impedes your waters from proceeding calmly or silently. Nothing speeds up your descent; there is no inrush from a whirlpool whence waters are borne headlong. With the same ebbing and flowing you extend as before your safe course, a very gentle stream. You will be free, an indication to late generations of the prince under whom this great glory was erected for you.

The Glowworm

Beneath a hedge and sometimes on the edge of a river bank there is a tiny reptile which glows by night and lies hidden by day. It has the appearance of a worm, but it derives its name from light; yet it is not clear from report of old whence it shines. Several believe that the light issues from its tail; nor are there lacking those who believe that it is its head that glows. For night which enkindles the stars above, gives to it also a scanty amount of light, matching its own measure. Perhaps nature in her prudence wanted to take this precaution lest anyone might trample with harsh foot upon the reptile: perhaps she wanted a tiny torch to be presented lest anyone stumble in the dark. Whether mother nature preferred the

haud frustra accensa est lux radiique dati.
ponite vos fastus, humiles nec spernite, magni;   15
    quando habet et minimum reptile quod niteat.

Bombyx

Fine sub Aprilis bombyx excluditur ovo,
    reptilis exiguo corpore vermiculus.
frondibus hinc mori, volvox dum fiat adultus,
    gnaviter incumbens dum satietur edit.
crescendo ad iustum cum iam maturuit aevum,   5
    incipit artifici stamine textor opus:
filaque condensans filis, orbem implicat orbi,
    et sensim in gyris conditus ipse latet.
inque cadi teretem formam se colligit, unde
    egrediens pennas papilionis habet.   10
fitque parens tandem foetumque reponit in ovis;
    hoc demum extremo munere functus, obit.
quotquot in hac nostra spirant animalia terra
    nulli est vel brevior vita vel utilior.

Apes

Gens frugi et prudens, operosa et provida, vitam
    quam placide peragunt quam sapienter apes!
urbis habent inter sese consortia; cuique
    stat sua pars operum, munia cuique sua.
nota domus sua cuique et parvae limina cellae,   5
    et sua de medio portio cuique cibi est.
hic esto populus, res esto haec publica, discat
    unde suos cives instituisse Plato.

Suicida

Musca meam volitat circum importuna lucernam,
    alasque amburit iam prope iamque suas.
saepe repello manu venientem, et "ineptula musca,
    quae te," inquam, "impellit tanta libido mori?"
illa tamen redit, et quanquam servare laboro,   5
    instat et in flammas exitiumque ruit.
"exiguam tibi nolo animam, quam proiicis, ultra
    servare; et si sis certa perire, peri!"

latter or the former purpose, it is not in vain that the light has been enkindled and rays provided. Lay aside your scorn, o mighty men, and do not spurn the lowly since even the tiniest reptile possesses that which glows.

The Silkworm

Toward the end of April the silkworm is hatched from an egg, a crawling little larva of tiny size. Industriously applying itself to the leaves of a mulberry tree until it becomes a mature creature, it eats until it is satiated. When it has now matured by growing to its appointed age, the weaver begins its work with artful loom: compressing threads upon threads, it entwines circle upon circle and gradually it buries itself in concealment in the rings. And it collects itself into the smooth shape of a cask, emerging from which it possesses the wings of a moth. At last it becomes a parent and places again its offspring in eggs. Having at last performed this final service, it dies. Of all the creatures that breathe in this earth of ours there is none that possesses a life that is briefer or more practical.

Bees

How, calmly, how wisely do bees, a prodigal and prudent brood, hard-working and provident, conduct their lives! They have cities divided amongst themselves; to each is established its own share of work; to each its own duties. Each knows its own homestead and the threshold of a small cell, and each has its own allocation of food from the common share. Let this be the people, let this be the republic from which Plato may learn to instruct his own citizens.

Suicide

A misguided fly flits around my lamp, and now, and again, it almost burns its wings. Frequently as it comes, I drive it away with my hand, and I say "Silly little fly, what is this great desire for death that compels you?" Nonetheless, it comes back, and even though I endeavour to save it, it persists, and rushes into the flames and into destruction. "No longer do I wish to save your tiny life which you are throwing away; and if you have resolved to die—die!"

Artis Est Celare Artem

Pulchra nec invitos vocat ad spectacula cives
    Fauxius, egregiae dexteritatis homo,
fallere spectantes quo non sollertior alter
    vel linguae insidiis vel levitate manus.
en! vobis (aperitque manum deceptor utramque)   5
    orbiculum! hei praesto!—fugit, abivit—adest.
est hic, est illic—nusquam est, et ubique—videte,
    in mensa—in loculis huius—in ore tuo.
tunc peram invertit, fraudemque exorsus ab ovo
    gallinam profert aligerumque gregem.   10
chartula (proh monstrum!) summi ad laquearia tecti
    subvolat et formam iussa capessit avis.
spectator laetus videt haec miracula rerum
    et stupet occulti captus amore doli.
multum habet ingenii, multum delusor et artis;   15
    qui, simul ac aperit se, nihil artis habet.

Levius Fit Patientia
Quicquid Corrigere Est Nefas

Clauditur in cavea laqueo quam prenderit auceps,
    et silet et fatum lugubre plorat avis.
nec placet angustus carcer, quam limite nullo
    aerias nuper iuverat ire vias.
nascitur et longo patientia crescit ab usu,   5
    nec iam quae dederat taedia carcer habet.
iam se solatur cantu captiva, nec ulla
    suavius in campis libera cantat avis.

Si Propius Stes,
Te Capiet Minus

Londini ad pontem prono cum labimur amne,
    quam tua dat turris dulce, Maria, melos!
ut servat iustum quaevis campana tenorem!
    pulsata ut variis contremit aura sonis!
nec mora nec requies: ripas concentibus implet,   5
    alternans hilares ingeminansque vices.
quo magis abscedis, tentat numerosior aurem
    musica; laetantur corda, salitque iecur.
talis ab harmonia surgit distante voluptas;
    sin turrim introeas, omnia clangor erit.   10

It Is a Mark of Art to Conceal Art

Fawkes, a man of outstanding dexterity, summons the citizens (nor are they unwilling) to his excellent shows; than whom no other is more clever in deceiving his spectators either through verbal trickery or through his sleight of hand. Behold (the illusionist opens up both his hands) a little ball! Hey presto! It has fled, it has departed, it is present. It is here, it is there—it is nowhere, and everywhere—behold, it is on the table, in his pocket, on your face. Then he turns a bag upside down; and as the beginnings of his deception he produces from an egg a chicken and a flock of winged creatures. A little piece of paper (oh, an omen!) flies upwards to the roof-tops, and when ordered, assumes the shape of a bird. The spectator watches these marvels with pleasure, and is stunned, captivated by his passion for the hidden trick. The illusionist has a great deal of ingenuity and a great deal of skill; but as soon as he reveals himself, he has no skill.

Whatever It Is Wrong to Correct
Becomes Lighter Through Patience

Enclosed in a cage a bird, which a fowler has caught in a noose, is both silent and laments its grievous fate. And the narrow prison fails to please one who had recently delighted in unlimited flight through the airy ways. Patience is born and increases from long accustomation, and no longer has the prison the tedium which it had. Now the prisoner consoles itself with song, and no free bird sings more sweetly in the fields.

The Closer You Stand,
The Less Will You Be Captivated

When we glide downstream to London bridge, what sweet music does your tower, Mary, produce! How each bell preserves its proper tone! How the breeze trembles, struck by the different sounds! There is neither delay nor respite: it fills the riverbanks with harmonies, alternating and redoubling in cheerful succession. The more you withdraw, the more rhythmically does the music play upon the ear; hearts are gladdened and the seat of feelings leaps for joy. Such is the pleasure that arises from distant harmony; if you enter the tower, all will be a din.

Innocens Praedatrix

Sedula per campos nullo defessa labore
   in cella ut stipet mella vagatur apis;
purpureum vix florem opifex praetervolat unum,
   innumeras inter quas alit hortus opes;
herbula gramineis vix una innascitur agris   5
   thesauri unde aliquid non studiosa legit.
a flore ad florem transit, mollique volando
   delibat tactu suave quod intus habent.
omnia delibat, parce sed et omnia, furti
   ut ne vel minimum videris indicium.   10
omnia degustat tam parce ut gratia nulla
   floribus, ut nullus diminuatur odor.
non ita praedantur modice bruchique et erucae;
   non, ista hortorum maxima pestis, aves;
non ita raptores corvi, quorum improba rostra   15
   despoliant agros effodiuntque sata.
succos immiscens succis, ita suaviter omnes
   temperat ut dederit chymia nulla pares.
vix furtum est illud dicive iniuria debet
   quod cera et multo melle rependit apis.   20

Ignavum Fucos Pecus A Praesepibus Arcent

Per Batavum plateas (ita, gens operosa, cavetis)
   mendicus nemo, nemo vagatur iners.
non caecus, non claudus iners; modo sint tibi, claude,
   qui prosint oculi; sint tibi, caece, manus.
non operum immunis puer est, non grandior aevo,   5
   sed sua stant puero, stant sua pensa seni.
o prudens hominum respublica! natio vestra
   in terris usquam si siet, Utopia est.

An Innocent Plunderer

The busy bee wanders through fields, indefatigable by any toil, in order to cram honey in a cell: scarcely does the worker fly past a single purple flower among the countless resources which the garden nurtures; scarcely is a single little plant born in the grassy fields whence in her keenness she does not extract some source of treasure. She passes from flower to flower and as she flies she tastes with gentle touch whatever sweetness they possess inside. She tastes everything, but everything in moderation, so that you cannot see even the least indication of theft. She tastes everything so sparingly that no grace, no fragrance, is detracted from the flowers. Locusts and caterpillars do not plunder so moderately; nor birds, that greatest pestilence of gardens: not thus rapacious crows, whose wanton beaks despoil fields, and dig up seeds. Mixing juices with juices, so sweetly does it temper them all that no chemist has produced its like. Hardly ought that to be called a theft or an injustice for which the bee compensates by wax and much honey.

From the Homestead They Ward Off Drones, a Lazy Brood

Through the streets of Holland (thus do you beware, o hard-working people) no one wanders as a beggar, no one as idle. The blind man, the lame man is not idle, provided that you, o lame man, have eyes, and you, o blind man, hands, that may be of use to you. No boy, no one more advanced in age, is without a share of work. But every boy, every old man have their own allotted span of work. O prudent republic of men! Your nation, if ever it exists upon earth, is Utopia.

APPENDIX 2

BOURNE AND COWPER

William Cowper

The Glow-Worm

Beneath the hedge or near the stream
  A worm is known to stray,
That shows by night a lucid beam,
  Which disappears by day.

Disputes have been, and still prevail,   5
  From whence his rays proceed;
Some give that honour to his tail,
  And others to his head.

But this is sure—the hand of night
  That kindles up the skies,   10
Gives him a modicum of light
  Proportion'd to his size.

Perhaps indulgent Nature meant
  By such a lamp bestow'd
To bid the traveller as he went   15
  Be careful where he trod:

Nor crush a worm, whose useful light
  Might serve, however small,
To show a stumbling stone by night,
  And save him from a fall.   20

Whate'er she meant, this truth divine
  Is legible and plain,
'Tis power almighty bids him shine,
  Nor bids him shine in vain.

Ye proud and wealthy, let this theme   25
  Teach humbler thoughts to you,
Since such a reptile has its gem,
  And boasts its splendour too.

The Jackdaw

There is a bird who, by his coat
And by the hoarseness of his note,
  Might be supposed a crow;
A great frequenter of the church,
Where bishop-like he finds a perch,   5
  And dormitory too.

Above the steeple shines a plate,
That turns and turns to indicate
  From what point blows the weather.
Look up—your brains begin to swim,   10
'Tis in the clouds—that pleases him,
  He chooses it the rather.

Fond of the speculative height,
Thither he wings his airy flight,
  And thence securely sees   15
The bustle and the raree-show,
That occupy mankind below,
  Secure and at his ease.

You think, no doubt, he sits and muses
On future broken bones and bruises,   20
  If he should chance to fall.
No; not a single thought like that
Employs his philosophic pate,
  Or troubles it at all.

He sees that this great roundabout—   25
The world, with all its motley rout,
  Church, army, physic, law,
Its customs and its bus'nesses,—
Is no concern at all of his,
  And says—what says he?— Caw.   30

Thrice happy bird! I too have seen
Much of the vanities of men;
  And, sick of having seen 'em,
Would cheerfully these limbs resign
For such a pair of wings as thine,   35
  And such a head between 'em.

The Cricket

Little inmate, full of mirth,
Chirping on my kitchen hearth,
Wheresoe'er be thine abode,
Always harbinger of good,
Pay me for thy warm retreat   5
With a song more soft and sweet;
In return thou shalt receive
Such a strain as I can give.

Thus thy praise shall be exprest,
Inoffensive, welcome guest!   10
While the rat is on the scout,
And the mouse with curious snout,
With what vermin else infest
Ev'ry dish, and spoil the best;
Frisking thus before the fire,   15
Thou hast all thine heart's desire.

Though in voice and shape they be
Form'd as if akin to thee,
Thou surpassest, happier far,
Happiest grasshoppers that are;   20
Theirs is but a summer's song,
Thine endures the winter long,
Unimpair'd, and shrill, and clear,
Melody throughout the year.

Neither night nor dawn of day   25
Puts a period to thy play:
Sing then—and extend thy span
Far beyond the date of man.
Wretched man, whose years are spent
In repining discontent,   30
Lives not, aged though he be,
Half a span, compared with thee.

The Parrot

In painted plumes superbly drest,
A native of the gorgeous east,
　By many a billow tost;
Poll gains at length the British shore,
Part of the captain's precious store—　　　　　5
　A present to his toast.

Belinda's maids are soon preferr'd
To teach him now and then a word,
　As poll can master it;
But 'tis her own important charge,　　　　　10
To qualify him more at large,
　And make him quite a wit.

Sweet Poll! his doating mistress cries,
Sweet Poll! the mimic bird replies,
　And calls aloud for sack.　　　　　15
She next instructs him in the kiss;
'Tis now a little one, like Miss,
　And now a hearty smack.

At first he aims at what he hears;
And, list'ning close with both his ears,　　　　　20
　Just catches at the sound;
But soon articulates aloud,
Much to the amusement of the crowd,
　And stuns the neighbours round.

A querulous old woman's voice　　　　　25
His hum'rous talent next employs—
He scolds, and gives the lie.
And now he sings, and now is sick—
Here, Sally, Susan, come, come quick,
　Poor Poll is like to die!　　　　　30

Belinda and her bird! 'tis rare
To meet with such a well match'd pair,
　The language and the tone,
Each character in ev'ry part
Sustain'd with so much grace and art,　　　　　35
　And both in unison.

When children first begin to spell,
And stammer out a syllable,

We think them tedious creatures;
But difficulties soon abate,   40
When birds are to be taught to prate,
And women are the teachers.

On the Picture of a Sleeping Child

Sweet babe, whose image here express'd
    Does thy peaceful slumbers show;
Guilt or fear, to break thy rest,
    Never did thy spirit know.

Soothing slumbers, soft repose,   5
    Such as mock the painter's skill,
Such as innocence bestows,
    Harmless infant, lull thee still!

Reciprocal Kindness The Primary Law of Nature

Androcles from his injur'd lord, in dread
Of instant death, to Lybia's desert fled.
Tir'd with his toilsome flight, and parch'd with heat,
He spied at length a cavern's cool retreat;
But scarce had giv'n to rest his weary frame,   5
When, hugest of his kind, a lion came:
He roar'd approaching; but the savage din
To plaintive murmurs chang'd,—arrived within,
And with expressive looks, his lifted paw
Presenting, aid implored from whom he saw.   10
The fugitive, through terror at a stand,
Dar'd not awhile afford his trembling hand,
But bolder grown at length, inherent found
A pointed thorn, and drew it from the wound.
The cure was wrought; he wiped the sanious blood,   15
And firm and free from pain the lion stood.
Again he seeks the wilds, and day by day
Regales his inmate with the parted prey:
Nor he disdains the dole, though unprepar'd,
Spread on the ground, and with a lion shar'd.   20
But thus to live—still lost, sequester'd still—
Scarce seem'd his lord's revenge a heavier ill.
Home! native home! O might he but repair!
He must, he will, though death attends him there.
He goes, and doom'd to perish, on the sands   25

Of the full theatre unpitied stands!
When lo! the selfsame lion from his cage
Flies to devour him, famish'd into rage.
He flies, but viewing in his purpos'd prey
The man, his healer, pauses on his way,   30
And, soften'd by remembrance into sweet
And kind composure, crouches at his feet.
  Mute with astonishment, th' assembly gaze;
But why, ye Romans? Whence your mute amaze?
All this is nat'ral: nature bade him rend   35
An enemy; she bids him spare a friend.

Strada's Nightingale

The shepherd touch'd his reed; sweet Philomel
  Essay'd, and oft essay'd to catch the strain,
And treasuring, as on her ear they fell,
  The numbers, echo'd note for note again.

The peevish youth, who ne'er had found before   5
  A rival of his skill, indignant heard,
And soon (for various was his tuneful store)
  In loftier tones defied the simple bird.

She dar'd the task, and rising, as he rose,
  With all the force that passion gives inspir'd,   10
Return'd the sounds awhile, but in the close
  Exhausted fell, and at his feet expir'd.

Thus strength, not skill prevail'd. O fatal strife,
  By thee, poor songstress, playfully begun;
And, O sad victory, which cost thy life,   15
  And he may wish that he had never won!

Ode on the Death of a Lady
Who Lived One Hundred Years, and Died
On Her Birthday, 1728

Ancient dame, how wide and vast
  To a race like ours appears,
Rounded to an orb at last,
  All thy multitude of years!

We, the herd of human kind,   5
   Frailer and of feebler pow'rs;
We, to narrow bounds confin'd,
   Soon exhaust the sum of ours.

Death's delicious banquet—we
   Perish even from the womb,   10
Swifter than a shadow flee,
   Nourish'd, but to feed the tomb.

Seeds of merciless disease
   Lurk in all that we enjoy;
Some that waste us by degrees,   15
   Some that suddenly destroy.

And, if life o'erleap the bourn
   Common to the sons of men,
What remains, but that we mourn,
   Dream, and doat, and drivel then?   20

Fast as moons can wax and wane
   Sorrow comes; and while we groan,
Pant with anguish and complain,
   Half our years are fled and gone.

If a few (to few 'tis given),   25
   Lingering on this earthly stage,
Creep and halt with steps unev'n
   To the period of an age;

Wherefore live they, but to see
   Cunning, arrogance, and force;   30
Sights lamented much by thee,
   Holding their accustom'd course?

Oft was seen, in ages past,
   All that we with wonder view;
Often shall be to the last;   35
   Earth produces nothing new.

Thee we gratulate, content,
   Should propitious Heav'n design
Life for us as calmly spent,
   Though but half the length of thine.   40

The Silk Worm

Theeams of April, ere it goes,
A worm, scarce visible, disclose;
All winter long content to dwell
The tenant of his native shell.
The same prolific season gives   5
The sustenance by which he lives,
The mulb'ry leaf, a simple store,
That serves him—till he needs no more!
For, his dimensions once complete,
Thenceforth none ever sees him eat;   10
Tho', till his growing time be past,
Scarce ever is he seen to fast.
That hour arriv'd, his work begins.
He spins and weaves, and weaves and spins;
Till circle upon circle, wound   15
Careless around him and around,
Conceals him with a veil, tho' slight,
Impervious to the keenest sight.
Thus self-inclos'd, as in a cask,
At length he finishes his task;   20
And, tho' a worm when he was lost,
Or caterpillar at the most,
When next we see him, wings he wears,
And in papilio-pomp appears;
Becomes oviparous; supplies,   25
With future worms and future flies,
The next ensuing year;—and dies!
Well were it for the world, if all
Who creep about this earthly ball,
Though shorter-liv'd than most he be,   30
Were useful in their kind as he.

The Innocent Thief

Not a flower can be found in the fields,
    Or the spot that we till for our pleasure,
From the largest to least, but it yields
    The bee, never-wearied, a treasure.

Scarce any she quits unexplor'd   5
    With a diligence truly exact;

Yet, steal what she may for her hoard,
  Leaves evidence none of the fact.

Her lucrative task she pursues,
  And pilfers with so much address,   10
That none of their odour they lose,
  Nor charm by their beauty the less.

Not thus inoffensively preys
  The canker-worm, in-dwelling foe!
His voracity not thus allays   15
  The sparrow, the finch, or the crow.

The worm, more expensively fed,
  The pride of the garden devours;
And birds peck the seed from the bed,
  Still less to be spar'd than the flow'rs.   20

But she with such delicate skill
  Her pillage so fits for her use,
That the chymist in vain with his still
  Would labour the like to produce.

Then grudge not her temperate meals,   25
  Nor a benefit blame as a theft;
Since, stole she not all that she steals,
  Neither honey nor wax would be left.

The Tears of a Painter

Apelles, hearing that his boy
Had just expir'd—his only joy!
Altho' the sight with anguish tore him,
Bade place his dear remains before him.
He seiz'd his brush, his colours spread;   5
And—"Oh! my child, accept,"—he said,
"('Tis all that I can now bestow,)
This tribute of a father's woe!"
Then, faithful to the two-fold part,
Both of his feelings and his art,   10
He clos'd his eyes with tender care,
And form'd at once a fellow pair.
His brow with amber locks beset,
And lips he drew not livid yet;
And shaded all that he had done   15

To a just image of his son.
  Thus far is well. But view again
The cause of thy paternal pain!
Thy melancholy task fulfil!
It needs the last, last touches still.   20
Again his pencil's pow'r he tries,
For on his lips a smile he spies:
And still his cheek unfaded shows
The deepest damask of the rose.
Then, heedful to the finish'd whole,   25
With fondest eagerness he stole,
Till scarce himself distinctly knew
The cherub copied from the true.
  Now, painter, cease! Thy task is done.
Long lives this image of thy son;   30
Nor short-lived shall the glory prove,
Or of thy labour or thy love.

APPENDIX 3

BOURNE AND LAMB

Charles Lamb

On a Sepulchral Statue of An Infant Sleeping

Beautiful Infant, who dost keep
Thy posture here, and sleep'st a marble sleep,
May the repose unbroken be,
Which the fine Artist's hand hath lent to thee,
While thou enjoy'st along with it   5
That which no art, or craft, could ever hit,
Or counterfeit to mortal sense,
The heaven-infused sleep of Innocence!

The Rival Bells

A tuneful challenge rings from either side
Of Thames' fair banks. Thy twice six Bells, Saint Bride,
Peal swift and shrill; to which more slow reply
The deep-toned eight of Mary Overy.
Such harmony from the contention flows,   5
That the divided ear no preference knows;
Betwixt them both disparting Music's State,
While one exceeds in number, one in weight.

Epitaph On A Dog
(1820)

Poor Irus' faithful wolf-dog here I lie,
That wont to tend my old blind master's steps,
His guide and guard; nor, while my service lasted,
Had he occasion for that staff, with which
He now goes picking out his path in fear   5
Over the highways and crossings, but would plant
Safe in the conduct of my friendly string,
A firm foot forward still, till he had reach'd
His poor seat on some stone, nigh where the tide
Of passers-by in thickest confluence flow'd: 10
To whom with loud and passionate laments

From morn to eve his dark estate he wail'd.
Nor wail'd to all in vain: some here and there,
The well disposed and good, their pennies gave.
I meantime at his feet obsequious slept; 15
Not all-asleep in sleep, but heart and ear
Prick'd up at his least motion, to receive
At his kind hand my customary crumbs,
And common portion in his feast of scraps;
Or when night warn'd us homeward, tired and spent 20
With our long day, and tedious beggary.
These were my manners, this my way of life,
Till age and slow disease me overtook,
And sever'd from my sightless master's side.
But lest the grace of so good deeds should die, 25
Through tract of years in mute oblivion lost,
This slender tomb of turf hath Irus rear'd,
Cheap monument of no ungrudging hand,
And with short verse inscribed it, to attest,
In long and lasting union to attest, 30
The virtues of the Beggar and his Dog.

The Ballad Singers

Where seven fair Streets to one tall Column draw,
Two Nymphs have ta'en their stand, in hats of straw;
Their yellower necks huge beads of amber grace,
And by their trade they're of the Sirens' race:
With cloak loose-pinn'd on each, that has been red, 5
But long with dust and dirt discoloured
Belies its hue; in mud behind, before,
From heel to middle leg becrusted o'er.
One a small infant at the breast does bear;
And one in her right hand her tuneful ware, 10
Which she would vend. Their station scarce is taken,
When youths and maids flock round. His stall forsaken,
Forth comes a Son of Crispin, leathern-capt,
Prepared to buy a ballad, if one apt
To move his fancy offers. Crispin's sons 15
Have, from uncounted time, with ale and buns
Cherish'd the gift of Song, which sorrow quells;
And, working single in their low-rooft cells,
Oft cheat the tedium of a winter's night
With anthems warbled in the Muses' spight. 20

Who now hath caught the alarm? the Servant Maid
Hath heard a buzz at distance; and, afraid
To miss a note, with elbows red comes out.
Leaving his forge to cool, Pyracmon stout
Thrusts in his unwash'd visage. He stands by,   25
Who the hard trade of Porterage does ply
With stooping shoulders. What cares he? he sees
The assembled ring, nor heeds his tottering knees,
But pricks his ears up with the hopes of song.
So, while the Bard of Rhodope his wrong   30
Bewail'd to Proserpine on Thracian strings,
The tasks of gloomy Orcus lost their stings,
And stone-vext Sisyphus forgets his load.
Hither and thither from the sevenfold road
Some cart or waggon crosses, which divides   35
The close-wedged audience; but, as when the tides
To ploughing ships give way, the ship being past,
They re-unite, so these unite as fast.
The older Songstress hitherto hath spent
Her elocution in the argument   40
Of their great Song in prose; to wit, the woes
Which Maiden true to faithless Sailor owes—
Ah! "Wandering He!"—which now in loftier verse
Pathetic they alternately rehearse.
All gaping wait the event. This Critic opes   45
His right ear to the strain. The other hopes
To catch it better with his left. Long trade
It were to tell, how the deluded Maid
A victim fell. And now right greedily
All hands are stretching forth the songs to buy,   50
That are so tragical; which She, and She,
Deals out, and sings the while; nor can there be
A breast so obdurate here, that will hold back
His contribution from the gentle rack
Of Music's pleasing torture. Irus' self,   55
The staff-propt Beggar, his thin-gotten pelf
Brings out from pouch, where squalid farthings rest.
And boldly claims his ballad with the best.
An old Dame only lingers. To her purse
The penny sticks. At length, with harmless curse,   60
"Give me," she cries. "I'll paste it on my wall,
While the wall lasts, to show what ills befal
Fond hearts seduced from Innocency's way;
How Maidens fall, and Mariners betray."

To David Cook,
Of the Parish of Saint Margaret's, Westminster, Watchman

For much good-natured verse received from thee,
A loving verse take in return from me.
"Good morrow to my masters," is your cry;
And to our David "twice as good," say I.
Not Peter's monitor, shrill chanticleer,   5
Crows the approach of dawn in notes more clear,
Or tells the hours more faithfully. While night
Fills half the world with shadows of affright,
You with your lantern, partner of your round,
Traverse the paths of Margaret's hallow'd bound.   10
The tales of ghosts which old wives' ears drink up,
The drunkard reeling home from tavern cup,
Nor prowling robber, your firm soul appal;
Arm'd with thy faithful staff thou slight'st them all.
But if the market gard'ner chance to pass,   15
Bringing to town his fruit, or early grass,
The gentle salesman you with candour greet,
And with reit'rated "good mornings" meet.
Announcing your approach by formal bell,
Of nightly weather you the changes tell;   20
Whether the Moon shines, or her head doth steep
In rain-portending clouds. When mortals sleep
In downy rest, you brave the snows and sleet
Of winter; and in alley, or in street,
Relieve your midnight progress with a verse.   25
What though fastidious Phoebus frown averse
On your didactic strain—indulgent Night
With caution hath seal'd up both ears of Spite,
And critics sleep while you in staves do sound
The praise of long-dead Saints, whose Days abound   30
In wintry months; but Crispen chief proclaim:
Who stirs not at that Prince of Coblers' name?
Profuse in loyalty some couplets shine,
And wish long days to all the Brunswick line!
To youths and virgins they chaste lessons read;   35
Teach wives and husbands how their lives to lead;
Maids to be cleanly, footmen free from vice;
How death at last all ranks doth equalise;
And, in conclusion, pray good years befal,
With store of wealth, your "worthy masters all."   40
For this and other tokens of good will,

On boxing day may store of shillings fill
Your Christmas purse; no householder give less,
When at each door your blameless suit you press:
And what you wish to us (it is but reason)   45
Receive in turn—the compliments o'th'season!

The Female Orators

Nigh London's famous Bridge, a Gate more famed
Stands, or once stood, from old Belinus named,
So judged Antiquity; and therein wrongs
A name, allusive strictly to two Tongues.
Her School hard by the Goddess Rhetoric opes,   5
And gratis deals to Oyster-wives her Tropes.
With Nereid green, green Nereid disputes,
Replies, rejoins, confutes, and still confutes.
One her coarse sense by metaphors expounds,
And one in literalities abounds;   10
In mood and figure these keep up the din:
Words multiply, and every word tells in.
Her hundred throats here bawling Slander strains;
And unclothed Venus to her tongue gives reins
In terms, which Demosthenic force outgo,   15
And baldest jests of foul-mouth'd Cicero.
Right in the midst great Ate keeps her stand,
And from her sovereign station taints the land.
Hence Pulpits rail; grave Senates learn to jar;
Quacks scold; and Billinsgate infects the Bar.   20

APPENDIX 4

BOURNE AND ADDISON

Bourne and Addison

In view of the paucity of biographical information on Bourne, his literary and perhaps his personal links with Joseph Addison are not easy to determine. That Bourne was aware of Addison's Latin poetry is a virtual certainty, even if his own terse epigrammatic style differs greatly from the essentially epic and mock-epic nature of Addison's Latin poems, which are largely Virgilian in nature.[1] Most of these were composed between 1689 and 1694 with several seeing their first appearance in print in the pirated *Examen Poeticum Duplex* (London, 1698).[2] It was in response to this that Addison issued just six months later the *Musae Anglicanae* (1699), an edition that he quite pointedly described as a "genuine one, printed by the permission of its authors."[3] As noted previously, Bourne produced in 1741 his own edition of the *Musae Anglicanae*.[4] In this (the fifth edition of the anthology) he retained Addison's Latin poems[5] while simultaneously expanding the range of the collection to include a wealth of Cambridge as well as Oxford poets.[6]

Some twenty-four years earlier, however, Bourne had apparently addressed a Latin poem to Addison upon the latter's recovery from sickness. The verses survive only in *The Life of Joseph Addison* by Lucy Aikin,[7] who does not cite the source. Having quoted Addison's Letter to Mr Wortley Montagu (28 September 1717) in which he describes himself as "having been confined to my chamber for some time by a dangerous fit of sickness,"[8] Aikin continues:

> The attack which he mentions in his letter to Mr Wortley, was evidently an alarming one, since his recovery from it was thought worthy of serious commemoration in Latin verse by the classic pen of Vincent Bourne, that usher of Westminster school since immortalized in the reminiscences, the praises, and the translations of the poet of the Task.[9]

---

[1] See Haan, *Vergilius Redivivus: Studies in Joseph Addison's Latin Poetry*, passim.

[2] See Haan, *Vergilius Redivivus: Studies in Joseph Addison's Latin Poetry*, 5–7.

[3] *Musarum Anglicanarum Analecta* (Oxford, 1699), II, a2^r: *Praefatio: sed illud et genuinum et auctorum permissu impressum*. See Haan, *Vergilius Redivivus: Studies in Joseph Addison's Latin Poetry*, 5.

[4] See Introduction, 10.

[5] Thus Bourne reprints Addison's *Pax Gulielmi, Barometri Descriptio, Proelium Inter Pygmaeos et Grues Commissum, Resurrectio Delineata, Sphaeristerium, Ad. D. D. Hannes, Machinae Gesticulantes*, and *Ad D.T. Burnettum*.

[6] See Introduction, 10.

[7] Lucy Aikin, *The Life of Joseph Addison* (London, 1843), II, 213–214.

[8] Aikin, *The Life of Joseph Addison*, II, 202.

[9] Aikin, *The Life of Joseph Addison*, II, 213–214.

O carum Musis quisquis fuit ille Machaon
    qui Musis potuit restituisse decus,
qui tibi languenti vires animamque reduxit
    visuram inferni iam prope regna dei,
qui nobis tristes elegos et lugubre carmen   5
    mutari plectro iam meliore facit!
o longum maneas, si quid pia vota valebunt,
    praesidium Aonii deliciaeque chori.
hanc fata incolumem servent, quando altera vita
    servari Musis tam pretiosa nequit.   10
sint seri luctus, et sint ea funera sera
    quae nemo poterit dicere sera nimis.

      Sic vovet, Honoratissime Domine,
        Tui Nominis amantissimus
          Vincentius Bourne
        Collegii Trinitatis Alumnus
    Datum Cantabrigiae 7 Cal Sept 1717[10]

O, whoever that Machaon was, who was able to restore to the Muses one who was dear to the Muses, one who was their glory; who has brought back to you, who were languishing, strength and life when you were already near to the point of beholding the kingdom of the infernal deity; who causes sad elegies and a song of mourning to be exchanged by us for a better plectrum!

O may you remain for long, if pious prayers have any force, the protection and the favorite of the Aonian chorus. May the fates preserve this life unharmed since no other life can be preserved that is so dear to the Muses. May grief be late, and late may that death be which no one will be able to call too late.

Thus prays, o most Honourable Lord, Vincent Bourne, Alumnus of Trinity College, Cambridge, most affectionate of your name: Cambridge, 7 Sept 1717.[11]

---

[10] Text is that of Aikin, *Life of Joseph Addison*, II, 213–214. I have modernized spelling and punctuation.

[11] Translation is mine.

BIBLIOGRAPHY

1. MANUSCRIPTS

BL Add 19268.
BL Add 32689 f. 296.
BL Add 32713 f. 428.

2. BOURNE: EDITIONS

Carmina Comitalia Cantabrigiensia, ed. Vincent Bourne (London, 1721).
In Obitum Roussaei Collegio Trinitatis Servi a Cubiculis Anno 1721 Editio Altera (London, 1726).
Poematia, Latine Partim Reddita, Partim Scripta: a V. Bourne, Collegii Trinitatis Apud Cantabrigienses Aliquando Socio (London, 1734).
Poematia, Latine Partim Reddita, Partim Scripta: a V. Bourne, Collegii Trinitatis Apud Cantabrigienses Aliquando Socio Tertio Edita Adiectis ad Calcem Quibusdam Novis (London, 1743).
Poematia, Latine Partim Reddita, Partim Scripta: a V. Bourne, Collegii Trinitatis Apud Cantabrigienses Aliquando Socio (London, 1750).
Poematia Latine Partim Reddita Partim Scripta a Vicentio Bourne, ed. John Mitford (London, 1840).

3. OTHER PRIMARY TEXTS AND ANTHOLOGIES

AESOP, *Fables*, trans. Laura Gibbs (Oxford: Oxford University Press, 2002).
ANACREON, in *Greek Lyric, II: Anacreon, Anacreontea, Choral Lyric From Olympus to Alman*, trans. D.A. Campbell (Harvard: Loeb Classical Library, 1988).
APOLLONIUS RHODIUS, *The Argonautica*, trans. R.C. Seaton (Harvard: Loeb Classical Library, 1930).
ASCHAM, Roger, *The Scholemaster*, ed. Edward Arber (London: Constable, 1923).
BALESTIERI, Domenico, *Lagrime in Morte di Un Gatto* (Milan, 1741).
BLAKE, William, *The Complete Works*, ed. Geoffrey Keynes (London and New York: Random House: The Nonesuch Press, 1939).
BRINSLEY, John, *Ludus Literarius or The Grammar School*, ed. E.T. Campagnac (Liverpool and London: Liverpool University Press, 1917).
BULLOKAR, William, *Aesops Fables in True Orthography* (London, 1585).
BUSBY, Richard, *A Short Institution of Grammar* (Cambridge, 1647).
—————, *A Short Institution of Grammar For the Use of the Lower Forms in the King's School at Westminster* (London, 1776).
CANELETTO, Antonio, *Westminster Bridge: London on Lord Mayor's Day* (1747).
Carmina Illustria Poetarum Italorum, ed. G.G. Bottari (Florence, 1719–1726).
CATULLUS, *The Poems*, ed. Kenneth Quinn (London: University Press, 1970; rpt. Bristol: Bristol Classical Press, 1996).
CICERO, *Opera* (Harvard: Loeb Classical Library, 1939).
COWLEY, Abraham, *Anacreon Done into English Out of the Original Greek* (Oxford, 1683).

COWPER, William, *Poetical Works*, ed. H.S. Milford (Oxford: Oxford University Press, 1971).

————, *The Letters and Prose Writings*, ed. James King and Charles Ryskamp (Oxford: Oxford University Press, 1986).

CRASHAW, Richard, *The Poems, English, Latin and Greek*, ed. L.C. Martin (Oxford: Oxford University Press, 1927).

CREYGHTON, Robert, *Iter Occidentale* (*Musae Anglicanae*, I, 133–136).

DEAN, Henry, *The Whole Art of Legerdemain: or Hocus Pocus in Perfection. By which the meanest Capacity may perform the Whole Art without a Teacher. Together with the Use of all the Instruments belonging thereto. To which is now added, Abundance of New and Rare Inventions, the like never before in Print but much desired by many* (London, 1763).

DICKENS, Charles, *The Christmas Books*, ed. Michael Slater (Harmondsworth: The Penguin English Library, 1971).

DILLINGHAM, William, *Campanae Undellenses* (*Musae Anglicanae*, I, 244–248).

————, *Sphaeristerium Suleianum* (*Musae Anglicanae*, I, 109–112).

DIODORUS SICULUS, trans. C.H. Oldfather (Harvard: Loeb Classical Library, 1939).

DRYDEN, John, *The Poems*, ed. Paul Hammond (London and New York: Longman, 1995).

Examen Poeticum Duplex (London, 1698).

FLORIAN, Jean Pierre Claris de, *Fables* (Paris: Paulin, 1846).

FORD, John, *Lover's Melancholy*, ed. R.F. Hill (Manchester: Manchester University Press, 1985).

GAY, John, *Trivia, Or The Art of Walking the Streets of London*, in *John Gay: Poetry and Prose*, ed. V.A. Dearing with C.E. Beckwith (Oxford: Oxford University Press, 1974).

GELLIUS, Aulus, *Noctes Atticae*, ed. P.K. Marshall (Oxford: Oxford University Press, 1968).

GRAY, Thomas, *Poems*, in *The Poems of Thomas Gray, William Collins, Oliver Goldsmith*, ed. Roger Lonsdale (London and New York: Longman, 1992).

HAZLITT, William, *The Spirit of The Age* (Menston: Scolar Press, 1971).

HERRICK, Robert, *Poetical Works*, ed. L.C. Martin (Oxford: Oxford University Press, 1965).

HOGARTH, William, *The Bad Taste of the Town* (1724).

————, *The Enraged Musician* (1741).

HOOD, Thomas, *Complete Poetical Works*, ed. Walter Jerrold (London: Oxford University Press, 1906).

HOOLE, Charles, *A New Discovery of the Olde Arte of Teaching Schoole*, ed. E.T. Campagnac (London: Constable and Liverpool: Liverpool University Press, 1913).

HORACE, *Opera*, ed. Stephanus Borzsák (Leipzig: Teubner, 1984).

Iusta Edovardo King (Cambridge, 1638).

JOHNSON, Samuel, *Lives of the Poets*, ed. Arthur Waugh (London: Trübner, 1896).

KEATS, John, *The Works* (Denmark: The Wordsworth Poetry Library, 1994).

LAMB, Charles, *The Essays of Elia*, in *The Works of Charles and Mary Lamb*, ed. E.V. Lucas (London: Methuen, 1903), II.

————, *The Letters*, ed. Alfred Ainger (London: Macmillan, 1904).

LILY, William, *A Short Introduction to Grammar* (London, 1549).

LUCRETIUS, *De Rerum Natura*, ed. Cyril Bailey; rev. Louis Roberts (Oxford: Oxford University Press, 1977).

LUDLUM, Robert, *The Bourne Identity* (New York: Richard Marek Publishing, 1980).

——————, *The Bourne Supremacy* (New York: Random House, 1986).

Lusus Westmonasterienses (Westminster, 1730).

Lusus Westmonasterienses, sive Epigrammatum et Poematum Minorum Delectus: Quibus Adiicitur Nunc Primum Edita Solitudo Regia (London, 1740).

MACAULAY, Thomas Babington, "Life and Writings of Addison," in *Critical and Historical Essays* (London, 1877).

MARVELL, Andrew, *The Poems*, ed. Nigel Smith (London: Longman, 2003).

MILTON, John, *Complete Shorter Poems*, ed. John Carey (London and New York: Longman, 1971; rev. 1997).

——————, *Paradise Lost*, ed. Alastair Fowler (London and New York: Longman, 1971; rev. 1998).

Musarum Anglicanarum Analecta (Oxford, 1699).

ORWELL, George, *Nineteen Eighty-Four*, ed. Bernard Crick (Oxford: Oxford University Press, 1984).

OVID, *Metamorphoses*, trans. F.J. Miller (Harvard: Loeb Classical Library, 1916).

Pietas Academiae Oxoniensis (Oxford, 1738).

PLINY, the Elder, *Natural History*, trans. H. Rackham (Harvard: Loeb Classical Library, 1938).

POPE, Alexander, *Correspondence*, ed. George Sherburn (Oxford: Oxford University Press, 1956).

——————, *The Poems*, ed. John Butt (London: Methuen, 1940).

——————, *The Dunciad*, ed. James Sutherland in *The Poems of Alexander Pope* (London: Methuen and New Haven: Yale University Press, 1965).

——————, *The Rape of the Lock*, ed. Cynthia Wall (Boston and New York: Bedford Cultural Editions, 1998).

PRIOR, Matthew, *Carmen Saeculare* (London, 1699).

Prolusiones Academicae, Oratoriae, Historicae, Poeticae R.P. Famiani Stradae Romani e Societate Iesu ... Coloniae Agrippinae (Rome, 1617).

PROPERTIUS, *Carmina* (Oxford: Oxford University Press, 1960).

QUINTILIAN, *Institutiones Oratoriae* (Oxford: Oxford University Press, 1970).

Round about our Coal Fire, or Christmas Entertainments (London, 1746).

Selecta Poemata Archibaldi Pitcarnii ... et Aliorum, ed. Robert Freebairn (Edinburgh, 1727).

SERVIUS, *Grammatici Qui Feruntur in Vergilii Carmina Commentarii*, eds. George Thilo and Herman Hagen (Leipzig: Teubner, 1887).

SHAKESPEARE, William, *The Complete Sonnets and Poems*, ed. Colin Burrow (Oxford: Oxford University Press, 2002).

SHELLEY, Percy Bysshe, *The Complete Poetical Works*, ed. Neville Rogers (Oxford: Oxford University Press, 1972).

SMITH, Charlotte, *Conversations Introducing Poetry* (London, 1804).

——————, *The Poems*, ed. Stuart Curran (Oxford: Oxford University Press, 1993).

SMOLLETT, Tobias, *The Adventures of Peregrine Pickle* (Oxford: Oxford University Press, 1925).

STRABO, *The Geography*, trans. H.L. Jones (Harvard: Loeb Classical Library, 1969).

Strada's Musical Duel ... In Latine, Much Enlarg'd in English (London, 1671).

STRODE, William, *The Academy of Pleasure* (London, 1656).

SWIFT, Jonathan, *The Poems*, ed. Harold Williams (Oxford: Oxford University Press, 1958).

TATE, Nahum, ed. *Poems by Several Hands, and On Several Occasions* (London, 1685).

TIBULLUS, *Carmina*, ed. George Luck (Stuttgart: Teubner, 1988).

TWICHELL, Chase, *The Snow Watcher* (Princeton: Ontario Review Press, 1998).

VASARI, Giorgio, *Lives of the Painters, Sculptors and Architects*, trans. G.C. de Vere with an introduction and notes by David Ekserdjian (London: Everymans Library Classics, 1996).

VIDA, Marco Girolamo, *Poemata Quae Extant Omnia* (London, 1732).

VILVAIN, Robert, *Enchiridion Epigrammatum Latino-Anglicum: An Epitome of Essais, Englished Out of Latin Etc.* (London, 1654).

VIRGIL, *Opera*, ed. R.A.B. Mynors (Oxford: Oxford University Press, 1969).

————, *Aeneidos Liber Quintus*, ed. R.D. Williams (Oxford: Oxford University Press, 1960).

————, *Georgics*, ed. R.A.B. Mynors (Oxford: Oxford University Press, 1990).

WORDSWORTH, William, *Lyrical Ballads*, ed. Michael Mason (London and New York: Longman, 1992).

————, *Shorter Poems, 1807–1820*, ed. C.H. Ketcham (Ithaca and London: Cornell University Press, 1989).

4.   WORKS OF REFERENCE

The Gentleman's Magazine (Edinburgh, 1731-1868).

Oxford Dictionary of National Biography, eds. H.C.G. Matthew and Brian Harrison (Oxford: Oxford University Press, 2004).

Oxford English Dictionary, prepared by J.A. Simpson and E.S.C. Weiner (Oxford: Oxford University Press, 1989).

Oxford Latin Dictionary, ed. P.G.W. Glare (Oxford: Oxford University Press, 1982).

The Register of St Margaret's, Westminster, ed. L.E. Tanner (London: Harleian Society 64 [1935] and 88 [1968]).

5.   SECONDARY LITERATURE

AIKIN, Lucy, *The Life of Joseph Addison* (London: Longman, 1843).

BARCHIESI, Alessandro, "The Uniqueness of the *Carmen Saeculare* and its Tradition," in *Traditions and Contexts in the Poetry of Horace*, eds. Tony Woodman and Denis Feeney (Cambridge: Cambridge University Press, 2002), 107–123.

BEATTIE, J.M., *Policing and Punishment in London 1600–1750: Urban Crime and the Limits of Terror* (Oxford: Oxford University Press, 2001).

BERMAN, Jeffrey, *Narcissism and the Novel* (New York: University Press, 1990).

BLOOM, Gina, "Localising Disembodied Voice in Sandys's 'Narcissus and Echo,'" in G.V. Stanivukovic, ed. *Ovid and the Renaissance Body* (New York and London: University of Toronto Press, 2001), 129–154.

BRADNER, Leicester, *Musae Anglicanae: A History of Anglo-Latin Poetry 1500–1925* (New York and London: Oxford University Press, 1940).

————, Review of J.W. Binns, ed. *The Latin Poetry of English Poets* (London, 1974), *Renaissance Quarterly* 29.2 (1976), 293–295.

BROWN, Pamela Allen, "Jonson among the Fishwives," *Ben Jonson Journal* 6 (1999), 89–108.

CAHOON, Leslie, "The Parrot and the Poet: The Function of Ovid's Funeral Elegies," *Classical Journal* 80 (1984–85), 27–35.

CLARK, D.L., *John Milton at St Paul's School* (New York: Columbia University Press, 1948; repr. Hamden, 1964).

COPLEY, F.O., *Exclusus Amator: A Study in Latin Love Poetry* (Baltimore: American Philological Association, 1956).

COTTON, Judith, "Kent's Hermitage for Queen Caroline at Richmond," *Architecture* 2 (1974), 181–191.

DIGGLE, James, Review of J.W. Binns, ed. *The Latin Poetry of English Poets* (London, 1974), *Times Higher Literary Supplement* (13 Sept. 1974).

DUNDES, Alan, "Couvade in Genesis," *Parsing Through Customs: Essays by a Freudian Folklorist* (Madison: University of Wisconsin Press, 1987), 145–166.

DURING, Simon, *Modern Enchantments: The Cultural Power of Secular Magic* (Harvard and London: Harvard University Press, 2002).

EDGECOMBE, Rodney, "A Reading of Gray's "Ode on the death of a Favourite Cat, Drowned in a Tub of Gold Fishes,'" *English Studies in Africa* 26.2 (1983), 99–104.

FOUCAULT, Michel, *The History of Sexuality, Volume I: An Introduction*, trans. Robert Hurley (New York: Routledge, 1990).

GALINSKY, G.K., "The Hercules-Cacus Episode in *Aeneid* VIII," *American Journal of Philology* 87 (1966), 18–51.

GEORGE, D.B., "An Etymological Reading of Thomas Gray's 'Ode on the Death of a Favourite Cat,'" *Classical Journal* 82.4 (1987), 329–330.

GILMORE, John, "Parrots, Poets and Philosophers: Language and Empire in the Eighteenth Century," *Entertext* 2.2 (2003), 84–102.

GREENBLATT, Stephen, *Renaissance Self-Fashioning From More to Shakespeare* (Chicago and London: University of Chicago Press, 1984).

HAAN, Estelle, *From Academia to Amicitia: Milton's Latin Writings and the Italian Academies* (Transactions of the American Philosophical Society 88.6 [Philadelphia, 1998]).

——————, *Andrew Marvell's Latin Poetry: From Text to Context* (Collection Latomus 275: Brussels, 2003).

——————, *Thomas Gray's Latin Poetry: Some Classical, Neo-Latin and Vernacular Contexts* (Collection Latomus 257: Brussels, 2000).

——————, *Vergilius Redivivus: Studies in Joseph Addison's Latin Poetry* (Transactions of the American Philosophical Society 95.2 [Philadelphia, 2005]).

——————, "The Adorning of My Native Tongue: Linguistic Metamorphosis in Milton," *Metaphrastes or Gained in Translation: Essays in Honour of Robert H. Jordon*, ed. Margaret Mullett (Belfast: Belfast Byzantine Texts and Translations, 2004), 111–127.

——————, "Marvell's Bilingualism and Renaissance Pedagogy," *Proceedings of the International Andrew Marvell Conference*, ed. Gilles Sambras (Reims, 2007).

HAND, W.D., "American Analogues of the Couvade," *Studies in Folklore*, ed. W. Edson (Indiana: Indiana University Press, 1957), 213–229.

HARRIS, A.T., *Policing the City: Crime and Legal Authority in London 1780–1840* (Ohio: Ohio State University Press, 2004).

HARRISON, A.T., "Echo and her Medieval Sisters," *The Centennial Review* 26.4 (1982), 324–340.

HARTLAND, E.S.,"Birth (Introduction)," *Encyclopedia of Religion and Ethics*, ed. James Hastings (New York: Scribner's, 1928).

INWOOD, Stephen, *A History of London* (London: Macmillan, 1998).

JOSÉ, J.G.A.M., "*Hercules exempli gratia:* de Hercules-Cacus-episode in Vergilius *Aeneis* 8.185–305," *Lampas* 23 (1990), 50–73.

KELLY, Philippa, "Surpassing Glass: Shakespeare's Mirrors," *Early Modern Literary Studies* 8.1 (May 2002), 2, 1–32.

KEYNES, Geoffrey, "The Library of Cowper," *Transactions of the Cambridge Bibliographical Society*, 1959–1961.

LACAN, Jacques, "The Mirror Stage as Formative of the Function of the I as Revealed in Psychoanalytic Experience," *Ecrits, A Selection* (1949), trans. Alan Sheridan, 1–7, in Philip Rice and Patricia Waugh, eds. *Modern Literary Theory: A Reader* (London: Oxford University Press, 2002), 189–195.

LEVINAS, Emanuel, *Totality and Infinity*, trans. Alphonso Lingis (1969), 194–202, in Philip Rice and Patricia Waugh, eds. *Modern Literary Theory: A Reader* (London: Oxford University Press, 2002), 422–429.

LUNDELL, Torborg, "Couvade in Sweden: Customs for New Fathers," *Scandinavian Studies* 3.22 (1999), 93–104.

MARKS, Herbert, "Echo and Narcissism," *University of Toronto Quarterly* 51.3 (1992), 334–354.

MELCHIOR-BONNET, Sabine, *The Mirror: A History*, trans. K.H. Jewitt (New York: Routledge, 2001).

MILLER, J.F., "Propertius 3.2 and Horace," *Transactions of the American Philological Association* 113 (1983), 289–299.

MONEY, D.K., *The English Horace: Anthony Alsop and the Tradition of British Latin Verse* (Oxford: Oxford University Press, 1998).

PALMER, D.J., "*Twelfth Night* and the Myth of Echo and Narcissus," *Shakespeare Survey* 32 (1979), 73–78.

POSTLETHWAITE, Nigel, and CAMPBELL, Gordon, eds., "Edward King, Milton's *Lycidas*: Poems and Documents," *Milton Quarterly* 28.4 (1994), 77–111.

PUTNAM, M.C.J., *Horace's Carmen Saeculare: Ritual Magic and the Poet's Art* (New Haven and London: Yale University Press, 2002).

RAY, R.H., "Marvell's 'To His Coy Mistress' and Sandys's translation of Ovid's *Metamorphoses*," *Review of English Studies* 44 (1993), 386–389.

REYNOLDS, Elaine, *Before the Bobbies: The Night Watch and Police Reform in Metropolitan London 1720–1830* (Stanford: Stanford University Press, 1998).

ROTH, H.L., "On the Signification of Couvade," *Journal of the Anthropological Institute of Great Britain and Ireland* 22 (1893), 204–243.

RUBINO, C.A., "Monuments and Pyramids: Death and the Poet in Horace's *Carmen* 3.30," *Classical and Modern Literature* 5 (1985), 99–110.

SHEPARD, Leslie, *The Broadside Ballad: A Study in Origins and Meaning* (London: H. Jenkins, 1942).

————, *The History of Street Literature: The Story of Broadside Ballads, Chapbooks, Proclamations, News-Sheets, Election Bills, Tracts, Pamphlets, Cocks, Catchpennies, and Other Ephemera* (Michigan: Singing Tree Press, 1973).

SHESGREEN, Sean, *Images of the Outcast: The Urban Poor in the Cries of London* (New Brunswick: Rutgers University Press, 2002).

SHUGER, Deborah, "The "I" of the Beholder: Renaissance Mirrors and the Reflexive Mind," in *Renaissance Culture and the Everyday*, ed. Patricia Fumerton and Simon Hunt (Philadelphia: Pennsylvania University Press, 1999), 19–36.

SIMPSON, C.J., "*Exegi Monumentum*: Building Imagery and Metaphor in Horace, *Odes* 1–3," *Latomus* 61 (2002), 57–66.

SPAAS, Lieve and SELOUS, Trista, eds. *Echoes of Narcissus* (New York: Berghahn Books, 2000).

STOREY, Mark, "The Latin Poetry of Vincent Bourne," in *The Latin Poetry of English Poets*, ed. J. W. Binns (London and Boston: Routledge, 1970), 121–149.

TERPENING, Ronnie H., *Charon and the Crossing: Ancient, Medieval and Renaissance Transformations of a Myth* (Lewisburg: Buckness University Press, 1985).

VAN VECHTEN, Carl, *The Tiger in the House* (New York: A.A. Knopf, 1922).

WOODMAN, Tony, "*Exegi monumentum*: Horace, *Odes* 3.30," in *Quality and Pleasure in Latin Poetry*, eds. Tony Woodman and David West (Cambridge: Cambridge University Press, 1974), 115–128.

INDEX NOMINUM

www.ingramcontent.com/pod-product-compliance
Lightning Source LLC
Chambersburg PA
CBHW080925100426
42812CB00007B/2368